INTERIOR CASTLE

THE ESSENTIAL WISDOM LIBRARY

The Tao Te Ching of Lao Tzu

Buddhism

The Bhagavad Gita

St. Francis of Assisi

The Kebra Nagast

The Kybalion

The Toltec Way

Orthodoxy

The Dhammapada

The Imitation of Christ

INTERIOR CASTLE

THE COMPLETE ORIGINAL EDITION

THE ESSENTIAL WISDOM LIBRARY

ST. TERESA OF AVILA

INTRODUCTION BY JON M. SWEENEY

ST. MARTIN'S
ESSENTIALS
NEW YORK

Published in the United States by St. Martin's Essentials,
an imprint of St. Martin's Publishing Group

INTRODUCTION. Copyright © 2023 by Jon M. Sweeney. All rights reserved.
Printed in the United States of America. For information, address
St. Martin's Publishing Group, 120 Broadway, New York, NY 10271.

www.stmartins.com

The Library of Congress Cataloging-in-Publication Data is available upon request.

ISBN 978-1-250-88884-6 (trade paperback)
ISBN 978-1-250-88885-3 (ebook)

Our books may be purchased in bulk for promotional, educational, or business use.
Please contact your local bookseller or the Macmillan Corporate and
Premium Sales Department at 1-800-221-7945, extension 5442, or by
email at MacmillanSpecialMarkets@macmillan.com.

This translation of *Interior Castle* was first published in 1906.
First St. Martin's Essentials Edition: 2023

10 9 8 7 6 5 4 3 2 1

This edition seeks to faithfully reproduce the original publication of the author's
work and so has maintained the original spelling and grammar throughout,
with only minor alterations for clarity or content.

Dedicated to

THE MARTYRED DAUGHTERS OF SAINT TERESA

THE BLESSED CARMELITES OF COMPIEGNE

BY THE DESCENDANTS

OF THEIR FELLOW PRISONERS

Stanbrook Abbey
Day of the Beatification
May 27, 1906

Contents

Introduction by Jon M. Sweeney   *1*

Introduction by Father Benedict Zimmerman   7

Preface   29

THE FIRST MANSIONS

1. Description of the Castle   35
2. The Human Soul   42

THE SECOND MANSIONS

1. War   57

THE THIRD MANSIONS

1. Fear of God   69
2. Aridity in Prayer   77

THE FOURTH MANSIONS

1. Sweetness in Prayer   89
2. Divine Consolations   99
3. Prayer of Quiet   106

THE FIFTH MANSIONS

1. Prayer of Union   121
2. Effects of Union   131
3. Cause of Union   141
4. Spiritual Espousals   150

THE SIXTH MANSIONS

1. Preparation for Spiritual Matrimony   161
2. The Wound of Love   172
   Introductory Note to Chapter 3   178
3. Locutions   182
4. Raptures   195
5. The Flight of the Spirit   206
6. Spiritual Jubilation   214
7. The Humanity of our Lord   224
8. Intellectual Visions   236
9. Imaginary Visions   244
10. Intellectual Visions Continued   256
11. The Dart of Love   261

THE SEVENTH MANSIONS

1. God's Presence Chamber   273
2. Spiritual Matrimony   281

3. Its Effects   290
4. Martha and Mary   299

Conclusion   311
Index   315

Introduction

Father Benedict Zimmerman, in his fine introduction to this spirituality classic, describes Teresa repeatedly as if she were known as a saint by her contemporaries. He, for instance, recounts this memory of a religious sister: "Entering one day [Teresa's] cell to deliver a message, the holy Mother was just beginning a new sheet of her book. While taking off her spectacles to listen to the message she was seized by a trance in which she remained for several hours. The nun, terrified at this, did not stir, but kept her eyes steadily on the Saint." This is no doubt true. In fact, there were also occasions when Teresa's sisters discovered her levitating slightly, so taken away was she in her prayer. But many of the nuns also thought she might be in trouble when she appeared in these ways. Like other great mystics throughout the history of religion—when it was perhaps possible to be one without optics—Teresa wasn't thought a saint so much as an addled woman.

As an abbess (spiritual leader and CEO of convents), Teresa

was often firm with fellow nuns, putting a stop to gossip, the misuse of funds, and bad confessors, even writing "terrible letters," as she called them—of reproof—when necessary. She often, in letters to priests, complained about some of the other nuns being too submissive, or lacking in humor. As a leader, she worried about debts and the policies of corrupt government officials. She was also sensitive to how personalities can clash in close quarters, remarking in one December 1579 letter about a prioress that was moved from one convent to another: "I tell you that if she were to return, the peace of this house would be completely destroyed." So, I ask you, does this sound like a mystic detached from reality?

Yet she could become transfixed. Look only at the famous Bernini sculpture of her heart being pierced by a divine spear and the almost erotic gaze of love on her face at that moment. She wrote—very hesitantly—of such experiences.

This is her masterwork, written, as I say, hesitantly. It has inspired millions of people over the centuries, many of them far away from the confines of a Catholic religious house. Some years ago, for instance, the motivational teacher and spiritual writer Caroline Myss wrote a book about the influence of this book of Teresa's upon her. Writing from what she called "a transreligious perspective," and in "a search for cosmic, unifying truths," Myss called hers "a guide to your soul," and all of that made sense because that's what *Interior Castle*—penned by a sixteenth-century (1515–1582) Carmelite nun—was always meant to be.*

---

* Caroline Myss, *Entering the Castle: Finding the Inner Path to God and Your Soul's Purpose* (New York: Free Press, 2008), 9.

The metaphor of a castle, and its mansions, are her way of explaining, by comparison, what she experienced in herself in prayer: God and soul together. By "soul" she does not mean the intellect, or what we usually call the mind. She means that word which we use much less than our grandparents did, to indicate the inexhaustible, eternal, personal, and unique center of identity of ourselves in relationship to our Creator.

"There are many rooms in this castle," she begins so simply. Then, a little while later, "There are very different ways of being in this castle."

Her reflections on prayer are deeply personal; she recognizes that her experiences will not match your own, and that hers have been obtained by grace, which means God's gift given without regard for her worthiness. "I am like a parrot which has learnt to talk," she says, "only knowing what it has been taught or has heard." This is really different from the preacher who asks you for money saying that God has given him some private revelation—because Teresa assumes no authority at all. It is to her reader to try—if we dare—what worked for her, to see how true it is.

Making her way through the mansions of this interior castle, Teresa is often in darkness. I imagine the interior castle as a poorly lit place. Over the centuries, the theologians have most often set sail with Saint Paul, emphasizing how God "commanded light to shine out of darkness" (2 Corinthians 4:6), and the theologian's (Father Zimmerman's) introduction to our volume, here, is no different. But what they often neglect is the love a mystic such as Teresa has for darkness itself, and how its night sea has a beauty all its own. That mysterious dark offers a person of faith more than any rainbow or rising sun.

A few final notes are needed before you get started. First,

the gender singularity in this work is refreshingly not male. You'll encounter many instances of "sisters" and "my daughters," reminding you to whom Teresa was originally speaking and writing. That's okay. We can all be, in absorbing this wisdom a half-millennium later, like nuns in a Spanish convent.

Another factor that may feel distancing between you and Teresa is how real the devil seemed to be in her life and experience. This is not so for most people in our time. I encourage you simply to consider the many ways that Teresa describes this devilish activity around her. There are "vipers and poisonous creatures" that need to be avoided. They take the form of negative thoughts—encouraging us to despair when joys cease, or people criticize us, or they lie by suggesting that our penances and disciplines will get us nowhere. These—and others—are "the devil's wiles!" We should still beware of them all.

Lastly, it will be interesting to some to know that this book bears the mark of other nuns, those who translated it from the Spanish a little more than a century ago: "Benedictines of Stanbrook," it says. They were located in Worcester, England, having arrived from Flanders following imprisonment at the hands of French Revolution enthusiasts. These nuns printed the early editions of the book as well. They ran a letterpress! My old hardback copy reads on the final page after the epilogue, "translated and printed by the Benedictines of Stanbrook A.D. MCMXXX." It was only in 2009 when they left the glorious Gothic buildings of Worcester for modern accommodations in North Yorkshire; but you can still visit the old abbey as a five-star hotel; stone cloisters and stained glass are now accompanied by "brasserie-style dining" and a wealth of other amenities, according to the website.

So follow through these gates, if you can, into these mansions of this castle that is right there inside you, even if it is not yet familiar to you. It is possible that, like Teresa, you will find that you (your soul)—as she says in one of the final mansions—"no longer feels solitary since it rejoices in such Company."

—Jon M. Sweeney
editor of *A Course in Christian Mysticism*
by Thomas Merton

Introduction

SAINT TERESA began to write the *Interior Castle* on June 2, 1577, Trinity Sunday, and completed it on the eve of St. Andrew, November 29, of the same year. But there was a long interruption of five months,* so that the actual time spent in the composition of this work was reduced to about four weeks—a fortnight for the first, and another fortnight for the second half of the book. The rapidity with which it was written is easily explained by the fact that the Saint had conceived its plan some time previously. On January 17, 1577, she had written to her brother, Don Lorenzo de Cepeda, at Avila: "I have asked the bishop—Don Alvaro Mendoza—for my book (the *Life*), because I shall perhaps complete it by adding those new favours our Lord has lately granted me. With these one may even compose a new work of considerable size, provided God grant me the grace of

---

* V. Mansions, ch. iv. 1.

explaining myself; otherwise the loss will be of small account."*
She never asked for permission to write anything, but waited
until she received a command from her superiors, which, in this
case, came from Father Jerome Gratian, superior of the Discalced Carmelites of the Provinces of Andalucia and Castille,
and from Don Alonzo Velasquez, canon of Toledo, afterwards
Bishop of Osma.† The Saint was not in good health at that
time; she repeatedly complains of noises in the head and other
infirmities, but, worst of all, she was weighed down by troubles and anxieties resulting from the action of the superiors of
the Order and of the Papal Nuncio against the nuns and friars
of the Reform. Matters became even more serious when, in
October, the nuns of the Incarnation of Avila proceeded to the
election of a new prioress. Notwithstanding the prohibition of
the provincial, fifty-five electors recorded their votes in favour
of the Saint and were immediately declared excommunicated.
The whole work of the Reform seemed on the brink of ruin;
the Saint, as well as all her friends, was in disgrace, subject to
obloquy and ill-treatment.

No trace of these trials is to be found in the *Interior Castle*.
Saint Teresa possessed the power of concentration of thought
in a marvellous degree. The early mornings and late evenings
were devoted to the composition of the book, while the rest of
the day was taken up by the affairs of the Order. Mother Mary
of the Nativity, a member of the community of Toledo, where

---

* Letters shortly to be published.

† The French Carmelite nuns in their new translation, *Œuvres complètes de Sainte
Térèse*, t. vi., Introduction, p. 5, quoting the *Año Teresiano*, t. vii. ad 7 July, and Father
Gratian's *Dilucidario*, as well as his additions to Ribera, show the exact share of Fr.
Gratian and Dr. Velasquez in the preliminaries of this work.

the book was begun, declared afterwards,* that she often saw her writing, generally after Communion, her face resplendent, with such rapidity and so absorbed in her occupation that she seemed undisturbed by, and in fact quite unconscious of, any noise that was made. Mother Mariana of the Angels† reports having heard from the same witness, that entering one day her cell to deliver a message, the holy Mother was just beginning a new sheet of her book. While taking off her spectacles to listen to the message she was seized by a trance in which she remained for several hours. The nun, terrified at this, did not stir, but kept her eyes steadily on the Saint. When she came to, it was seen that the paper, previously blank, was covered with writing. Noticing that her visitor had discovered it, Saint Teresa put the paper quietly in a box.

Another nun, Mary of St. Francis, left the following declaration: "I know that our holy Mother wrote four books, the *Life,* the *Way of Perfection,* the *Foundations,* and the *Mansions,* which I have seen her writing. Once, while she was composing the last-named work, I entered to deliver a message, and found her so absorbed that she did not notice me; her face seemed

---

* Fuente, *Obras de Santa Teresa de Jesús.* Edit. 1881, vol. vi. p. 278.

† *Ibid.* p. 178. A somewhat similar incident is reported by Mother Anne of the Incarnation (*Ibid.* p. 213), but it appears to be wrongly brought into connection with the composition of the *Castle.* The nun in question had belonged to the convent of St. Joseph at Segovia at an earlier period, but there is no evidence that St. Teresa visited this place in the course of the six months during which she composed this work. The Bollandists, indeed, maintain that it was commenced at Toledo, continued at Segovia and completed at Avila (n. 1541), but their sole authority for including Segovia is the passage in question, which, however, must refer to some other work of the Saint. The sister, passing St. Teresa's door, saw her writing, her face being lit up as by a bright light. She wrote very fast without making any corrections. After an hour, it being about midnight, she ceased and the light disappeared. The Saint then knelt down and remained in prayer for three hours, after which she went to sleep.

quite inflamed and most beautiful. After having listened to me she said: 'Sit down, my child, and let me write what our Lord has told me ere I forget it,' and she went on writing with great rapidity and without stopping.'"*

Mary of St. Joseph says she heard from Mary of the Nativity that Father Jerome Gratian commanded the Saint to write the *Mansions*; she, however, begged to be excused, because, so many books having been written by holy and learned men, there remained nothing for a woman to write. At length she yielded under obedience. This nun (Mary of the Nativity) was frequently in the Saint's cell while she was writing, and noticed her resplendent face and the almost preternatural velocity with which her hand travelled over the paper.†

Writing to Mother Mary of St. Joseph, Prioress of Seville, November 8, 1581, Saint Teresa gives her a message for Father Rodrigo Alvarez, S. J.: "Our father (Jerome Gratian, then provincial) tells me that he has handed you a book written by me, which perhaps you do not feel inclined to read yourself. Kindly read to Fr. Rodrigo Alvarez, at his next visit, the last Mansion, but under the seal of confession, as he asks this in his superior wisdom. This is only for you two. Tell him that the person he knows has arrived at this Mansion and enjoys the peace there described; that she is entirely at rest, and that some grave theologians have assured her that she is on a safe road. In case you could not read these pages to him do not send him the book, for it might lead to unpleasantness. Until I have his answer on this matter I will not write to him. Give him my compliments."

---

* Fuente, *l.c.* p. 223.

† *Ibid.* p. 255.

At the end of the original manuscript, before the epilogue (marked with Ihs.) there is a notice in Father Alvarez' handwriting to this effect: "The Mother Prioress of this convent of Seville has read to me this seventh Mansion, whither a soul may arrive in the present life. Let all the saints praise the infinite goodness of God, Who communicates Himself to His creatures so that they truly seek His glory and the salvation of their neighbour. What I feel and judge of this matter, is, that everything that has been read to me is conformable to Catholic truth and in accordance with Holy Scripture and the teaching of the Saints. Whosoever has read the doctrine of the Saints, such as the books of St. Gertrude, St. Catharine of Siena, or St. Bridget of Sweden, and other saints and spiritual writers, will clearly understand that the spirit of Mother Tireza (*sic*) of Jesus is true, since it leads to the same effects as are to be found in the saints; and because this is in truth my judgment and opinion, I have hereunto set my name, this, the 22nd day of February, 1582. P. Rodrigo Alvarez."*

The work was copied, probably under the supervision of the Saint, who introduced many changes; when completed the original was handed to Father Jerome Gratian and to the Dominican, Fray Diego de Yanguas, for approval. Both, particularly the former, made numerous corrections, which Fuente, not without reason, calls impertinent, scratching out whole sentences and adding others. The book thus revised must have enjoyed a certain celebrity, though not to the same extent as the *Life,* to which St. Teresa herself preferred it. Scarcely a week after its completion she wrote to Fr. Salazar, S. J.: "If Señor Carillo

---

* *Autograph,* fol. cx.

[Salazar himself] came, the person in question [the Saint] thinks he would find another jewel which in her opinion is superior to the former [the *Life*]. This one reflects nothing foreign to itself, but is resplendent in its own beauty. It is enriched with more delicate enamels than the former; the workmanship, too, is more perfect. For, as the person in question says, the jeweller was less experienced when he fashioned the previous one. Moreover, the gold of the new one is of better quality than that of the former, though the precious stones are not so well set. It has been done, as might be expected, according to the designs of the Jeweller Himself."[*] Later on she wrote to Fr. Jerome Gratian: "The book I have written since seems to me superior [to the *Life*]; at least I had more experience when I wrote it."[†]

One day, speaking with Mother Mary of Jesus on spiritual matters, she said that our Lord had communicated so much to her since she had reached what she described in the seventh Mansion—the spiritual Matrimony—that she did not consider it possible to advance further in this life, in the way of prayer, nor even to wish to do so.[‡]

The book was eagerly read by those who were able to obtain copies. At the archiepiscopal Seminary at Salamanca it was read publicly after dinner; the students, contrary to custom, sacrificing the recreation rather than miss so edifying an instruction. The result was that several entered the religious life, one becoming a Franciscan, two others, who had already taken their de-

---

[*] Dec. 7, 1577.

[†] Jan. 14, 1580.

[‡] Fuente, *Obras, l.c.* p. 275.

grees, joining the Discalced Carmelites.* We also know of a lady who became a Poor Clare through reading the *Interior Castle*.† The process of Beatification contains the following evidence of Don Francisco de Mora, architect to Philip III.: "The same prioress (of a convent of Dominican nuns) being concerned about my salvation gave me a book in manuscript, called *The Mansions*, by Mother Teresa, hoping I should derive some benefit from it. I fear this was not the case, but it made me acquainted with Teresa of Jesus, the foundress of the Discalced Carmelite nuns, of whom I had not yet heard, but for whom I now felt devotion."‡

In August 1586 it was decided to print Saint Teresa's works, the Augustinian Fray Luis de Leon being selected as editor, as he was unconcerned in the quarrels raging round the Reform. Accordingly, the manuscript of the *Interior Castle* was handed to him. On the first leaf he wrote the following note:

"Many passages of this book written by the holy Mother have been scored through, other words being substituted or notes being added in the margin. Most of these corrections are badly done, the original text being much better. It will be noticed that the holy Mother's sentences are superior and agree with the context, which is not the case with the corrections. These improvements and glosses may therefore be dispensed with. Having myself read and considered everything with great care, it appears to me that the reader, too, should have before him the words of the author who knew best what to say; for

---

* Fuente, *Obras, l.c.* p. 217.

† *Ibid.* p. 227.

‡ *Ibid.* p. 190.

this reason I have left out the additions, and have restored what has been changed, excepting only a few corrections made by the writer herself. I beg of the reader that he would in charity reverence the words and even the letters traced by so holy a hand, and strive to understand what has been written. He will then see that there was no need for corrections; should he fail to understand her, let him believe that the writer knew what she said, and that her words cannot be tampered with if they are not to lose their meaning; otherwise what was to the point will seem out of place. This is how books become corrupted, useless, and are finally lost."[*]

When Luis de Leon undertook the editing of St. Teresa's writings he received a long letter from Don Diego de Yepes, afterwards Bishop of Tarazona, a former friend and confessor of the Saint, in which he records his personal recollections. I shall only insert here what he says about the *Interior Castle:*

"This holy Mother desired to see the beauty of a soul in the state of grace, a thing greatly to be coveted both for the sake of seeing and of possessing it. While this desire lasted, she was commanded to write a treatise on prayer, of which she had much personal experience. On the eve of the Blessed Trinity, while considering what subject to choose for this treatise, God, Who disposes everything in due season, fulfilled her wish and furnished a suitable subject. He showed her a most beautiful globe of crystal, in the shape of a Castle, with seven rooms, the seventh, situated in the centre, being occupied by the King of glory, resplendent with the most exquisite brilliancy, which shone through and adorned the remaining rooms. The nearer

---

[*] *Autograph,* fol. 1.

these lay to the centre, the more did they partake of that wondrous light. It did not, however, penetrate beyond the crystal, for everything round about was a mass of darkness and impurity, full of toads and vipers and other venomous animals.

"She was still admiring this beauty which, by the grace of God dwells in the soul, when, lo! the light suddenly disappeared, and the crystal, wherein the King of glory was still residing, became opaque and as dark as coal, emitting an intolerable odour; the venomous animals, formerly held in check outside, obtained admittance into the Castle. The holy Mother wished that every one should behold this vision, for she thought that no one having seen the beauty and splendour of grace, which is forfeited by sin and replaced by such repulsive misery, would ever dare to offend God.

"She told me this vision on the same day, for in this as well as in other things she was so communicative that on the following morning she said to me: 'How I forgot myself yesterday! I cannot think how it could have happened. Those high aspirations of mine, and the affection I have for you must have caused me to go beyond all reasonable limits. God grant I may have derived some profit therefrom.' I promised her to say nothing about it during her lifetime, but since her death I should like to make it known to all men. From this vision she learnt four important matters.

"First, she came to understand this axiom, which in this form she had never heard of in her life,* that God is present in all things by His essence, presence, and power. As she was

---

* See *Life*, ch. xviii. 20. V. Mansions, ch. i. 9. The ignorance of the priest who had told her that God was only present by His grace, made a lasting impression on St. Teresa. She was first undeceived by a Dominican.

deeply humble and submissive and obedient to the doctrine of the Church and the teaching of the learned ministers of God, she never rested until her revelations had been approved of by her superiors and by theologians, and were shown to be conformable to Holy Scripture. She went so far as to say that if all the angels of heaven said one thing, and her superiors another, though she could not doubt that the former were true angels, yet she would hold what was told her by her superiors, because faith comes through these and there remains no room for deceit, whereas revelations coming from angels might be illusionary.

"With such regard for obedience, she asked me one day at Toledo—probably at the time when she saw the vision of the Castle—whether it was true that God was in all things by His power, presence, and essence, to which I replied in the affirmative, explaining it as best I could on the authority of St. Paul, particularly where he says 'the sufferings of this time are not worthy to be compared with the glory to come that shall be revealed in us.'* Laying stress on these words, 'shall be revealed in us,' she was so overjoyed that I was quite astonished. Though in a way it seemed to me a kind of curiosity, I could not help thinking there was some mystery about it, for she said: 'This is the very thing.'

"Secondly, she was greatly surprised at the malice of sin, since, notwithstanding the presence of God in these various ways, it prevents the soul from partaking of that powerful light.

"Thirdly, she derived such humility and self-knowledge from this vision, that from that moment she never thought of herself in all the good she was doing; for she learnt that all the

---

* Rom. viii. 18.

beauty of the soul emanates from that resplendent light, and that the powers of the soul and of the body are enlivened and strengthened by the Power established in the centre, whence comes all our good, so that we have but a small share in our good works. All the good she did, she from this moment referred to God as its principal author.

"Fourthly, she derived from it the subject of the book she was ordered to write on prayer, comparing the seven rooms of the Castle with as many degrees of prayer, whereby we enter within ourselves and draw nearer to God. So that, penetrating to the depths of our soul and gaining perfect self-knowledge, we reach the seventh room where God Himself dwells, with Whom we become united by as perfect a union as is possible in the present life, being made partakers of His light and love.

"I will say no more of this vision and the Mansions, because your Reverence must by now have seen this admirable book, and must know with what accuracy, with what majestic doctrine, with what lucid examples she describes the progress of the soul from the gate to the very centre. It is clearly seen in this treatise how she communicated with our Lord, and how His Majesty vouchsafed to place her in the centre and to unite her with Himself, as she puts it, by the bonds of matrimony and an inseparable union."*

After the publication of the *Interior Castle,* in 1588 at Salamanca, it became not only more widely known, but also more and more appreciated. Francis Suarez, the great theologian of the Society of Jesus, says in his deposition in the process of Beatification that he had read some of St. Teresa's works, particularly

---

* Fuente, *l.c.* pp. 131–133.

the *Mansions,* which contain an absolutely safe doctrine and give proof of a wonderful spirit of prayer and contemplation.[*]

Thomas Hurtado, professor of theology at Seville, speaks as follows:

"As often as I read the books of the holy Mother, I admire the wonderful manner in which God instructed her in mystical theology for the sake of souls giving themselves truly to familiar intercourse with His divine Majesty. But where I most regret my inability of expressing in fitting terms my sentiments towards this excellent teacher is when I look at, and refresh myself in, that Castle with its seven rooms; for there is seen the effect of infused knowledge such as St. Denis received from St. Hierotheus[†] and both from St. Paul, and which has been committed to writing in the famous book of *Mystical Theology.* Hence comes, as from a fountain-head, notwithstanding the obscurity (to our manner of thinking) of its language, the doctrine of the great masters of the spiritual life, such as Hugh of St. Victor, Bernard, Ruysbroek, Tauler, Gerson, and many others whom I pass by.

"Nevertheless, I will boldly say that no one has given us water more limpid from that Apostolical and Areopagitical well than the holy Mother Teresa, who, in her books, but chiefly in the *Mansions,* has cleared up in simple language the most difficult questions of this divine theology, and has brought forth light from darkness, as it is written: '(He) commanded light

---

[*] Fuente, *l.c.* p. 184.

[†] Allusion to the famous *Mystical Theology* attributed to Dionysius the Areopagite, and long considered the chief authority on this subject.

to shine out of darkness."* Who has ever been able to show as clearly as our Saint how God takes possession of the soul, how He unites Himself with its substance, whence comes to the intellect the light of faith, to the will the ardour of love, and to the senses the jubilation over His works? No one has ever turned theory into practice in a more convincing or more catholic manner. The most profound secrets of this supernatural wisdom are here treated with such ease, so amiably, so delightfully, they are illustrated by such nice and homely examples, that instead of awe-inspiring obscurity we find lovely flowers and the sweetness of love, through which, as through an avenue, the soul passes onwards. When God made known His exalted doctrine to St. Dionysius and other mystical writers, He made use of their own language and pen. But St. Teresa in the *Mansions* is like the light of dawn whose rays are not intercepted by the clouds of this world; like a soft rain from above, whereby the soul grows and profits by its communications with God. Until the teaching of this great doctor became known it seemed as though God were inaccessible, being surrounded by darkness, through which Moses and some other persons had to pass when approaching Him;† but they neither explained the manner nor showed the way whereby they came to the enjoyment of the sweetness of the Spouse. Now, however, this way is clear and patent to all, having been pointed out in the *Mansions,* in language so straight and so methodical, and no longer such as could not be understood or required further explanation. In

---

* 2 Cor. iv. 6.

† The example of Moses is scarcely to the point (cf. Exod. xxxiii. 11, and Num. xii. 7, 8).

my opinion this holy writer derived not only the substance of her teaching from infused knowledge, but even the words with which she explains it."*

Likewise Don Alvaro de Villegas, canon of Toledo, expressed his opinion that the *Way of Perfection* and the *Interior Castle* contain "heavenly doctrine." The weight of the subject-matter, the propriety of the comparisons, the force of expressions, the consistency of the teaching, the sweetness of her well-chosen, vivid words, the clearness of the arguments, all this proves that she was guided by her heavenly Spouse, in Whom are hidden the treasures of the wisdom of God; and that the Holy Ghost, Who more than once was seen resting on her head like a dove, was dictating these works. Villegas does not believe that any one could read them, as such books ought to be read, without becoming himself a master of the spiritual life. For they are like heavenly dew, rendering the soul fruitful in the matter of prayer.†

It would be a mistake to consider the *Interior Castle* a complete treatise of mystical theology. Like St. Teresa's other works, it is intensely personal: she describes the road by which she has been led, being well aware that others may be led in a different way. In the heavenly Father's house there are many mansions, not only seven, and many paths lead to them. What gives the work such high value is, that it is the result of a most searching inquiry into the various phases whereby a soul is gradually transformed into the likeness of God Himself. Here St. Teresa is always at her best. She takes nothing for granted, even her own

---

* Fuente, *l.c.* pp. 330–332.

† Fuente, *l.o.* p. 334. These testimonies could easily be multiplied.

personal experiences are admitted only after having been fully investigated and found to be consistent one with the other, and conformable to the teaching of the Church and the words of Holy Scripture.

Mystical theology is generally divided into three parts, respectively called the purgative, the illuminative, and the unitive life. In the first, man is cleansed from sin and habitual imperfection by the use of the sacraments and by voluntary mortification of the passions. The mind is purified by sedulous meditation on the last end and on the Life and Passion of Christ, which must ever be the great model of the Christian. This first portion of the way to heaven can be covered by the help of the ordinary means of grace, without any direct and extraordinary intervention of divine power.

The second part differs in many ways from the first. It comprises the passive purification of the soul and the passive enlightenment of the mind. By sending it keen interior and exterior trials and sufferings, God completes the cleansing of the soul in a manner far surpassing any voluntary effort of man. By raising it to the stage of contemplation He gives it fresh light on the mysteries of our Redemption. The mind is then no longer compelled to strain the memory, the reason, and the will, in order to dwell upon the great truths of religion and to derive some personal benefit therefrom, for these truths are now more or less permanently before it and fill it with holy thoughts, sometimes giving it consolation in trouble, at other times striking a warning note against imperfection. Again, the subtraction of sensible consolation, and the interior aridity arising therefrom, leaves a terrible blank in the soul, showing it that, without God's help, it is mere nothingness. This apparent estrangement from God is the keenest trial that can befall a soul, but also the most powerful means of cleansing it from the least, the most subtle imperfections.

Emerging from this state of probation, the soul enters upon the third stage, in which, though perhaps in the midst of severe suffering and sharp persecution, it knows itself to be a privileged child of God, to Whom it is united by perfect conformity of the will. Such phenomena as revelations, visions, locutions, and even more wonderful manifestations, like the wound of love, spiritual betrothal and nuptials, are incidental rather than essential to the second and third stages. Some great contemplatives have never experienced anything of the kind, while, on the other hand, some of these occurrences may sometimes have been merely the work of an exuberant imagination, or even the result of diabolical illusion. They should therefore never be wished for, or cherished, but rather shunned and ignored, in as far as that is possible. If they are real and come from God, they will do their work without the co-operation of the soul. The danger of self-deception is so great that a person labouring under such phenomena should offer every resistance, and that the spiritual director should exercise the utmost vigilance. St. Teresa is very eloquent on this point, and undeceived many would-be contemplatives, while her disciple, St. John of the Cross, is even more thorough-going in the deprecation of spiritual favours. Among the numerous marks whereby the trained theologian may discriminate between real and imaginary phenomena, there is one about which St. Teresa speaks with wonderful clearness. If they proceed from hysteria the imagination alone is active and the higher powers of the soul are torpid; if, however, they come from God, the intellect and the will are so intensely active, that the lower powers and even the body lose all strength for the time being.

It will be noticed that the first two Mansions belong to the purgative life, the third and fourth to the illuminative, and the remaining three to the unitive life. Compared with similar works, the treatment of the first stage must be called meagre. True, in her *Life* and in the *Way of Perfection* St. Teresa has dealt with this subject somewhat more fully. Indeed, the last-named work was designed as a treatise on Christian Ascetics, dealing with the purgation of the soul by mortification and the enlightenment of the mind by meditation. There, too, appears the first idea of the *Mansions,** and Fuente remarks that the passage in question may be taken for the parting of the ways between the two works. However, this is not the only, nor, indeed, the chief reason why Saint Teresa is so reticent about the preliminary stage of the contemplative life. The fact is that she herself did not pass through these experiences. By God's grace she was preserved from childhood from grievous sin and gross imperfection. Though she never grows tired of bewailing her faults and unfaithfulness, these avowals must be taken *cum grano salis*. While yet a child, she sometimes gave way to vanity in dress and wasted her time in reading romances. As a young religious, she was sought after by friends and relatives who took pleasure in her attractive conversation. This proved further loss of time and caused distractions. Owing to acute suffering, she for some years left off the practice of mental prayer, though she faithfully performed all her religious obligations, as far as her weak state of health allowed. This is all. The war of the

---

* *Way of Perf.* ch. xx. 1.

flesh against the spirit, the insubordination of the lower parts of nature, the fickleness of the will, which so often thwart the most noble aspirations of a soul, were unknown to her. Under these circumstances, we cannot be surprised to find her entering upon the journey towards God at a point which in many cases marks but the closing stage.

As to the remaining parts of this book, it will be seen from the parallel passages that they cover much the same ground as her *Life* and the *Relations*. With her singular gift of introspection and analysis, the Saint studied her own case from every point of view, so as to make sure that her extraordinary experiences were due to no illusion, and offered no obstacle to the safety of her soul. Although the *Interior Castle* contains little that we do not already know from her other works, it is superior to them by reason of its logical order and the masterly treatment of the most recondite matters of mystical theology. While ostensibly dealing with general facts, St. Teresa in reality records her personal experiences. How definite these were, how little room there remained for the freaks of the imagination, will appear from the fact that she nearly always repeats the very words she had used in her *Life* and in the other reports of her interior progress, although she did not have these writings before her eyes, nor had she ever seen them since they first left her hands. Every one of her experiences must have produced a profound impression to be remembered so minutely after an interval of years.

There is that in the *Interior Castle* which reminds one of Dante's *Paradiso*. In the one and the other, the soul, purified from earthly dross, is gradually being invested with new and glorious qualities, and is being led through regions unknown, until it arrives at the very threshold of the throne of God. Not even the boldest imagination could have designed so wonderful a picture of a soul adorned with graces at once so varied and so true. In one case we know, the poet has drawn abundantly from the treasury of the Angelical Doctor, putting in verse the conclusions of the scholastic theologian. In the other case we can follow, chapter by chapter, the influence of the teaching of St. Thomas Aquinas. St. Teresa had never studied it herself, but her directors and confessors were deeply versed in it and solved her doubts and perplexities on the lines of the greatest of the schoolmen. The *Interior Castle* might almost be considered a practical illustration of certain parts of the *Summa theologica*,* as it describes the progress of the soul through every stage of perfection. When we have reached the second chapter of the seventh Mansion there remains but one thing: the Beatific Vision, and this is reserved for the next life.

After the publication of the *Interior Castle* by Luis de Leon, the manuscript came into the possession of Father Jerome Gratian, who, after having made a copy of it which is still extant, presented the original, on the occasion of a visit to the convent of Seville, to Don Pedro Cereso Pardo, a great friend of the Saint, and a benefactor of the convent. When his only daughter took the habit there, the precious manuscript was part of her dowry. Doña Juana de Mendoza, Duchess of Beguiar, a novice in the same convent, had it bound in silver and precious stones. It is still there,† and the present writer had the privilege of seeing it.

---

* S. Theol. 2da 2dæ, qq. 171–184.

† Bollandists, *Acta,* n. 1495. See also *Impressions in Spain.* By Lady Herbert. London, 1867, p. 171.

It comprises a hundred and thirteen leaves in folio, but orginally there must have been some more leaves which at a later period have been torn out. These, it is presumed, contained the headings of the chapters. Unlike the *Life* and the *Foundations,* the text of the *Castle* is divided only by figures, without indication of the contents of each chapter, but the arguments which have come down to us are so entirely similar to those of the two works named, that it is impossible to consider them otherwise than the genuine work of the author. In the present translation they have been inserted in their proper places.

On the occasion of the tercentenary of Saint Teresa's death, a photo-lithographic edition of the original was published under the direction of Cardinal Lluch, Carmelite of the old observance, Archbishop of Seville:

El Castillo Ynterior ó Tratado de las Moradas,
escrito por Sta. Teresa de Jesús.
Litografía de Juan Moyano (Seville) *1882.*

The present translation, the third in English,* has been made directly from this autograph edition. It has been thought

---

* The first translation is to be found in the *Works of the Holy Mother St. Teresa of Jesus* (third part). Printed in the year MDCLXXV. pp. 137–286. It bears the title: *The Interiour Castle: or, Mansions.* As to the authors of this translation—Abraham Woodhead and another, whose name is not known—see my book *Carmel in England,* p. 342, note. It is stated there that the third part, containing the *Way of Perfection* and the *Castle,* has no title-page. This is true with regard to the copy I had before me when writing that book. The one I have now is more complete. The second translation, by the Rev. John Dalton, appeared in 1852 and has been repeatedly reprinted. It was dedicated to Bishop Ullathorne. Of foreign translations it will be sufficient to mention the one by Cyprien de la Nativité, in *Œuvres de la Sainte Mère Térèse de Jésus,* Paris, 1657, and the new one in *Œuvres* already mentioned.

advisable that, as far as the genius of the language allows it, the wording of the author should be strictly adhered to, and that not even a shade of her expression should be sacrificed. For Teresa is not only a saint whose every word is telling, but she is a classic in her own language who knows how to give expression to her deepest thoughts. Having compared word for word the translation with the original, I am in a position to affirm that this programme has been faithfully carried out. For the footnotes—with few exceptions—as well as for the Index, I am responsible.* It seemed to me important to point out all the parallel passages from the various works of the Saint. Only by this means can it be seen how consistent Saint Teresa is in all her writings.† It would have been easy to multiply quotations from the works of other writers on mystical theology. Thus, the influence of the *Imitation of Christ* and of the *Life of our Lord* by Ludolphus the Carthusian can be distinctly traced in the *Interior Castle*. Both these works, as well as some Spanish books, were held in such esteem by St. Teresa, that she ordered the prioress of her convents to keep them at the disposal of the nuns. As there is a limit to footnotes, I have contented myself with such references as seemed to me conducive to the elucidation of the doctrine laid down in this treatise.

In conclusion I venture to express the hope that this new

---

* Page 81 was already printed when the new translation of *Saint Peter of Alcantara*, edited by George Seymour Hollings, appeared.

† The present translation ought to dispose of the reservations expressed by an able critic in his otherwise valuable appreciation of the works of the Saint. See *Santa Teresa*, by Alexander Whyte, D.D. London, 1898, p. 32.

translation will be found helpful by those who feel called to a higher life.

Benedict Zimmerman,
Prior, O. C. D.
St. Luke's Priory
Wincanton, Somerset
July 1, 1905, and *December* 25, 1911

Preface

This treatise, styled the Interior Castle, *was written by Teresa of Jesus, Nun of our Lady of Carmel, for her Sisters and Daughters, the Discalced Carmelite Nuns.*

Rarely has obedience laid upon me so difficult a task as this of writing about prayer; for one reason, because I do not feel that God has given me either the power or the desire for it, besides which, during the last three months I have suffered from noises and a great weakness in my head that have made it painful for me to write even on necessary business.*

However, as I know the power obedience has of making things easy which seem impossible, my will submits with a good grace, although nature seems greatly distressed, for God has not given me such strength as to bear, without repugnance, the constant struggle against illness while performing many different duties. May He, Who has helped me in other more difficult matters, aid me with His grace in this, for I trust in His mercy. I think I have but little to say that has not already

---

* "I am always suffering from my head." Letter of June 28, 1577.

been put forth in my other works written under obedience; in fact, I fear this will be but repetition of them. I am like a parrot which has learnt to talk; only knowing what it has been taught or has heard, it repeats the same thing over and over again. If God wishes me to write anything new, He will teach it me, or bring back to my memory what I have said elsewhere. I should be content even with this, for as I am very forgetful, I should be glad to be able to recall some of the matters about which people say I have spoken well, lest they should be altogether lost. If our Lord will not even grant me this, still, if I weary my brains and increase my headache by striving to obey, I shall gain in merit, though my words should be useless to any one. So I begin this work on the Feast of the Blessed Trinity in the year 1577, in the Convent of St. Joseph of Carmel at Toledo, where I am living, and I submit all my writings to the judgment of those learned men by whose commands I undertake them. That it will be the fault of ignorance, not malice, if I say anything contrary to the doctrine of the Holy Roman Catholic Church, may be held as certain. By God's goodness I am, and always shall be, faithful to the Church, as I have been in the past. May He be for ever blessed and glorified. Amen.

He who bids me write this, tells me that the nuns of these convents of our Lady of Carmel need some one to solve their difficulties about prayer: he thinks that women understand one another's language best and that my Sisters' affection for me would make them pay special attention to my words, therefore it is important for me to explain the subject clearly to them. Thus I am writing only to my Sisters; the idea that any one else could benefit by what I say would be absurd. Our Lord will be doing me a great favour if He enables me to help but one of the nuns to praise Him a little better; His Majesty knows well that I have no other aim. If anything is to the point, they will understand that it does not originate from me and there is no reason to attribute it to me, as with my scant understanding and skill I could write nothing of the sort, unless God, in His mercy, enabled me to do so.

THE FIRST MANSIONS

1

Description of the Castle

This chapter treats of the beauty and dignity of our souls and makes a comparison to explain this. The advantage of knowing and understanding this and the favours God grants to us is shown, and how prayer is the gate of the spiritual castle.

1. (Plan of this book). WHILE I was begging our Lord to-day to speak for me, since I knew not what to say nor how to commence this work which obedience has laid upon me, an idea occurred to me which I will explain, and which will serve as the foundation for all that I am about to write.

2. (The Interior Castle). I thought of the soul as resembling a castle,* formed of a single diamond or a very transparent crystal,† and containing many rooms, just as in heaven there are many mansions.‡ If we reflect, Sisters, we shall see that

---

* *Way of Perf.* ch. xxviii. 9.

† In her *Life* St. Teresa likened God to a diamond (ch. xl. 14); and elsewhere (ch. xi. 10) the soul to a garden wherein our Lord takes His delight.

‡ St. John xiv. 2: "In domo Patris mei mansiones multæ sunt" St. John of the Cross uses the same comparison: "If the soul shall overcome the devil in the first combat,

the soul of the just man is but a paradise, in which, God tells us, He takes His delight.* What, do you imagine, must that dwelling be in which a King so mighty, so wise, and so pure, containing in Himself all good, can delight to rest? Nothing can be compared to the great beauty and capabilities of a soul; however keen our intellects may be, they are as unable to comprehend them as to comprehend God, for, as He has told us, He created us in His own image and likeness.†

3. (Our culpable self-ignorance). As this is so, we need not tire ourselves by trying to realise all the beauty of this castle, although, being His creature, there is all the difference between the soul and God that there is between the creature and the Creator; the fact that it is made in God's image teaches us how great are its dignity and loveliness. It is no small misfortune and disgrace that, through our own fault, we neither understand our nature nor our origin. Would it not be gross ignorance, my daughters, if, when a man was questioned about his name, or country, or parents, he could not answer? Stupid as this would be, it is unspeakably more foolish to care to learn nothing of our nature except that we possess bodies, and only to realise vaguely that we have souls, because people say so and it is a doctrine of faith. Rarely do we reflect upon what gifts our souls may possess, Who dwells within them, or how extremely precious they are. Therefore we do little

---

it shall then pass on to the second; and if it shall be victorious there also, it shall then pass on to the third; and then through the seven mansions, the seven degrees of love, until the Bridegroom shall bring it to the 'cellar of wine' or perfect charity" (*Ascent of Mount Carmel*, bk. ii. ch. xi. 7.)

* Prov. viii. 31: "Deliciæ meæ esse cum filiis hominum."

† Gen. i. 26: "Faciamus hominem ad imaginem et similitudinem nostram."

to preserve their beauty; all our care is concentrated on our bodies, which are but the coarse setting of the diamond, or the outer walls of the castle.*

4. (God dwells in the centre of the soul). Let us imagine, as I said, that there are many rooms in this castle, of which some are above, some below, others at the side; in the centre, in the very midst of them all, is the principal chamber in which God and the soul hold their most secret intercourse.† Think over this comparison very carefully; God grant it may enlighten you about the different kinds of graces He is pleased to bestow upon the soul. No one can know all about them, much less a person so ignorant as I am. The knowledge that such things are possible will console you greatly should our Lord ever grant you any of these favours; people themselves deprived of them can then at least praise Him for His great goodness in bestowing them on others. The thought of heaven and the happiness of the saints does us no harm, but cheers, and urges us to win this joy for ourselves, nor will it injure us to know that during this exile God can communicate Himself to us loathsome worms; it will rather make us love Him for such immense goodness and infinite mercy.

---

* *Way of Perf.* ch. xxviii. 5.

† St. John of the Cross on the words in his stanza: "In the inner cellar of my Beloved have I drunk." "Here the soul speaks of that sovereign grace of God in taking it into the house of His love, which is the union or transformation of love in God. . . . The cellar is the highest degree of love to which the soul can attain in this life, and is therefore said to be the inner. It follows from this that there are other cellars not so interior; that is, the degrees of love by which souls reach to this, the last. These cellars are seven in number, and the soul has entered them all when it has in perfection the seven gifts of the Holy Ghost, so far as it is possible for it. . . . Many souls reach and enter the first cellar, each according to the perfection of its love, but the last and inmost cellar is entered by few in this world, because therein is wrought the perfect union with God, the union of the spiritual marriage" (*A Spiritual Canticle*, stanza xxvi. 1–3).

5. (Why all souls do not receive certain favours?). I feel sure that vexation at thinking that during our life on earth God can bestow these graces on the souls of others shows a want of humility and charity for one's neighbour, for why should we not feel glad at a brother's receiving divine favours, which do not deprive us of our own share? Should we not rather rejoice at His Majesty thus manifesting His greatness wherever He chooses?* Sometimes our Lord acts thus solely for the sake of showing His power, as He declared when the Apostles questioned whether the blind man whom He cured had been suffering for his own or his parents' sins.† God does not bestow these favours on certain souls because they are more holy than others who do not receive them, but to manifest His greatness, as in the case of St. Paul and St. Mary Magdalen, and that we may glorify Him in His creatures.

6. (Reasons for speaking of these favours). People may say such things appear impossible and it is best not to scandalise the weak in faith by speaking about them. But it is better that the latter should disbelieve us, than that we should desist from enlightening souls which receive these graces, that they may rejoice and may endeavour to love God better for His favours, seeing He is so mighty and so great. There is no danger here of shocking those for whom I write by treating of such matters, for they know and believe that God gives even greater proofs of His love. I am certain that if any one of you doubts the truth of this, God will never allow her to learn it

---

* St. Matt. xx. 15: "Aut non licet mihi quod volo facere? an oculus tuus nequam est quia ego bonus sum?"

† St. John ix. 2: "Quis peccavit, hic aut parentes ejus, ut cæcus nasceretur?"

by experience, for He desires that no limits should be set to His work: therefore never discredit them because you are not thus led yourselves.

7. (The entrance of the castle). Now let us return to our beautiful and charming castle and discover how to enter it. This appears incongruous: if this castle is the soul, clearly no one can have to enter it, for it is the person himself: one might as well tell some one to go into a room he is already in! There are, however, very different ways of being in this castle; many souls live in the courtyard of the building where the sentinels stand, neither caring to enter farther, nor to know who dwells in that most delightful place, what is in it and what rooms it contains.

8. (Entering into oneself.) Certain books on prayer that you have read advise the soul to enter into itself,* and this is what I mean. I was recently told by a great theologian that souls without prayer are like bodies, palsied and lame, having hands and feet they cannot use. Just so, there are souls so infirm and accustomed to think of nothing but earthly matters, that there seems no cure for them. It appears impossible for them to retire into their own hearts; accustomed as they are to be with the reptiles and other creatures which live outside the castle, they have come at last to imitate their habits. Though these souls are by their nature so richly endowed, capable of communion even with God Himself, yet their case seems hopeless. Unless they endeavour to understand and remedy their most miserable plight, their minds will become, as it

---

* *Imitation*, bk. 11. ch. 1: "Regnum Dei intra vos est." The *Imitation* is one of the books which according to St. Teresa's *Constitutions* (§ 7) every Prioress was bound to provide for her convent.

were, bereft of movement, just as Lot's wife became a pillar of salt for looking backwards in disobedience to God's command.*

9. (Prayer.) As far as I can understand, the gate by which to enter this castle is prayer and meditation. I do not allude more to mental than to vocal prayer, for if it is prayer at all, the mind must take part in it. If a person neither considers to Whom he is addressing himself, what he asks, nor what he is who ventures to speak to God, although his lips may utter many words, I do not call it prayer.† Sometimes, indeed one may pray devoutly without making all these considerations through having practised them at other times. The custom of speaking to God Almighty as freely as with a slave—caring nothing whether the words are suitable or not, but simply saying the first thing that comes to mind from being learnt by rote by frequent repetition—cannot be called prayer: God grant that no Christian may address Him in this manner. I trust His Majesty will prevent any of you, Sisters, from doing so. Our habit in this Order of conversing about spiritual matters is a good preservative against such evil ways.

10. (Those who dwell in the first mansion). Let us speak no more of those crippled souls, who are in a most miserable and dangerous state, unless our Lord bid them rise, as He did the palsied man who had waited more than thirty years at the pool of Bethsaida.‡ We will now think of the others who at

---

* Gen. xix. 26: "Respiciensque uxor ejus post se, versa est in statuam salis."

† *Way of Perf.* ch. xxi. 6, ch. xxix. 4.

‡ St. John v. 5: "Erat autem quidam homo ibi triginta et octo annos habens in infirmitate sua."

last enter the precincts of the castle; they are still very worldly, yet have some desire to do right, and at times, though rarely, commend themselves to God's care. They think about their souls every now and then; although very busy, they pray a few times a month, with minds generally filled with a thousand other matters, for where their treasure is, there is their heart also.* Still, occasionally they cast aside these cares; it is a great boon for them to realise to some extent the state of their souls, and to see that they will never reach the gate by the road they are following.

11. (Entering). At length they enter the first rooms in the basement of the castle, accompanied by numerous reptiles† which disturb their peace, and prevent them seeing the beauty of the building; still, it is a great gain that these persons should have found their way in at all.

12. (Difficulties of the subject). You may think, my daughters, that all this does not concern you, because, by God's grace, you are farther advanced; still, you must be patient with me, for I can explain myself on some spiritual matters concerning prayer in no other way. May our Lord enable me to speak to the point; the subject is most difficult to understand without personal experience of such graces. Any one who has received them will know how impossible it is to avoid touching on subjects which, by the mercy of God, will never apply to us.

---

* St. Matt. vi. 21: "Ubi enim est thesaurus tuus ibi est et cor tuum."

† Many an ancient castle was provided with a bear-garden where rare animals were kept for the amusement of the inhabitants. This may have supplied the material for St. Teresa's comparison.

2

The Human Soul

Describes the hideous appearance of a soul in mortal sin as revealed by God to some one: offers a few remarks on self-knowledge: this chapter is useful, as it contains some points requiring attention. An explanation of the Mansions.

1. (Effects of mortal sin). BEFORE going farther, I wish you to consider the state to which mortal sin* brings this magnificent and beautiful castle, this pearl of the East, this tree of life, planted beside the living waters of life† which symbolise God Himself. No night can be so dark, no gloom nor blackness can compare to its obscurity. Suffice it to say that the sun in the centre of the soul, which gave it such splendour and beauty, is totally eclipsed, though the spirit is as fitted to enjoy God's presence as is the crystal to reflect the sun.‡

2. (It prevents the soul gaining merit). While the soul is in mor-

---

* *Life,* ch. xxxviii. 31, ch. xl. 15.

† Ps. i. 3: "Et erit tanquam lignum quod plantatum est secus decursus aquarum."

‡ *Way of Perf.* ch. xxviii. 9.

tal sin nothing can profit it; none of its good works merit an eternal reward, since they do not proceed from God as their first principle, and by Him alone is our virtue real virtue. The soul separated from Him is no longer pleasing in His eyes, because by committing a mortal sin, instead of seeking to please God, it prefers to gratify the devil, the prince of darkness, and so comes to share his blackness. I knew a person to whom our Lord revealed the result of a mortal sin* and who said she thought no one who realised its effects could ever commit it, but would suffer unimaginable torments to avoid it. This vision made her very desirous for all to realise this truth, therefore I beg you, my daughters, to pray fervently to God for sinners, who live in blindness and do deeds of darkness.

3. (The soul compared to a tree). In a state of grace the soul is like a well of limpid water, from which flow only streams of clearest crystal. Its works are pleasing both to God and man, rising from the River of Life, beside which it is rooted like a tree. Otherwise it would produce neither leaves nor fruit, for the waters of grace nourish it, keep it from withering from drought, and cause it to bring forth good fruit. But the soul by sinning withdraws from this stream of life, and, growing beside a black and fetid pool, can produce nothing but disgusting and unwholesome fruit. Notice that it is not the fountain and the brilliant sun which lose their splendour and beauty, for they are placed in the very centre of the soul and cannot be deprived of their lustre. The soul is like a crystal in

---

* In this as in most other cases when the Saint speaks of "a person she knows," she means herself. *Life*, ch. xl. 15.

the sunshine over which a thick black cloth has been thrown, so that however brightly the sun may shine the crystal can never reflect it.

4. (Disorder of the soul in mortal sin). O souls, redeemed by the Blood of Jesus Christ, take these things to heart; have mercy on yourselves! If you realise your pitiable condition, how can you refrain from trying to remove the darkness from the crystal of your souls? Remember, if death should take you now, you would never again enjoy the light of this Sun. O Jesus! how sad a sight must be a soul deprived of light! What a terrible state the chambers of this castle are in! How disorderly must be the senses—the inhabitants of the castle—the powers of the soul—its magistrates, governors, and stewards—blind and uncontrolled as they are! In short, as the soil in which the tree is now planted is in the devil's domain, how can its fruit be anything but evil? A man of great spiritual insight once told me he was not so much surprised at such a soul's wicked deeds as astonished that it did not commit even worse sins. May God in His mercy keep us from such great evil, for nothing in this life merits the name of evil in comparison with this, which delivers us over to evil which is eternal.

5. (Vision of a sinful soul). This is what we must dread and pray God to deliver us from, for we are weakness itself, and unless He guards the city, in vain shall we labour to defend it.* The person of whom I spoke† said that she had learnt two things from the vision granted her. The first was, a great fear of of-

---

* Ps. cxxvi. 1: "Nisi Dominus custodierit civitatem frustra vigilat qui custodit eam."

† *Life*, ch. xxxviii. 33; ch. xl. 15, 16.

fending God; seeing how terrible were the consequences, she constantly begged Him to preserve her from falling into sin. Secondly, it was a mirror to teach her humility, for she saw that nothing good in us springs from ourselves but comes from the waters of grace near which the soul remains like a tree planted beside a river, and from that Sun which gives life to our works. She realised this so vividly that on seeing any good deed performed by herself or by other people she at once turned to God as to its fountain head—without Whose help she well knew we can do nothing—and broke out into songs of praise to Him. Generally she forgot all about herself and only thought of God when she did any meritorious action.

6. (Profit of realising these lessons). The time which has been spent in reading or writing on this subject will not have been lost if it has taught us these two truths; for though learned, clever men know them perfectly, women's wits are dull and need help in every way. Perhaps this is why our Lord has suggested these comparisons to me; may He give us grace to profit by them!

7. (Prayer). So obscure are these spiritual matters that to explain them an ignorant person like myself must say much that is superfluous, and even alien to the subject, before coming to the point. My readers must be patient with me, as I am with myself while writing what I do not understand; indeed, I often take up the paper like a dunce, not knowing what to say, nor how to begin. Doubtless there is need for me to do my best to explain these spiritual subjects to you, for we often hear how beneficial prayer is for our souls; our Constitutions oblige us to pray so many hours a day, yet tell us nothing of

what part we ourselves can take in it and very little of the work God does in the soul by its means.* It will be helpful, in setting it before you in various ways, to consider this heavenly edifice within us, so little understood by men, near as they often come to it. Our Lord gave me grace to understand something of such matters when I wrote on them before, yet I think I have more light now, especially on the more difficult questions. Unfortunately I am too ignorant to treat of such subjects without saying much that is already well known.

8. (Beauty of the Castle). Now let us turn at last to our castle with its many mansions. You must not think of a suite of rooms placed in succession, but fix your eyes on the keep, the court inhabited by the King.† Like the kernel of the palmito,‡ from which several rinds must be removed before coming to the eatable part, this principal chamber is surrounded by many others. However large, magnificent, and spacious you imagine this castle to be, you cannot exaggerate it; the capacity of the soul is beyond all our understanding, and the Sun within this palace enlightens every part of it.

9. (Self-knowledge). A soul which gives itself to prayer, either much or little, should on no account be kept within narrow bounds. Since God has given it such great dignity, permit it

---

* *Life,* ch. x. 2 *sqq. Constitut.* 2, 6.

† *Way of Perf.* ch. xxviii. 1.

‡ The palmito here referred to is not a palm, but a shrub about four feet high and very dense with leaves, resembling palm leaves. The poorer classes and principally children dig it up by the roots, which they peel of its many layers until a sort of kernel is disclosed, which is eaten, not without relish, and is somewhat like a filbert in taste. See St. John of the Cross, *Ascent of Mount Carmel,* bk. ii. ch. xiv. 3.

to wander at will through the rooms of the castle, from the lowest to the highest. Let it not force itself to remain for very long in the same mansion, even that of self-knowledge. Mark well, however, that self-knowledge is indispensable, even for those whom God takes to dwell in the same mansion with Himself. Nothing else, however elevated, perfects the soul which must never seek to forget its own nothingness. Let humility be always at work, like the bee at the honeycomb, or all will be lost. But, remember, the bee leaves its hive to fly in search of flowers and the soul should sometimes cease thinking of itself to rise in meditation on the grandeur and majesty of its God. It will learn its own baseness better thus than by self-contemplation, and will be freer from the reptiles which enter the first room where self-knowledge is acquired. Although it is a great grace from God to practise self-examination, yet "too much is as bad as too little," as they say; believe me, by God's help, we shall advance more by contemplating the Divinity than by keeping our eyes fixed on ourselves, poor creatures of earth that we are.

10. (Gained by meditating on the divine perfections). I do not know whether I have put this clearly; self-knowledge is of such consequence that I would not have you careless of it, though you may be lifted to heaven in prayer, because while on earth nothing is more needful than humility. Therefore, I repeat, not only a *good* way, but the *best* of all ways, is to endeavour to enter first by the room where humility is practised, which is far better than at once rushing on to the others. This is the right road;—if we know how easy and safe it is to walk by it, why ask for wings with which to fly? Let us rather try to learn how to advance quickly. I believe we shall

never learn to know ourselves except by endeavouring to know God, for, beholding His greatness we are struck by our own baseness, His purity shows our foulness, and by meditating on His humility we find how very far we are from being humble.

11. (Advantage of such meditation). Two advantages are gained by this practice. First, it is clear that white looks far whiter when placed near something black, and on the contrary, black never looks so dark as when seen beside something white. Secondly, our understanding and will become more noble and capable of good in every way when we turn from ourselves to God: it is very injurious never to raise our minds above the mire of our own faults. I described how murky and fetid are the streams that spring from the source of a soul in mortal sin.* Thus (although the case is not really the same, God forbid! this is only a comparison), while we are continually absorbed in contemplating the weakness of our earthly nature, the springs of our actions will never flow free from the mire of timid, weak, and cowardly thoughts, such as: "I wonder whether people are noticing me or not! If I follow this course, will harm come to me? Dare I begin this work? Would it not be presumptuous? Is it right for any one as faulty as myself to speak on sublime spiritual subjects?† Will not people think too well of me, if I make myself singular? Extremes are bad, even in virtue; sinful as I am I shall only fall the lower. Perhaps I shall fail and be a source of scandal to good people; such a person as I am has no need of peculiarities."

---

* *Supra,* § 3.

† *Life,* ch. viii. 6, ch. x. 4, ch. xxiii. 3–5. *Way of Perf.* ch. xxxix. 1.

12. (Christ should be our model). Alas, my daughters, what loss the devil must have caused to many a soul by such thoughts as these! It thinks such ideas and many others of the same sort I could mention arise from humility. This comes from not understanding our own nature; self-knowledge becomes so warped that, unless we take our thoughts off ourselves, I am not surprised that these and many worse fears should threaten us. Therefore I maintain, my daughters, that we should fix our eyes on Christ our only Good, and on His saints; there we shall learn true humility, and our minds will be ennobled, so that self-knowledge will not make us base and cowardly. Although only the first, this mansion contains great riches and such treasures that if the soul only manages to elude the reptiles dwelling here, it cannot fail to advance farther. Terrible are the wiles and stratagems the devil uses to hinder people from realising their weakness and detecting his snares.

13. (The devil entraps beginners). From personal experience I could give you much information as to what happens in these first mansions. I will only say that you must not imagine there are only a few, but a number of rooms, for souls enter them by many different ways, and always with a good intention. The devil is so angry at this, that he keeps legions of evil spirits hidden in each room to stop the progress of Christians, whom, being ignorant of this, he entraps in a thousand ways. He cannot so easily deceive souls which dwell nearer to the King as he can beginners still absorbed in the world, immersed in its pleasures, and eager for its honours and distinctions. As the vassals of their souls, the senses and powers bestowed on them by God, are weak,

such people are easily vanquished, although desirous not to offend God.

14. (Our strength must come from God). Those conscious of being in this state must as often as possible have recourse to His Majesty, taking His Blessed Mother and the saints for their advocates to do battle for them, because we creatures possess little strength for self-defence. Indeed in every state of life all our help must come from God; may He in His mercy grant it us, Amen! What a miserable life we lead! As I have spoken more fully in other writings* on the ill that results from ignoring the need of humility and self-knowledge, I will treat no more about it here, my daughters, although it is of the first importance. God grant that what I have said may be useful to you.

15. (Sin blinds the soul). You must notice that the light which comes from the King's palace hardly shines at all in these first mansions; although not as gloomy and black as the soul in mortal sin, yet they are in semi-darkness, and their inhabitants see scarcely anything. I cannot explain myself; I do not mean that this is the fault of the mansions themselves, but that the number of snakes, vipers, and venomous reptiles from outside the castle prevent souls entering them from seeing the light. They resemble a person entering a chamber full of brilliant sunshine, with eyes clogged and half closed with dust. Though the room itself is light, he cannot see because of his self-imposed impediment. In the same way, these fierce

---

* *Life,* ch. xiii. 23. *Way of Perf.* ch. x. 4. *Castle,* M. iii. ch. ii. 8. *Concep.* ch. ii. 20. *Const.* 21.

and wild beasts blind the eyes of the beginner, so that he sees nothing but them.

16. (Worldliness). Such, it appears to me, is the soul which, though not in a state of mortal sin, is so worldly and preoccupied with earthly riches, honours, and affairs, that as I said, even if it sincerely wishes to enter into itself and enjoy the beauties of the castle, it is prevented by these distractions and seems unable to overcome so many obstacles. It is most important to withdraw from all unnecessary cares and business, as far as compatible with the duties of one's state of life, in order to enter the second mansion. This is so essential, that unless done immediately I think it impossible for any one ever to reach the principal room, or even to remain where he is without great risk of losing what is already gained; otherwise, although he is inside the castle, he will find it impossible to avoid being bitten some time or other by some of the very venomous creatures surrounding him.

17. (The world in the cloister). What then would become of a religious like ourselves, my daughters, if, after having escaped from all these impediments, and having entered much farther into the more secret mansions, she should, by her own fault, return to all this turmoil? Through her sins, many other people on whom God had bestowed great graces would culpably relapse into their wretched state. In our convents we are free from these exterior evils; please God our minds may be as free from them, and may He deliver us from such ills.

18. (Assaults of the devil). Do not trouble yourselves, my daughters, with cares which do not concern you. You must notice that the struggle with the demons continues through nearly

all the mansions of this castle. True, in some of them the guards, which, as I explained, are the powers of the soul, have strength for the combat, but we must be keenly on the watch against the devil's arts, lest he deceive us in the form of an angel of light. He creeps in gradually, in numberless ways, and does us much harm, though we do not discover it until too late.[*]

19. (Examples of the devil's arts). As I said elsewhere,[†] he works like a file, secretly and silently wearing its way: I will give you some examples to show how he begins his wiles. For instance: a nun has such a longing for penance as to feel no peace unless she is tormenting herself in some way.[‡] This is good in itself; but suppose that the Prioress has forbidden her to practise any mortifications without special leave, and the sister thinking that, in such a meritorious cause, she may venture to disobey, secretly leads such a life that she loses her health and cannot even fulfil the requirements of her rule— you see how this show of good ends. Another nun is very zealous about religious perfection; this is very right, but may cause her to think every small fault she sees in her sisters a serious crime, and to watch constantly whether they do anything wrong, that she may run to the Prioress to accuse them of it. At the same time, may be, she never notices her own short-comings because of her great zeal about other people's

---

[*] *Life,* ch. xxxi. 23.

[†] No doubt the Saint often used this excellent comparison in her verbal instructions, but it occurs nowhere else in her writings.

[‡] *Way of Perf.* ch. x. 5, ch xxxix. 4. *Rel.* iii. 12.

religious observance, while perhaps her sisters, not seeing her intention but only knowing of the watch she keeps on them, do not take her behaviour in good part.

20. (Perfection consists in charity). The devil's chief aim here is to cool the charity and lessen the mutual affection of the nuns, which would injure them seriously. Be sure, my daughters, that true perfection consists in the love of God and our neighbour, and the better we keep both these commandments, the more perfect shall we be. The sole object of our Rule and Constitutions is to help us to observe these two laws.

21. (Indiscreet zeal). Indiscreet zeal about others must not be indulged in; it may do us much harm; let each one look to herself. However, as I have spoken fully on this subject elsewhere,* I will not enlarge on it here, and will only beg you to remember the necessity of this mutual affection. Our souls may lose their peace and even disturb other people's if we are always criticising trivial actions which often are not real defects at all, but we construe them wrongly through ignorance of their motives. See how much it costs to attain perfection! Sometimes the devil tempts nuns in this way about the Prioress, which is still more dangerous. Great prudence is then required, for if she disobeys the Rule or Constitutions the matter must not always be overlooked, but should be mentioned to her;† if, after this, she does not amend, the Superior

---

* The Saint must frequently have spoken on the subject, but she never treated it more fully than in this place. *Way of Perf.* ch. xli. 7. *Life,* ch. xiii. 11, 14 *sqq.*

† *Way of Perf.* ch. ii. 3. *Visit.* 20–22, 34, 36.

of the Order should be informed of it. It is true charity to speak in this case, as it would be if we saw our sisters commit a grave fault; to keep silence for fear that speech would be a temptation against charity, would be that very temptation itself.*

22. (Danger of detraction). However, I must warn you seriously not to talk to each other about such things, lest the devil deceive you. He would gain greatly by your doing so, because it would lead to the habit of detraction; rather, as I said, state the matter to those whose duty it is to remedy it. Thank God, our custom here of keeping almost perpetual silence gives little opportunity for such conversation, still, it is well to stand ever on our guard.

---

* "It is terrible to think what harm a Prioress can do! For although the Sisters witness things which scandalise them (of which there are plenty here!), yet they think it would be sinning against obedience to see any harm in them" (Letter to Father Gratian, written at Malagon, at the beginning of December, 1579).

THE SECOND MANSIONS

1

War

Treats of the great importance of perseverance in order to enter the last mansions, and of the fierce war the devil wages against us. How essential it is to take the right path from the very commencement of our journey. A method of action which has proved very efficacious.

1. (Souls in the second chapter). Now let us consider which are the souls that enter the second mansions, and what they do there. I do not wish to enlarge on this subject, having already treated it very fully elsewhere,* for I could not avoid repeating myself, as my memory is very bad. If I could state my ideas in another form they would not weary you, for we never tire of reading books on this subject, numerous as they are.

2. (Their state). In this part of the castle are found souls which have begun to practise prayer; they realize the importance of their not remaining in the first mansions, yet often lack

---

* *Life,* ch. xiii. 1 *sqq. Way of Perf.* ch. xx.–xxix.

determination to quit their present condition by avoiding occasions of sin, which is a very perilous state to be in.

3. (Their sufferings). However, it is a great grace that they should sometimes make good their escape from the vipers and poisonous creatures around them and should understand the need of avoiding them. In some way these souls suffer a great deal more than those in the first mansions, although not in such danger, as they begin to understand their peril and there are great hopes of their entering farther into the castle. I say that they suffer a great deal more, for those in an earlier stage are like deaf-mutes and are not so distressed at being unable to speak, while the others, who can hear but cannot talk, find it much harder. At the same time, it is better not to be deaf, and a decided advantage to hear what is said to us.

4. (They cannot get rid of their imperfections). These souls hear Our Lord calling them, for as they approach nearer to where His Majesty dwells He proves a loving Neighbour, though they may still be engaged in the amusements and business, the pleasures and vanities of this world. While in this state we continually fall into sin and rise again, for the creatures amongst whom we dwell are so venomous, so vicious, and so dangerous, that it is almost impossible to avoid being tripped up by them. Yet such are the pity and compassion of this Lord of ours, so desirous is He that we should seek Him and enjoy His company, that in one way or another He never ceases calling us to Him. So sweet is His voice, that the poor soul is disconsolate at being unable to follow His bidding at once, and therefore, as I said, suffers more than if it could not hear Him.

5. (How God calls these souls). I do not mean that divine com-

munications and inspirations received in this mansion are the same as those I shall describe later on; God here speaks to souls through words uttered by pious people, by sermons or good books, and in many other such ways. Sometimes He calls souls by means of sickness or troubles, or by some truth He teaches them during prayer, for tepid as they may be in seeking Him, yet God holds them very dear.

6. (Perseverance is essential). Do not think lightly, Sisters, of this first grace, nor be downcast if you have not responded immediately to Our Lord's voice, for His Majesty is willing to wait for us many a day and even many a year, especially when He sees perseverance and good desires in our hearts. Perseverance is the first essential; with this we are sure to profit greatly. However, the devils now fiercely assault the soul in a thousand different ways: it suffers even more than ever, because formerly it was mute and deaf, or at least could hear very little, and offered but feeble resistance, like one who has almost lost all hope of victory.

7. (Temptations of the devil). Here, however, the understanding being more vigilant and the powers more on the alert, we cannot avoid hearing the fighting and cannonading around us. For now the devils set on us the reptiles, that is to say, thoughts about the world and its joys which they picture as unending; they remind us of the high esteem men held us in, of our friends and relations; they tell us how the penances which souls in this mansion always begin to wish to perform would injure our health: in fine, the evil spirits place a thousand impediments in the way.

8. (Delusion of earthly joys). O Jesus! What turmoil the devils cause in the poor soul! How unhappy it feels, not knowing

whether to go forward or to return to the first mansion! On the other hand, reason shows it the delusion of overrating worldly things, while faith teaches what alone can satisfy its cravings. Memory reminds the soul how all earthly joys end, recalling the death of those who lived at ease; how some died suddenly and were soon forgotten, how others, once so prosperous, are now buried beneath the ground and men pass by the graves where they lie, the prey of worms,* while the mind recalls many other such incidents.

9. (God alone to be loved). The will inclines to love Our Lord and longs to make some return to Him Who is so amiable, and Who has given so many proofs of His love, especially by His constant presence with the soul, which this faithful Lover never quits, ever accompanying it and giving it life and being. The understanding aids by showing that however many years life might last, no one could ever wish for a better friend than God; that the world is full of falsehood, and that the worldly pleasures pictured by the devil to the mind were but troubles and cares and annoyances in disguise.

10. (Reasons for continuing the journey). Reason convinces the soul that as outside its interior castle are found neither peace nor security, it should cease to seek another home abroad, its own being full of riches that it can enjoy at will. Besides, it is not every one who, like itself, possesses all he needs within

---

* "How many, thinking to live long, have been deceived and unexpectedly have been snatched away! How often hast thou heard that such a one was slain by the sword; another drowned; another, falling from on high, broke his neck; this man died at the table; that other came to his death while he was at play. . . . Thus death is the end of all; and man's life passeth suddenly like a shadow" (*Imitation*, bk. 1. ch. xxiii. 7). The edition of the *Imitation* known to St. Teresa under the title of *Contemptus Mundi* was translated by Luis de Granada, printed at Seville in 1536, at Lisbon in 1542, and at Alcalá in 1548. See *Life*, ch. xxxix. 21, note.

his own dwelling, and above all, such a Host, Who will give it all it can desire, unless, like the prodigal son, it choose to go astray and feed with the swine.* Surely these arguments are strong enough to defeat the devil's wiles! But, O my God, how the force of worldly habits, and the example of others who practise them, ruin everything! Our faith is so dead that we trust less to its teaching than to what is visible, though, indeed, we see that worldly lives bring nothing but unhappiness. All this results from those venomous thoughts I described, which, unless we are very careful, will deform the soul as the sting of a viper poisons and swells the body.

11. (Warfare of the devil). When this happens, great care is evidently needed to cure it, and only God's signal mercy prevents its resulting in death. Indeed, the soul passes through severe trials at this time, especially when the devil perceives from a person's character and behaviour that she is likely to make very great progress, for then all hell will league together to force her to turn back. O my Lord! what need there is here that, by Thy mercy, Thou shouldst prevent the soul from being deluded into forsaking the good begun! Enlighten it to see that its welfare consists in perseverance in the right way, and in withdrawing from bad company.

12. (Importance of choice of friends). It is of the utmost importance for the beginner to associate with those who lead a spiritual life,† and not only with those in the same mansion as herself, but with others who have travelled farther into the

---

* St. Luke xv. 16: "Et cupiebat implere ventrem suum de siliquis quas porci manducabant."

† *Life,* ch. vii. 33–37; ch. xvi. 12; ch. xxx. 6. *Way of Perf.* ch. vi. 1; vii. 4.

castle, who will aid her greatly and draw her to join them. The soul should firmly resolve never to submit to defeat, for if the devil sees it staunchly determined to lose life and comfort and all that he can offer, rather than return to the first mansion, he will the sooner leave it alone.

13. (Valour required). Let the Christian be valiant; let him not be like those who lay down to drink from the brook when they went to battle (I do not remember when).* Let him resolve to go forth to combat with the host of demons, and be convinced that there is no better weapon than the cross. I have already said,† yet it is of such importance that I repeat it here: let no one think on starting of the reward to be reaped: this would be a very ignoble way of commencing such a large and stately building. If built on sand it would soon fall down.‡ Souls who acted thus would continually suffer from discouragement and temptations, for in these mansions no manna rains;§ farther on, the soul is pleased with all that comes, because it desires nothing but what God wills.

14. (Presumption of expecting spiritual consolations at first). What a farce it is! Here are we, with a thousand obstacles, drawbacks, and imperfections within ourselves, our virtues so newly born that they have scarcely the strength to act (and God grant that they exist at all!), yet we are not ashamed to

---

* With Gideon. Jud. vii. 5: "Qui lingua lambuerint aquas, sicut solent canes lambere, separabis eos seorsum."

† *Life*, ch. xi. 16.

‡ St. Matt. vii. 26, 27: "Qui ædificavit domum suam super arenam . . . et fuit ruina illius magna."

§ Ps. lxxvii. 24: "Pluit illis manna ad manducandum." *Way of Perf.* ch. x. 4.

expect sweetness in prayer and to complain of feeling dry-ness.[*]

15. (In the Cross is strength). Do not act thus, sisters; embrace the cross your Spouse bore on His shoulders; know that your motto should be: "Most happy she who suffers most if it be for Christ!"[†] All else should be looked upon as secondary: if our Lord give it you, render Him grateful thanks. You may imagine you would be resolute in enduring external trials if God gave you interior consolations: His Majesty knows best what is good for us; it is not for us to advise Him how to treat us, for He has the right to tell us that we know not what we ask.[‡] Remember, it is of the greatest importance—the sole aim of one beginning to practise prayer should be to endure trials, and to resolve and strive to the utmost of her power to conform her own will to the will of God.[§] Be certain that in this consists all the greatest perfection to be attained in the spiritual life, as I will explain later. She who practises this most perfectly will receive from God the highest reward and is the farthest advanced on the right road. Do not imagine that we have need of a cabalistic formula or any other occult or mysterious thing to attain it—our whole welfare consists in doing the will of God. If we start with the false principle of wishing God to follow our will and to lead us in the way we think best, upon what firm foundation can this spiritual edifice rest?

---

[*] *Life*, ch. xii. 5.

[†] *Way of Perf.* ch. xvii. 6, ch. xxiii. 1.

[‡] St. Matt. xx. 22: "Nescitis quid petatis."

[§] *Way of Perf.* ch. xvi. 2. *Found.* ch. v. 2, 3. *Life*, ch. iv. 11, ch. xi. 20.

16. (Our falls should raise us higher). Let us endeavour to do our best: beware of the poisonous reptiles—that is to say, the bad thoughts and aridities which are often permitted by God to assail and torment us so that we cannot repel them. Indeed, perchance we feel their sting! He allows this to teach us to be more on our guard in the future and to see whether we grieve much at offending Him. Therefore if you occasionally lapse into sin, do not lose heart and cease trying to advance, for God will draw good even out of our falls, like the merchant who sells theriac, who first takes poison, then the theriac, to prove the power of his elixir.* This combat would suffice to teach us to amend our habits if we realised our failings in no other way, and would show us the injury we receive from a life of dissipation. Can any evil be greater than that we find at home? What peace can we hope to find elsewhere, if we have none within us? What friends or kindred can be so close and intimate as the powers of our soul, which, whether we will or no, must ever bear us company? These seem to wage war on us as if they knew the harm our vices had wrought them. "Peace, peace be unto you," my sisters, as our Lord said, and many a time proclaimed to His Apostles.†
Believe me, if we neither possess nor strive to obtain this peace at home, we shall never find it abroad.

17. (Confidence and perseverance). By the Blood which our Lord shed for us, I implore those who have not yet begun to enter into themselves, to stop this warfare: I beg those already

---

* A drug greatly in vogue until recent times. It was composed of all the essences supposed to contain life-giving and life-preserving qualities of animals and plants.

† St. Luke xxiv. 36. St. John xx. 19.

started in the right path, not to let the combat turn them back from it. Let them reflect that a relapse is worse than a fall, and see what ruin it would bring. They should confide in God's mercy, trusting nothing in themselves; then they will see how His Majesty will lead them from one mansion to another, and will set them in a place where these wild beasts can no more touch or annoy them, but will be entirely at their mercy and merely objects of ridicule. Then, even in this life, they will enjoy a far greater happiness than they are able even to desire.

18. (Recollection). As I said at the beginning of this work, I have explained elsewhere* how you should behave when the devil thus disturbs you. I also told you that the habit of recollection is not to be gained by force of arms, but with calmness, which will enable you to practise it for a longer space of time.† I will say no more now, except that I think it very helpful for those of you who are beginners to consult persons experienced in such matters, lest you imagine that you are injuring yourselves by leaving your prayer to perform any necessary duties. This is not the case; our Lord will direct such things to our profit, although we may have no one to counsel us.‡ The only remedy for having given up a habit of recollection is to recommence it, otherwise the soul will continue to lose it more and more every day, and God grant it may realise its danger.

19. (Why we must practise prayer). You may think, that if it is so

---

* *Life,* ch. xix. 8. *Way of Perf.* ch. xxiii. 3.

† *Way of Perf.* ch. xix. 3.

‡ *Way of Perf.* ch. xxiii. 3.

very injurious to desist, it would have been better never to have begun, and to have remained outside the castle. But, as I began by saying, and as God Himself declares: "He that loves danger shall perish by it,"[*] and the door by which we must enter this castle is prayer. Remember, we *must* get to heaven, and it would be madness to think we could do so without sometimes retiring into our souls so as to know ourselves, or thinking of our failings and of what we owe to God, or frequently imploring His mercy. Our Lord also says, "No man cometh to the Father but by Me"[†] (I am not sure whether this quotation is correct, but I think so), and, "He that seeth Me seeth the Father also."[‡]

20. (Meditation kindles love). If we never look up at Him and reflect on what we owe Him for having died for us, I do not understand how we can know Him, or perform good deeds in His service. What value is there in faith without works? And what are they worth if they are not united to the merits of Jesus Christ, our only Good? What would incite us to love our Lord unless we thought of Him? May He give us grace to understand how much we cost Him; that "the servant is not above his lord"[§]; that we must toil for Him if we would enjoy His glory; and that prayer is a necessity to prevent us from constantly falling into temptation.[¶]

---

[*] Ecclus. iii. 27: "Qui amat periculum in illo peribit."

[†] St. John xiv. 6: "Nemo venit ad Patrem nisi per Me."

[‡] St. John xiv. 9: "Qui videt Me videt et Patrem."

[§] St. Matt. x. 24: "Nec servus super dominum suum."

[¶] St. Matt. xxvi. 41: "Orate ut non intretis in tentationem."

THE THIRD MANSIONS

1

Fear of God

Treats of the insecurity of life in this exile, however high we may be raised, and of how we must always walk in fear. Contains some good points.

1. (Souls in the Third Mansions). As for those who, by the mercy of God, have vanquished in these combats and persevered until they reached the third mansions, what can we say to them but "Blessed is the man that feareth the Lord"?* It is no small favour from God that I should be able to translate this verse into Spanish so as to explain its meaning, considering how dense I usually am in such matters. We may well call these souls blessed, for, as far as we can tell, unless they turn back on their course they are on the safe road to salvation. Now, my sisters, you see how important it is for them to conquer in their former struggles, for I am convinced that our Lord will henceforth never cease to keep them in security of conscience, which is no small boon.

---

* Ps. cxi: "Beatus vir qui timet Dominum."

2. (Insecurity of this life). I am wrong in saying "security," for there is no security in this life; understand that in such cases I always imply: "If they do not cease to continue as they have begun." What misery to live in this world! We are like men whose enemies are at the door, who must not lay aside their arms, even while sleeping or eating, and are always in dread lest the foe should enter the fortress by some breach in the walls. O my Lord and my All! How canst Thou wish us to prize such a wretched existence? We could not desist from longing and begging Thee to take us from it, were it not for the hope of losing it for Thy sake or devoting it entirely to Thy service—and above all, because we know it is Thy will that we should live. Since this is so, "Let us die with Thee!"* as St. Thomas said, for to be away from Thee is but to die again and again, haunted as we are by the dread risk of losing Thee for ever!

3. (Our danger of falling from grace). This is why I say, daughters, that we ought to ask our Lord as our boon to grant us one day to dwell in safety with the Saints, for with such fears, what pleasure can she enjoy whose only pleasure is to please God? Remember, many Saints have felt this as we do, and were even far more fervent, yet fell into grave sin, and we cannot be sure that God would stretch forth His hand to raise us from sin again to do such penance as they performed. This applies to extraordinary grace.† Truly, my daughters, I feel such terror as I tell you this, that I know not how to

---

* St. John xi. 16; "Eamus et nos ut moriamur cum eo." [Lazarus!]

† These last words, in the margin, but in the handwriting of the Saint, were scored through by one of the censors, but Fr. Luis de Leon wrote underneath (as he did in other cases), "Nothing to be scratched out."

write it, nor even how to go on living, when I reflect upon it as I very often do. Beg of His Majesty, my daughters, to abide within me, for otherwise, what security could I feel, after a life so badly spent as mine has been?

4. (The Saint bewails her past life). Do not grieve at knowing this. I have often seen you troubled when I spoke about it, for you wish that my past had been a very holy one, in which you are right—indeed, I wish the same myself. But what can be done, now that I have wasted it entirely through my own fault? I have no right to complain that God withheld the aid I needed to fulfil your wishes. It is impossible for me to write this without tears and great shame, when I see that I am explaining these matters to those capable of teaching me. What a hard task has obedience laid upon me! God grant that, as I do it for Him, it may be of some service to you; therefore beg Him to pardon me for my miserable presumption.

5. (Our Lady's patronage). His Majesty knows that I have nothing to rely upon but His mercy; as I cannot cancel the past, I have no other remedy but to flee to Him, and to confide in the merits of His Son and of His Virgin Mother, whose habit, unworthy as I am, I wear as you do also. Praise Him, then, my daughters, for making you truly daughters of our Lady, so that you need not blush for my wickedness as you have such a good Mother. Imitate her; think how great she must be and what a blessing it is for you to have her for a patroness, since my sins and evil character have brought no tarnish on the lustre of our holy Order.

6. (Fear necessary even for religious). Still I must give you one warning: be not too confident because you are nuns and the daughters of such a Mother. David was very holy, yet you

know what Solomon became.* Therefore rely not on your enclosure, on your penitential life, nor on your continual exercise of prayer and constant communion with God, nor trust in having left the world, or in the idea that you hold its ways in horror. All this is good, but is not enough, as I have already said, to remove all fear; therefore meditate on this text and often recall it:"Blessed is the man that feareth the Lord."†

7. (St. Teresa's contrition). I do not recollect what I was saying, and have digressed very much: for when I think of myself, my mind cannot soar to higher things, but is like a bird with broken wings; so I will leave this subject for the present.

8. (Characteristics of those in the Third Mansions). To return to what I began to explain about the souls which have entered the third mansions. God has shown them no small favour, but a very great one, in enabling them to pass through the first difficulties. Thanks to His mercy I believe there are many such people in the world: they are very desirous not to offend His Majesty even by venial sins, they love penance and spend hours in meditation, they employ their time well, exercise themselves in works of charity to their neighbours, are well-ordered in their conversation and dress, and those who own a household govern it well. This is certainly to be desired, and there appears no reason to forbid their entrance to the last mansions; nor will our Lord deny it them if they desire it, for this is the right disposition for receiving all His favours.

9. (The rich young man in the Gospel). O Jesus! can any one

---

* St. Teresa wrote "Solomon"; Fr. Gratian corrected "Absalom," and Fr. Luis de Leon restored the original text.

† Ps. cxi. 1.

declare that they do not desire this great blessing, especially after they have passed through the chief difficulties? No; no one can! We all say we desire it, but there is need of more than that for the Lord to possess entire dominion over the soul. It is not enough to say so, any more than it was enough for the young man when our Lord told him what he must do if he desired to be perfect.* Since I began to speak of these dwelling-rooms I have him constantly before my mind, for we are exactly like him; this very frequently produces the great dryness we feel in prayer, though sometimes it proceeds from other causes as well. I am not speaking of certain interior sufferings, which give intolerable pain to many devout souls through no fault of their own; from these trials, however, our Lord always delivers them with much profit to themselves. I also except people who suffer from melancholy and other infirmities. But in these cases, as in all others, we must leave aside the judgments of God.

10. (Reason of aridities in prayer). I hold that these effects usually result from the first cause I mentioned; such souls know that nothing would induce them to commit a sin (many of them would not even commit a venial sin advertently), and that they employ their life and riches well. They cannot, therefore, patiently endure to be excluded from the presence of our King, Whose vassals they consider themselves, as indeed they are. An earthly king may have many subjects, yet all do not enter his court. Enter then, enter, my daughters, into your interior; pass beyond the thought of your own petty works, which are no more, nor even as much, as Christians

---

* St. Matt. xix. 21.

are bound to perform: let it suffice that you are God's servants, do not pursue so much as to catch nothing.* Think of the saints, who have entered the Divine Presence, and you will see the difference between them and ourselves.

11. (Humility). Do not ask for what you do not deserve, nor should we ever think, however much we may have done for God, that we merit the reward of the saints, for we have offended Him. Oh, humility, humility! I know not why, but I am always tempted to think that persons who complain so much of aridities must be a little wanting in this virtue. However, I am not speaking of severe interior sufferings, which are far worse than a want of devotion.

12. (Tepidity). Let us try ourselves, my sisters, or let our Lord try us; He knows well how to do so (although we often pretend to misunderstand Him). We will now speak of these well-ordered souls. Let us consider what they do for God and we shall see at once what little right we have to murmur against His Majesty. If we turn our backs on Him and go away sorrowfully like the youth in the Gospel† when He tells us what to do to be perfect, what can God do? for He must proportion the reward to our love for Him. This love, my daughters, must not be the fabric of our imagination; we must prove it by our works. Yet do not suppose that our Lord has need of any works of ours; He only expects us to manifest our goodwill.‡

13. (We must give all to God). It seems to us we have done ev-

---

* Proverbially, like "having too many irons in the fire."

† St. Mark x. 22. *Way of Perf.* ch. xvii. 5.

‡ *Rel.* ix. 15.

erything, by taking the religious habit of our own will, and renouncing worldly things and all our possessions for God (although they may have been but the nets of St. Peter,* yet they seemed much to us, for they were our all). This is an excellent disposition: if we continue in it and do not return, even in desire, to the company of the reptiles of the first rooms, doubtless, by persevering in this poverty and detachment of soul, we shall obtain all for which we strive. But, mark this,—it must be on one condition—that we "hold ourselves for unprofitable servants,"† as we are told either by St. Paul or by Christ, and that we do not consider that our Lord is bound to grant us any favours, but that, as we have received more from Him, we are the deeper in His debt.

14. (Our debt). How little is all we can do for so generous a God, Who died for us, Who created us, Who gives us being, that we should not think ourselves happy to be able to acquit ourselves of part of the debt we owe Him for having served us, without asking Him for fresh mercies and favours? I am loth to use this expression, yet so it is, for He did nothing else during the whole time He lived in this world but serve us.

15. (Consolations and aridities). Think well, my daughters, over some of the points I have treated, although confusedly, for I do not know how to explain them better. Our Lord will make you understand them, that you may reap humility from your dryness, instead of the disquietude the devil strives to cause by it. I believe that where true humility exists, although God should never bestow consolations, yet He gives a peace

---

* St. Matt. iv. 20: "Relictis retibus secuti sunt eum."

† St. Luke xvii. 10: "Servi inutiles sumus, quod debuimus facere fecimus."

and resignation which make the soul happier than are others with sensible devotion. These consolations, as you have read, are often given by the Divine Majesty to the weakest souls who, I suppose, would not exchange them for the fortitude of Christians serving God in aridities: we love consolations better than the cross! Do Thou, O Lord, Who knowest all truth, so prove us that we may know ourselves.

2

Aridity in Prayer

Continues the same subject and speaks of aridities in prayer and their results: of the necessity of trying ourselves and how our Lord proves those who are in these mansions.

1. (Imperfections of dwellers in the first three mansions). I HAVE known some, in fact, I may say numerous souls, who have reached this state, and for many years lived, apparently, a regular and well-ordered life, both of body and mind. It would seem that they must have gained the mastery over this world, or at least be extremely detached from it, yet if His Majesty sends very moderate trials they become so disturbed and disheartened as not only to astonish but to make me anxious about them. Advice is useless; having practised virtue for so long they think themselves capable of teaching it, and believe that they have abundant reason to feel miserable.

2. (Our trials show us our weakness). The only way to help them is to compassionate their troubles; indeed, one cannot but feel sorry at seeing people in such an unhappy state. They must not be argued with, for they are convinced they suffer

only for God's sake, and cannot be made to understand they are acting imperfectly, which is a further error in persons so far advanced. No wonder that they should feel these trials for a time, but I think they ought speedily to overcome their concern about such matters. God, wishing His elect to realise their own misery, often temporarily withdraws His favours: no more is needed to prove to us in a very short time what we really are.*

3. (Humility learnt by our faults). Souls soon learn in this way; they perceive their faults very clearly, and sometimes the discovery of how quickly they are overcome by but slight earthly trials is more painful than the subtraction of God's sensible favours. I consider that God thus shows them great mercy, for though their behaviour may be faulty, yet they gain greatly in humility. Not so with the people of whom I first spoke; they believe their conduct is saintly, and wish others to agree with them. I will give you some examples which will help us to understand and to try ourselves, without waiting for God to try us, since it would be far better to have prepared and examined ourselves beforehand.

4. (Love of money). A rich man, without son or heir, loses part of his property,† but still has more than enough to keep himself and his household. If this misfortune grieves and disquiets him as though he were left to beg his bread, how can our Lord ask him to give up all things for His sake? This man will tell you he regrets losing his money because he wished to bestow it on the poor.

---

* *Way of Perf.* ch. xxxviii. 7.

† *Way of Perf.* ch. xxxviii, 10. *Concep.* ch. ii. 11, 12. *Life,* ch. xi. 3.

5. (Liberty of spirit). I believe His Majesty would prefer me to conform to His will, and the peace of soul while attending to my interests, to such charity as this. If this person cannot resign himself because God has not raised him so high in virtue, well and good: let him know that he is wanting in liberty of spirit; let him beg our Lord to grant it him, and be rightly disposed to receive it. Another person has more than sufficient means to live on, when an opportunity occurs for acquiring more property: if it is offered him, by all means let him accept it; but if he must go out of his way to obtain it and then continues working to gain more and more— however good his intention may be (and it must be good, for I am speaking of people who lead prayerful and good lives), he cannot possibly enter the mansions near the King.

6. (On bearing contempt). Something of the same sort happens if such people meet with contempt or want of due respect. God often gives them grace to bear it well, as He loves to see virtue upheld in public, and will not have it condemned in those who practise it, or else because these persons have served Him faithfully, and He, our supreme Good, is exceedingly good to us all; nevertheless, these persons are disturbed, and cannot overcome or get rid of the feeling for some time.[*] Alas! have they not long meditated on the pains our Lord endured and how well it is for us to suffer, and have even longed to do so? They wish every one were as virtuous as they are; and God grant they do not consider other people to blame for their troubles and attribute merit to themselves!

7. (Detachment proved by trials). You may think, my daughters,

---

[*] *Way of Perf.* ch. xxxviii. 12.

that I have wandered from the subject, for all this does not concern you: nothing of the sort occurs to us here, where we neither own nor wish for any property, nor endeavour to gain it, and no one does us any wrong. The instances I have mentioned do not coincide exactly, yet conclusions applicable to us may be drawn from them, which it would be neither well nor necessary to mention. These will teach you whether you are really detached from all you have left; trifling occasions often occur, although perhaps not quite of the same kind, by which you can prove to yourselves whether you have obtained the mastery over your passions.

8. (Virtue and humility are the essentials). Believe me, the question is not whether we wear the religious habit or not, but whether we strive to practise the virtues and to submit our will in all things to the will of God. The object of our life must be to do what He requires of us: let us not ask that *our* will may be done, but *His*. If we have not yet attained to this, let us be humble, as I said above. Humility is the ointment for our wounds; if we have it, although perhaps He may defer His coming for a time, God, Who is our Physician, will come and heal us.

9. (Perfection requires detachment). The penances performed by the persons I spoke of are as well regulated as their life, which they value very highly because they wish to serve our Lord with it—in which there is nothing to blame—so they are very discreet in their mortifications lest they should injure their health. Never fear they will kill themselves: they are far too sensible! Their love is not strong enough to overcome their reason; I wish it were—that they might not be content

to creep on their way to God: a pace that will never bring them to their journey's end!

10. (We should try to make rapid progress). We seem to ourselves to be making progress, yet we become weary, for, believe me, we are walking through a mist; it will be fortunate if we do not lose ourselves. Do you think, my daughters, if we could travel from one country to another in eight days, that it would be well to spend a year on the journey, through wind, snow, and inundations and over bad roads?* Would it not be better to get it over at once, for it is full of dangers and serpents? Oh, how many striking instances could I give you of this! God grant that I have passed beyond this state myself: often I think that I have not.

11. (Leave our cares in God's hands). All things obstruct us while prudence rules our actions; we are afraid of everything and therefore fear to make progress—as if we could reach the inner chambers while others made the journey for us! As this is impossible, sisters, for the love of God let us exert ourselves, and leave our reason and our fears in His hands, paying no attention to the weaknesses of nature which might retard us. Let our Superiors, to whom the charge belongs, look after our bodies; let our only care be to hasten to our Lord's presence—for though there are few or no indulgences to be obtained here, yet regard for health might mislead us and it would be none the better for our care, as I know well.

12. (Humility more necessary than corporal penances). I know,

---

* St. Teresa very probably had in her mind her journey to make a foundation at Seville, when the boat, which was crossing the Guadalquivir, narrowly escaped being carried down the river by the current. *Found.* ch. xxiv. 6.

too, that our bodies are not the chief factors in the work we have before us; they are accessory: extreme humility is the principal point. It is the want of this, I believe, that stops people's progress. It may seem that we have made but little way: we should believe that is the case, and that our sisters are advancing much more rapidly than we are. Not only should we wish others to consider us the worst of all; we should endeavour to make them think so. If we act in this manner, our soul will do well; otherwise we shall make no progress and shall always remain the prey to a thousand troubles and miseries. The way will be difficult and wearisome without self-renunciation, weighed down as we are by the burden and frailties of human nature, which are no longer felt in the more interior mansions.

13. (Consolations rarely received until the fourth mansions). In these third mansions the Lord never fails to repay our services, both as a just and even as a merciful God, Who always bestows on us far more than we deserve, giving us greater happiness than could be obtained from any earthly pleasures and amusements. I think He grants few consolations here, except, perhaps, occasionally to entice us to prepare ourselves to enter the last mansions by showing us their contents. There may *appear* to you to be no difference except in name between sensible devotion and consolations, and you may ask why I distinguish them. I think there *is* a very great difference, but I may be mistaken.

14. (Advantages of hearing them). This will be best explained while writing of the fourth mansion, which comes next, when I must speak of the consolations received there from our Lord. The subject may appear futile, yet may prove useful

by urging souls who know what each mansion contains to strive to enter the best. It will solace those whom God has advanced so far; others, who thought they had reached the summit, will be abashed, yet if they are humble they will be led to thank God.

15. (Perfection consists in love, not in reward). Those who do not receive these consolations may feel a despondency that is uncalled for, since perfection does not consist in consolation but in greater love; our reward will be in proportion to this, and to the justice and sincerity of our actions. Perhaps you wonder, then, why I treat of these interior favours and their nature. I do not know; ask him who bade me write this. I must obey Superiors, not argue with them, which I have no right to do.

16. (St. Teresa's joy at seeing other souls favoured). I assure you that when I had neither received these favours,* nor understood them by experience, or ever expected to (and rightly so, for I should have felt reassured if I had known or even conjectured that I was pleasing to God in any way), yet when I read of the mercies and consolations that our Lord grants to His servants, I was delighted and praised Him fervently. If such a wretch as myself acted thus, how much more would the humble and good glorify Him! I think it is worth while to explain these subjects and show what consolations and delights we lose through our own fault, if only for the sake of moving a single soul to praise God once.

17. (These graces should be striven for). When these joys are from God they come laden with love and strength, which aid

---

* *Life,* ch. xii. 2. *Rel.* vii. 3.

the soul on its way and increase its good works and virtues. Do not imagine that it is unimportant whether you try to obtain these graces or no; if you are not to blame, the Lord is just: what He refuses in one way, His Majesty will give you in another, as He knows how; His secret ways are very mysterious, and doubtless He will do what is best for you.

18. (Obedience and direction). Souls who by God's mercy are brought so far (which, as I said, is no small mercy, for they are likely to ascend still higher) will be greatly benefited by practising prompt obedience. Even if they are not in the religious state, it would be well if they, like certain other people, were to take a director,* so as never to follow their own will, which is the cause of most of our ills. They should not choose one of their own turn of mind† (as the saying goes), who is over-prudent in his actions, but should select one thoroughly detached from worldly things; it is very helpful to consult a person who has learnt and can teach this. It is encouraging to see that trials which seemed to us impossible to submit to are possible to others, and that they bear them sweetly. Their flight makes us try to soar, like nestlings taught by the elder birds, who, though they cannot fly far at first, little by little imitate their parents: I know the great benefit of this. However determined such persons may be not to offend our Lord, they must not expose themselves to temptation: they are still near the first mansions to which they might easily return. Their strength is not yet established on a solid foundation like that of souls exercised in sufferings, who know how little cause

---

* *Life,* ch. xiii. 29.

† *Rel,* vii. 18.

there is to fear the tempests of this world and care nothing for its pleasures: beginners might succumb before any severe trial. Some great persecution, such as the devil knows how to raise to injure us, might make beginners turn back; while zealously trying to withdraw others from sin, they might succumb to the attacks made upon them.

19. (Misguided zeal for others). Let us look at our own faults, and not at other people's. People who are extremely correct themselves are often shocked at everything they see;* however, we might often learn a great deal that is essential from the very persons whom we censure. Our exterior comportment and manners may be better—this is well enough, but not of the first importance. We ought not to insist on every one following in our footsteps, nor to take upon ourselves to give instructions in spirituality when, perhaps, we do not even know what it is. Zeal for the good of souls, though given us by God, may often lead us astray, sisters; it is best to keep our rule, which bids us ever to live in silence and in hope.† Our Lord will care for the souls belonging to Him; and if we beg His Majesty to do so, by His grace we shall be able to aid them greatly. May He be for ever blessed!

---

* *Way of Perf.* ch. vii. 6. *Castle,* M. i. ch. ii. 20, 21.

† Isa. xxx. 15: "In silentio et in spe erit fortitudo vestra." *Rule,* § 13.

THE FOURTH MANSIONS

1

Sweetness in Prayer

How sweetness and tenderness in prayer differ from consolations. Explains how advantageous it was (for St. Teresa) to understand that the imagination and the understanding are not the same thing. This chapter is useful for those whose thoughts wander much during prayer.

1. (Graces received in this mansion). Now that I commence writing about the fourth mansions, it is requisite, as I said,* to commend myself to the Holy Ghost and to beg Him henceforth to speak for me, that I may be enabled to treat these matters intelligibly. Henceforth they begin to be supernatural and it will be most difficult to speak clearly about them, unless His Majesty undertakes it for me, as He did when I explained the subject (as far as I understood it) somewhat about fourteen years ago.† I believe I now possess more light about the favours God grants some souls, but that is different from

---

* First Mansions, ch. i. 1.

† *Life,* ch. xii. 11.

being able to elucidate them.* May His Majesty enable me to do so if it would be useful, but not otherwise.

2. (Mystic favours). As these mansions are nearer the King's dwelling they are very beautiful, and so subtle are the things seen and heard in them, that, as those tell us who have tried to do so, the mind cannot give a lucid idea of them to those inexperienced in the matter. People who have enjoyed these favours, especially if it was to any great extent, will easily comprehend me.

3. (Temptations bring humility and merit). Apparently a person must have dwelt for a long time in the former mansions before entering these; although in ordinary cases the soul must have been in the last one spoken of, yet, as you must often have heard, there is no fixed rule, for God gives when, how, and to whom He wills†—the goods are His own, and His choice wrongs no one.‡ The poisonous reptiles rarely come into these rooms, and, if they enter, do more good than harm. I think it is far better for them to get in and make war on the soul in this state of prayer; were it not tempted, the devil might sometimes deceive it about divine consolations, thus injuring it far more. Besides, the soul would benefit less, because all occasions of gaining merit would be withdrawn, were it left continually absorbed in God. I am not confident that this absorption is genuine when it always remains in the same state, nor does it appear to me possible for the Holy

---

* *Life,* ch. xvii. 7.

† Philippus a SS. Trinitate, *Summa Theologiæ Mysticæ,* pars iii. tract. i. disc. iii. art. 2. *Life,* ch. xv. 11, ch. xxii. 22, 23. *Way of Perf.* ch. xvi. 4, ch. xli. 2. *Concep.* ch. v. 3.

‡ S. Matt. xx. 15: "Aut non licet mihi quod volo facere?"

Ghost to dwell constantly within us, to the same extent, during our earthly exile.

4. (Sensible devotion and natural joys). I will now describe, as I promised, the difference between sweetness in prayer and spiritual consolations. It appears to me that what we acquire for ourselves in meditation and petitions to our Lord may be termed "sweetness in devotion."* It is natural, although ultimately aided by the grace of God. I must be understood to imply this in all I say, for we can do nothing without Him. This sweetness arises principally from the good work we perform, and appears to result from our labours: well may we feel happy at having thus spent our time. We shall find, on consideration, that many temporal matters give us the same pleasure—such as unexpectedly coming into a large fortune, suddenly meeting with a dearly-loved friend, or succeeding in any important or influential affair which makes a sensation in the world. Again, it would be felt by one who had been told her husband, brother, or son was dead, and who saw him return to her alive. I have seen people weep from such happiness, as I have done myself. I consider both these joys and those we feel in religious matters to be natural ones. Although there is nothing wrong about the former, yet those produced by devotion spring from a more noble source—in short, they begin in ourselves and end in God. Spiritual consolations, on the contrary, arise from God, and our nature feels them and

---

* .*Way of Perf.* ch. xix. 8. *Castle,* M. iv.ch. ii. 4. The first three mansions of the *Interior Castle* correspond with the "first water," or the prayer of Meditation, explained in chapters xi.–xiii. of the *Life;* the fourth mansion, or the prayer of Quiet, to the second water, *Life,* ch. xiv. and xv.; the fifth mansion, or the prayer of Union, with the third water, *Life,* ch. xvi. and xvii.; and the sixth mansion, ecstasy, etc., with the fourth water, *Life,* ch. xviii.–xxi.

rejoices as keenly in them, and indeed far more keenly, than in the others I described.

5. (Sweetness in devotion). O Jesus! how I wish I could elucidate this point! It seems to me that I can perfectly distinguish the difference between the two joys, yet I have not the skill to make myself understood; may God give it me! I remember a verse we say at Prime at the end of the final Psalm; the last words are:"Cum dilatasti cor meum"—"When Thou didst dilate my heart."* To those with much experience, this suffices to show the difference between sweetness in prayer and spiritual consolations; other people will require more explanation. The sensible devotion I mentioned does not dilate the heart, but generally appears to narrow it slightly; although joyful at seeing herself work for God, yet such a person sheds tears of sorrow which seem partly produced by the passions. I know little about the passions of the soul, or I could write of them more clearly and could better define what comes from the sensitive disposition and what is natural, having passed through this state myself, but I am very stupid. Knowledge and learning are a great advantage to every one.

6. (St. Teresa's experience of it). My own experience of this delight and sweetness in meditation was that when I began to weep over the Passion I could not stop until I had a severe headache;† the same thing occurred when I grieved over my sins: this was a great grace from our Lord. I do not intend to inquire now which of these states of prayer is the better, but I wish I knew how to explain the difference between the

---

* Ps. cxviii. 32. *Way of Perf.* ch. xxviii. 11.

† *Life,* ch. iii. 1.

two. In that of which I speak, the tears and good desires are often partly caused by the natural disposition, but although this may be the case, yet, as I said, these feelings terminate in God. Sensible devotion is very desirable if the soul is humble enough to understand that it is not more holy on account of these sentiments, which cannot always with certainty be ascribed to charity, and even then are still the gift of God.

7. (Love of God, and how to foster it). These feelings of devotion are most common with souls in the first three mansions, who are nearly always using their understanding and reason in making meditations. This is good for them, for they have not been given grace for more; they should, however, try occasionally to elicit some acts such as praising God, rejoicing in His goodness and that He is what He is: let them desire that He may be honoured and glorified. They must do this as best they can, for it greatly inflames the will. Let them be very careful, when God gives these sentiments, not to set them aside in order to finish their accustomed meditation. But, having spoken fully on this subject elsewhere,* I will say no more now. I only wish to warn you that to make rapid progress and to reach the mansions we wish to enter, it is not so essential to *think* much as to *love* much: therefore you must practise whatever most excites you to this. Perhaps we do not know what love is, nor does this greatly surprise me. Love does not consist in great sweetness of devotion, but in a more fervent determination to strive to please God in all things, in avoiding, as far as possible, all that would offend Him, and in praying for the increase of the glory and honour

---

* *Life,* ch. xii. 2–4.

of His Son and for the growth of the Catholic Church. These
are the signs of love; do not imagine that it consists in never
thinking of anything but God, and that if your thoughts wander a little all is lost.*

8. (Distractions). I, myself, have sometimes been troubled by this
turmoil of thoughts. I learnt by experience, but little more
than four years ago, that our thoughts, or it is clearer to call it
our imagination, are not the same thing as the understanding.
I questioned a theologian on the subject; he told me it was
the fact, which consoled me not a little. As the understanding
is one of the powers of the soul, it puzzled me to see it so
sluggish at times, while, as a rule, the imagination takes flight
at once, so that God alone can control it by so uniting us
to Himself† that we seem, in a manner, detached from our
bodies. It puzzled me to see that while to all appearance the
powers of the soul were occupied with God and recollected
in Him, the imagination was wandering elsewhere.

9. (They do not destroy divine union). Do Thou, O Lord, take
into account all that we suffer in this way through our ignorance. We err in thinking that we need only know that we
must keep our thoughts fixed on Thee. We do not understand
that we should consult those better instructed than ourselves,
nor are we aware that there is anything for us to learn. We
pass through terrible trials, on account of not understanding
our own nature, and take what is not merely harmless, but
good, for a grave fault. This causes the sufferings felt by many
people, particularly by the unlearned, who practise prayer.

---

* *Found.* ch. v. 2. *Way of Perf.* ch. xxxi. 6, 12. *Life,* ch. xv. 10, ch. xxx. 19.

† *Life,* ch. xv. 9, 10.

They complain of interior trials, become melancholy, lose their health, and even give up prayer altogether for want of recognising that we have within ourselves as it were, an interior world. We cannot stop the revolution of the heavens as they rush with velocity upon their course, neither can we control our imagination. When this wanders we at once imagine that all the powers of the soul follow it; we think everything is lost, and that the time spent in God's presence is wasted. Meanwhile, the soul is perhaps entirely united to Him in the innermost mansions, while the imagination is in the precincts of the castle, struggling with a thousand wild arid venomous creatures and gaining merit by its warfare. Therefore we need not let ourselves be disturbed, nor give up prayer, as the devil is striving to persuade us. As a rule, all our anxieties and troubles come from misunderstanding our own nature.

10. (St. Teresa's physical distractions). Whilst writing this I am thinking of the loud noise in my head which I mentioned in the Introduction, and which has made it almost impossible to obey the command given me to write this. It sounds as if there were a number of rushing waterfalls within my brain, while in other parts, drowned by the sound of the waters, are the voices of birds singing and whistling. This tumult is not in my ears, but in the upper part of my head, where, they say, is placed the superior part of the soul. I have long thought that this must be so because the flight of the spirit seems to take place from this part with great velocity. Please God I may recollect to explain the cause when writing of the latter mansions, this not being the proper place for it. It may be that God has sent this suffering in my head to help me to

understand the matter, for all this tumult in my brain does not interfere with my prayer, nor with my speaking to you, but the great calm and love and desires in my soul remain undisturbed and my mind is clear.

11. (How to treat distractions). How, then, can the superior part of the soul remain undisturbed if it resides in the upper part of the brain? I cannot account for it, but am sure that I am speaking the truth. This noise disturbs my prayer when unaccompanied with ecstasy, but when it is ecstatic I do not feel any pain, however great. I should suffer keenly were I forced to cease praying on account of these infirmities. We should not be distressed by reason of our thoughts, nor allow ourselves to be worried by them: if they come from the devil, he will let us alone if we take no notice of them; and if they are, as often happens, one of the many frailties entailed by Adam's sin, let us be patient and suffer them for the love of God. Likewise, since we must eat and sleep without being able to avoid it, much to our grief, let us acknowledge that we are human, and long to be where no one may despise us.*
Sometimes I recall these words, spoken by the Spouse in the Canticle;† truly never in our lives have we better reason to say them, for I think no earthly scorn or suffering can try us so severely as these struggles within our souls. All uneasiness or conflict can be borne while we have peace in ourselves, as I said; but if, while seeking for rest amidst the thousand trials of

---

* *Way of Perf.* ch. xxxiii. 8. *Life,* ch. xxi. 8. *Rel.* ii. 12.

† According to Fr. Gratian the Saint here refers to Cant. viii. 1: "Et. jam me nemo despiciat."

the world—knowing that God has prepared this rest for us—the obstacle is found in ourselves, the trial must needs prove painful and almost insufferable.

12. (They should be disregarded). Take us, therefore, O Lord, to where these miseries can no longer cause us to be despised, for sometimes it seems as if they mocked our souls. Even in this life God delivers us from them when we reach the last mansion, as by His grace I will show you. Everybody is not so violently distressed and assaulted by these weaknesses as I have been for many years,* on account of my wickedness, so that it seems as if I strove to take vengeance on myself.† Since I suffer so much in this way, perhaps you may do the same, so I shall continue to explain the subject to you in different ways, in order to find some means of making it clear. The thing is inevitable, therefore do not let it disturb or grieve you, but let the mill clack on while we grind our wheat; that is, let us continue to work with our will and intellect.

13. (Self-knowledge necessary). These troubles annoy us more or less according to the state of our health or in different circumstances. The poor soul suffers; although not now to blame, it has sinned at other times, and must be patient. We are so ignorant that what we have read and been told has not sufficed to teach us to disregard wandering thoughts, therefore I shall not be wasting time in instructing and consoling you about these trials. However, this will help you but little until God chooses to enlighten you, and additional measures are needed:

---

* *Way of Perf.* ch. xvii. 2.

† *Way of Perf.* ch. xxxi. 9.

His Majesty wishes us to learn by ordinary means to understand ourselves and to recognise the share taken in these troubles by our wandering imagination, our nature, and the devil's temptations, instead of laying all the blame on our souls.

2

Divine Consolations

*Continues the same subject, explaining by a comparison in what
divine consolations consist: and how we ought to try to prepare
ourselves to receive them, without endeavouring to obtain them.*

1. (Physical results of sensible devotion). GOD help me! how I
have wandered from my subject! I forget what I was speaking
about, for my occupations and ill-health often force me to
cease writing until some more suitable time. The sense will be
very disconnected; as my memory is extremely bad and I have
no time to read over what is written, even what I really understand is expressed very vaguely, at least I fear so. I think I said
that spiritual consolations are occasionally connected with the
passions. These feelings of devotion produce fits of sobbing; I
have even heard that sometimes they cause a compression of
the chest, and uncontrollable exterior motions violent enough
to cause bleeding at the nose and other painful effects.*

---

* "A clear description of an attack of hysteria with the significant remark that she herself had never experienced anything of the kind" (Dr. Goix, quoted by P. Grégoire,
La prétendue hystérie de Sainte Thérèse, Lyon, Vitte, 1895, p. 53).

2. (Effects of divine consolations). I can say nothing about this, never having experienced anything of the kind myself; but there appears some cause for comfort in it, because, as I said, all ends in the desire to please God and to enjoy His presence. What I call divine consolations, or have termed elsewhere the "prayer of quiet," is a very different thing, as those will understand who, by the mercy of God, have experienced them.

3. (The two fountains). To make the matter clearer, let us imagine we see two fountains with basins which fill with water. I can find no simile more appropriate than water by which to explain spiritual things, as I am very ignorant and have poor wits to help me.* Besides, I love this element so much that I have studied it more attentively than other things. God, Who is so great, so wise, has doubtless hidden secrets in all things He created, which we should greatly benefit by knowing, as those say who understand such matters. Indeed, I believe that in each smallest creature He has made, though it be but a tiny ant, are more wonders than can be comprehended. These two basins are filled in different ways; the one with water from a distance flowing into it through many pipes and waterworks, while the other basin is built near the source of the spring itself and fills quite noiselessly. If the fountain is plentiful, like the one we speak of, after the basin is full the water overflows in a great stream, which flows continually. No machinery is needed here, nor does the water run through aqueducts.

4. (They symbolise two kinds of prayer). Such is the difference

---

* *Way of Perf.* ch. xix. 5; also St. John of the Cross, *Ascent of Mount Carmel,* bk. ii. ch. xiv. 2, and xxi. 3.

between the two kinds of prayer. The water running through the aqueducts resembles sensible devotion, which is obtained by meditation. We gain it by our thoughts, by meditating on created things, and by the labour of our minds; in short, it is the result of our endeavours, and so makes the commotion I spoke of, while profiting the soul.* The other fountain, like divine consolations, receives the water from the source itself, which signifies God; as usual, when His Majesty wills to bestow on us any supernatural favours, we experience the greatest peace, calm, and sweetness in the inmost depths of our being; I know neither where, nor how.

5. (Divine consolations shared by body and soul). This joy is not, like earthly happiness, at once felt by the heart; after gradually filling it to the brim, the delight overflows throughout all the mansions and faculties, until at last it reaches the body. Therefore, I say it arises from God and ends in ourselves, for whoever experiences it will find that the whole physical part of our nature shares in this delight and sweetness. While writing this I have been thinking that the verse "Dilatasti cor meum," "Thou hast dilated my heart,"† declares that the heart is dilated. This joy does not appear to me to originate in the heart, but in some more interior part and, as it were, in the depths of our being. I think this must be the centre of the soul, as I have since learnt and will explain later on. I discover secrets within us which often fill me with astonishment: how many more must there be unknown to me! O my Lord and my God! how stupendous is Thy grandeur! We are like so

---

* *Life,* ch. x. 2.

† Ps. cxviii. 32. *Life,* ch. xvii. 14.

many foolish peasant lads: we think we know something of Thee, yet it must be comparatively nothing, for there are profound secrets even in ourselves of which we know naught. I say "comparatively nothing" in proportion with all the secrets hidden within Thee, yet how great are Thy mysteries that we are acquainted with and can learn even by the study of such of Thy works as we see!*

6. (The incense within the soul). To return to the verse I quoted, which may help to explain the dilation begun by the celestial waters in the depths of our being. They appear to dilate and enlarge us internally, and benefit us in an inexplicable manner, nor does even the soul itself understand what it receives. It is conscious of what may be described as a certain fragrance, as if within its inmost depths were a brazier sprinkled with sweet perfumes. Although the spirit neither sees the flame nor knows where it is, yet it is penetrated by the warmth, and scented fumes, which are even sometimes perceived by the body. Understand me, the soul does not feel any real heat or scent, but something far more subtle, which I use this metaphor to explain. Let those who have never experienced it believe that it really occurs to others: the soul is conscious of it and feels it more distinctly than can be expressed. It is not a thing we can fancy or gain by anything we can do; clearly it does not arise from the base coin of human nature, but from the most pure gold of Divine Wisdom. I believe that in this case the powers of the soul are not united to God, but are absorbed and astounded at the marvel before them. I may possibly be contradicting what I wrote else-

---

* *Life,* ch. xiv. 9. *Way of Perf.* ch. xxviii. 11.

where;* nor would this be surprising, for it was done about fifteen years ago, and perhaps God has given me since then a clearer insight into the matter. I may be entirely mistaken on the subject, both then and now, but never do I wilfully say what is untrue. No; by the mercy of God, I would rather die a thousand times than tell a falsehood: I speak of the matter as I understand it. I believe that in this case the will must in some way be united with that of God. The after effects on the soul, and the subsequent behaviour of the person, show whether this prayer was genuine or no: this is the best crucible by which to test it.

7. (Graces received in this prayer). Our Lord bestows a signal grace on the soul if it realises how great is this favour, and another greater still if it does not turn back on the right road. You are longing, my daughters, to enter into this state of prayer at once, and you are right, for, as I said, the soul cannot understand the value of the graces there bestowed by God upon it, nor the love which draws Him ever closer to it: we should certainly desire to learn how to obtain this favour. I will tell you what I know about it, setting aside certain cases in which God bestows these graces for no other reason than His own choice, into which we have no right to inquire.

8. (Such favours not to be sought after). Practise what I advised in the preceding mansions, then—humility, humility! for God lets Himself be vanquished by this and grants us all

---

* *Life,* ch. xiv. 3: "The faculties are not lost, neither are they asleep; the will alone is occupied in such a way that without knowing how it has become a captive it gives a simple consent to become the prisoner of God." *Ibid.* § 4: "The other two faculties help the will that it may render itself capable of the fruition of so great a good; nevertheless, it occasionally happens even when the will is in union that they hinder it very much." See also *Way of Perf.* ch. xxxi. 8.

we ask.* The first proof † that you possess humility is that you neither think you now deserve these graces and consolations from God, nor that you ever will as long as you live. You ask me: "How shall we receive them, if we do not try to gain them?" I answer, that there is no surer way to obtain them than the one I have told you, therefore make no efforts to acquire them, for the following reasons. The first is, that the chief means of obtaining them is to love God without self-interest. The second, that it is a slight lack of humility to think that our wretched services can win so great a reward. The third, that the real preparation for them is to desire to suffer and to imitate our Lord, rather than to receive consolations, for indeed we have all offended Him. The fourth reason is, that His Majesty has not promised to give us these favours in the same way as He has bound Himself to bestow eternal glory on us, if we keep His commandments. We can be saved without these special graces; He sees better than we do what is best for us and which of us love Him sincerely. I know for a certain truth, being acquainted with some who walk by the way of love (and therefore only seek to serve Jesus Christ crucified), that not only they neither ask for nor desire consolation, but they even beg Him not to give it them during this life: this is a fact. Fifthly, we should but labour in vain: this water does not flow through aqueducts, like that we first spoke of, and if the spring does not afford it, in vain shall we toil to obtain it. I mean, that though we may meditate and try our hardest, and though we shed tears to gain it, we

---

* *Way of Perf.* ch. xvi. 1. *Life,* ch. xxii. 16.

† Philippus a SS. Trinitate, *l.c.* art. 3.

cannot make this water flow. God alone gives it to whom He chooses, and often when the soul is least thinking of it. We are His, sisters, let Him do what He will with us, and lead us where He will. If we are really humble and annihilate ourselves, not only in our imagination (which often deceives us), but if we truly detach ourselves from all things, our Lord will not only grant us these favours but many others that we do not know even how to wish for. May He be for ever praised and blessed! Amen.

3

Prayer of Quiet

*Of the prayer of recollection which God generally gives the
soul before granting it that last described. Its effects: also those
of the prayer of divine consolations described in the last chapter.*

1. (The prayer of recollection compared to the inhabitants of
the castle). THE effects of divine consolations are very numerous: before describing them, I will speak of another kind
of prayer which usually precedes them. I need not say much
on this subject, having written about it elsewhere.* This is a

---

* *Life,* ch. xiv. 2. The Saint says in the second chapter of this mansion, § 5, and also
in a letter dated January 14, 1580, that when writing the *Interior Castle* she had more
experience in spiritual things than when she composed her former works. This is fully
borne out by the present chapter. In the corresponding part of her *Life* she practically
confounded the prayer of recollection with the prayer of quiet (the second state of
the soul). Likewise, in the *Way of Perfection,* ch. xxviii., she speaks of but one kind of
prayer of recollection and then passes on to the prayer of quiet. Here, however, she
mentions a second form of the prayer of recollection. See Philippus a SS. Trinitate,
pars iii. tract. 1, disc. iii. art. 1, "De oratione recollectionis" (page 81 of the third
vol. of the edition of 1874); "de secundo modo recollectionis" (*ibid.* p. 82); and art.
2, "De oratione quietis" (*ibid.* p. 84). Antonius a Spiritu Sancto, *Direct. Mystic.* tract.
iv. n. 78: "Duo sunt hujus recollectionis modi, primus quidem activus [reference to
the *Way of Perfection, l.c.*], secundus autem passivus [reference to this chapter of the
Fourth Mansion]." The former is not supernatural, in the sense that with special grace
from above it can be acquired; the second is altogether supernatural and more like

kind of recollection which, I believe, is supernatural. There is no occasion to retire nor to shut the eyes, nor does it depend on anything exterior; involuntarily the eyes suddenly close and solitude is found. Without any labour of one's own, the temple of which I spoke is reared for the soul in which to pray: the senses and exterior surroundings appear to lose their hold, while the spirit gradually regains its lost sovereignty. Some say the soul enters into itself; others, that it rises above itself. I can say nothing about these terms, but had better speak of the subject as I understand it. You will probably grasp my meaning, although, perhaps, I may be the only person who understands it. Let us imagine that the senses and powers of the soul (which I compared in my allegory to the inhabitants of the castle) have fled and joined the enemy outside. After long days and years of absence, perceiving how great has been their loss, they return to the neighbourhood of the castle, but cannot manage to re-enter it, for their evil habits are hard to break off; still, they are no longer traitors, and they wander about outside.

2. (The Shepherd recalls His flock into the castle). The King, Who holds His court within it, sees their good will, and out of His great mercy desires them to return to Him. Like a good shepherd, He plays so sweetly on His pipes, that although scarcely hearing it they recognise His call and no longer wander, but return, like lost sheep, to the mansions. So strong is this Pastor's power over His flock, that they abandon the worldly cares which misled them and re-enter the castle.

---

gratuitous grace (*ibid.* no. 80 and 81). On the meaning of "Solitude," "Silence," etc., see Anton. a Sp. S. *l.c.,* tract. 1, n. 78–82.

3. (This recollection supernatural). I think I never put this matter so clearly before. To seek God within ourselves avails us far more than to look for Him amongst creatures; Saint Augustine tells us how he found the Almighty within his own soul, after having long sought for Him elsewhere.* This recollection helps us greatly when God bestows it upon us. But do not fancy you can gain it by thinking of God dwelling within you, or by imagining Him as present in your soul: this is a good practice and an excellent kind of meditation, for it is founded on the fact that God resides within us;† it is not, however, the prayer of recollection, for by the divine assistance every one can practise this, but what I mean is quite a different thing. Sometimes, before they have begun to think of God, the powers of the soul find themselves within the castle. I know not by what means they entered, nor how they heard the Shepherd's pipe; the ears perceived no sound but the soul is keenly conscious of a delicious sense of recollec-

---

* Some editors of the *Interior Castle* think that St. Teresa refers to the following passage taken from the *Confessions* of St. Augustine: "Too late have I loved Thee, O Beauty, ever ancient yet ever new! too late have I loved Thee! And behold, Thou wert within me and I abroad, and there I searched for Thee, and, deformed as I was, I pursued the beauties that Thou hast made. Thou wert with me, but I was not with Thee. Those things kept me far from Thee, which, unless they were in Thee, could have had no being" (*St. Augustine's Confessions,* bk. x. ch. xxvii.). The *Confessions of St. Augustine* were first translated into Spanish by Sebastian Toscano, a Portuguese Augustinian. This edition, which was published at Salamanca in 1554, was the one used by St. Teresa. However, it is more probable that here and elsewhere (*Life,* ch. xli. 10; *Way of Perf.* ch. xxviii. 2) St. Teresa quotes a passage which occurs in a pious book entitled *Soliloquia,* and erroneously attributed to St. Augustine: "I have gone about the streets and the broad ways of the city of this world, seeking Thee, but have not found Thee, for I was wrong in seeking without for what was within" (ch. xxxi.). This treatise, which is also quoted by St. John of the Cross, *Spiritual Canticle,* stanza i. 7, and *Ascent of Mount Carmel,* bk. i. ch. v. 1, appeared in a Spanish translation at Valladolid in 1515, at Medina del Campo in 1553, and at Toledo in 1565.

† *Life,* ch. xiv. 7, 8; ch. xviii. 20.

tion experienced by those who enjoy this favour, which I cannot describe more clearly.

4. (It prepares us for higher favours). I think I read somewhere that the soul is then like a tortoise or sea-urchin, which retreats into itself. Those who said this no doubt understood what they were talking about; but these creatures can withdraw into themselves at will, while here it is not in our power to retire into ourselves, unless God gives us the grace. In my opinion, His Majesty only bestows this favour on those who have renounced the world, in *desire* at least, if their state of life does not permit their doing so in *fact*. He thus specially calls them to devote themselves to spiritual things; if they allow Him power to act freely He will bestow still greater graces on those whom He thus begins calling to a higher life. Those who enjoy this recollection should thank God fervently: it is of the highest importance for them to realise the value of this favour, gratitude for which would prepare them to receive still more signal graces. Some books advise that as a preparation for hearing what our Lord may say to us we should keep our minds at rest, waiting to see what He will work in our souls.* But unless His Majesty has begun to suspend our faculties, I cannot understand how we are to stop thinking, without doing ourselves more harm than good. This point has been much debated by those learned in spiritual matters; I confess my want of humility in having been unable to yield to their opinion.†

5. (The mind must act until God calls it to recollection by love).

---

* *Life,* ch. xii. 8.

† *Life,* ch. xiv. 10.

Some one told me of a certain book written on the subject by the saintly Friar Peter of Alcantara (as I think I may justly call him); I should have submitted to his decision, knowing that he was competent to judge, but on reading it I found he agreed with me that the mind must act until called to recollection by love, although he stated it in other words.* Possibly I may be mistaken, but I rely on these reasons. Firstly, he who reasons less and tries to do least, does most in spiritual matters. We should make our petitions like beggars before a powerful and rich Emperor; then, with downcast eyes, humbly wait. When He secretly shows us He hears our prayers, it is well to be silent, as He has drawn us into His presence; there would then be no harm in trying to keep our minds at rest (that is to say, if we can). If, however, the King makes no sign of listening or of seeing us, there is no need to stand inert, like a dolt, which the soul would resemble if it continued inactive. In this case its dryness would greatly increase, and the imagination would be made more restless than before by its very effort to think of nothing. Our Lord wishes us at such a time to offer Him our petitions and to place ourselves in His presence; He knows what is best for us.

6. (The soul should here abandon itself into God's hands). I be-

---

* See St. Peter of Alcantara's work on meditation, *Tratado de la Oración y Meditación*, published at Lisbon between 1556 and 1560 and at Medina del Campo 1563. Translated into English by Giles Willoughby (and lately by George Seymour Hollings). P. 1, 8th document (p. 168): "As often as this spiritual sleep shall sweetly oppress any one—that is to say, when the understanding is drowned, as it were, in a sleep (but the will watching) let him quietly enjoy this delicate meat as long as it shall last. But when it is digested, let him return again to meditation, in which we must behave ourselves like a gardener, who, when he watereth a bed of his garden, after he hath once sprinkled it with water, expecteth a while until it be drunk in, then sprinkleth again, that at last it may thoroughly wet the earth that it may become more fruitful."

lieve that human efforts avail nothing in these matters, which His Majesty appears to reserve to Himself, setting this limit to our powers. In many other things, such as penances, good works, and prayers, with His aid we can help ourselves as far as human weakness will allow. The second reason is, that these interior operations being sweet and peaceful,* any painful effort does us more harm than good. By "painful effort" I mean any forcible restraint we place on ourselves, such as holding our breath.† We should rather abandon our souls into the hands of God, leaving Him to do as He chooses with us, as far as possible forgetting all self-interest and resigning ourselves entirely to His will. The third reason is, that the very effort to think of nothing excites our imagination the more. The fourth is, because we render God the most true and acceptable service by caring only for His honour and glory and forgetting ourselves, our advantages, comfort, and happiness. How can we be self-oblivious, while keeping ourselves under such strict control that we are afraid to move, or even to think, or to leave our minds enough liberty to desire God's greater glory and to rejoice in the glory which He possesses? When His Majesty wishes the mind to rest from working He employs it in another manner, giving it a light and knowledge far above any obtainable by its own efforts and absorbing it entirely into Himself. Then, though it knows not how, it is filled with wisdom such as it could never gain for itself by striving to suspend the thoughts. God gave us faculties for our use; each of them will receive its proper reward. Then do

---

* *Sap.* viii. 1: "Disponit omnia suaviter."

† *Life,* ch. xv. 1.

not let us try to charm them to sleep, but permit them to do their work until divinely called to something higher.*

7. (The prayer of recollection, and the distractions in prayer). In my opinion, when God chooses to place the soul in this mansion it is best for it to do as I advised, and then endeavour, without force or disturbance, to keep free from wandering thoughts. No effort, however, should be made to suspend the intellect and imagination entirely from acting, for it is well to remember God's presence and to consider Who He is. If transported out of itself by its feelings, well and good; but let it not try to understand what is passing within it, for this favour is bestowed on the will which should be left to enjoy it in peace, only making loving aspirations occasionally. Although, in this kind of prayer, the soul makes no effort towards it, yet often, for a very short time, the mind ceases to think at all. I explained elsewhere why this occurs during this spiritual state.† On first speaking of the fourth mansions, I told you I had mentioned divine consolations before the prayer of recollection. The latter should have come first, as it is far inferior to consolations, of which it is the commencement.

---

* "The whole of the time in which our Lord communicates the simple, loving general attention of which I made mention before, or when the soul, assisted by grace, is established in that state, we must contrive to keep the understanding in repose, undisturbed by the intrusion of forms, figures, or particular knowledge, unless it were slightly and for an instant, and that with sweetness of love, to enkindle our souls the more. At other times, however, in all our acts of devotion and good works, we must make use of good recollections and meditations, so that we may feel an increase of profit and devotion; most especially applying ourselves to the life, passion, and death of Jesus Christ, our Lord, that our life and conduct may be an imitation of His" (St. John of the Cross, *Ascent of Mount Carmel*, bk. ii. ch. xxxii. 7).

† *Life,* ch. xv. 2.

Recollection does not require us to give up meditation, nor to cease using our intellect. In the prayer of quiet, when the water flows from the spring itself and not through conduits, the mind ceases to act; it is forced to do so, although it does not understand what is happening, and so wanders hither and thither in bewilderment, finding no place for rest. Meanwhile the will, entirely united to God, is much disturbed by the tumult of the thoughts: no notice, however, should be taken of them, or they would cause the loss of a great part of the favour the soul is enjoying. Let the spirit ignore these distractions and abandon itself in the arms of divine love: His Majesty will teach it how best to act, which chiefly consists in its recognising its unworthiness of so great a good and occupying itself in thanking Him for it.

8. (Liberty of spirit gained by consolations). In order to treat of the prayer of recollection, I passed over in silence the effects and symptoms to be found in souls thus favoured by God. Divine consolations evidently cause a dilation or enlargement of the soul that may be compared to water flowing from a spring into a basin which has no outlet, but is so constructed as to increase in size and proportion to the quantity poured into it. God seems to work the same effect by this prayer, besides giving many other marvellous graces, so preparing and disposing the soul to contain all He intends to give it. After interior sweetness and dilation the soul is not so restrained as formerly in God's service, but possesses much more liberty of spirit. It is no longer distressed by the terror of hell, for though more anxious than ever not to offend God, it has lost servile fear and feels sure that one day it will possess its Lord.

It does not dread the loss of health by austerities;* believing
that there is nothing it could not do by His grace, it is more
desirous than before of doing penance. Greater indifference
is felt for sufferings, because, faith being stronger, it trusts
that if borne for God He will give the grace to endure them
patiently. Indeed, such a one at times even longs for trials,
having a most ardent desire to do something for His sake.
As the soul better understands the Divine Majesty, it realises more vividly its own baseness. Divine consolation shows
it how vile are earthly pleasures; by gradually withdrawing
from them, it gains greater self-mastery. In short, its virtues
are increased and it will not cease to advance in perfection,
unless it turns back and offends God. Should it act thus, it
would lose everything, however high the state it may have
reached.

9. (The soul must be watchful). It is not to be supposed that
all these effects are produced merely by God's having shown
these favours once or twice. They must be received continually, for it is on their frequent reception that the whole
welfare of the soul depends. I strongly urge those who have
reached this state to avoid most carefully all occasions of offending God.† The soul is not yet fully established in virtue, but is like a new-born babe first feeding at its mother's
breast:‡ if it leaves her, what can it do but die? I greatly fear
that when a soul to whom God has granted this favour dis-

---

* *Life,* ch. xxiv. 2.

† *Way of Perf.* ch. xvi. 5. *Castle,* M. v. ch. i. 2, 3,; ch. ii. 4, 5; ch. iii. 2, 6, 12.

‡ *Way of Perf.* ch. xxxi. 7. *Concep.* ch. iv. 6.

continues prayer, except under urgent necessity, it will, unless it returns to the practice at once, go from bad to worse.

10. (The devil specially tempts such souls). I realise the danger of such a case, having had the grief of witnessing the fall of persons I knew, through their withdrawal from Him Who sought, with so much love, to make Himself their friend, as He proved by His treatment of them. I urgently warn such persons not to run the risk of sinning, for the devil would rather gain one of these souls than many to whom our Lord does not grant such graces,* as the former may cause him severe loss by leading others to follow their example, and may even render great service to the Church of God. Were there no other reason except that he saw the special love His Majesty bore these people, it would suffice to make Satan frantic to destroy God's work in them, so that they might be lost eternally. Therefore they suffer grievous temptations, and if they fall, they fall lower than others.

11. (False trances and raptures). You, my sisters, are free from such dangers, as far as we can tell: God keep you from pride and vainglory! The devil sometimes offers counterfeits of the graces I have mentioned: this can easily be detected—the effects being exactly contrary to those of the genuine ones.† Although I have spoken of it elsewhere,‡ I wish to warn you here of a special danger to which those who practise prayer are subject, particularly women, whose weakness of consti-tution makes them more liable to such mistakes. On account

---

* *Way of Perf.* ch. xl. 3.

† *Life,* ch. xx. 31.

‡ *Found.* ch. vi.

of their penances, prayers, and vigils, or even merely because of debility of health, some persons cannot receive spiritual consolation without being overcome by it. On feeling any interior joy, their bodies being languid and weak, they fall into a slumber—they call it spiritual sleep,—which is a more advanced stage of what I have described; they think the soul shares in it as well as the body, and abandon themselves to a sort of intoxication. The more they lose self-control, the more do their feelings get possession of them, because the frame becomes more feeble. They fancy this is a trance and call it one, but I call it nonsense; it does nothing but waste their time and injure their health.

12. (How to treat those deluded in this way). This state lasted with a certain person for eight hours, during which time she was neither insensible, nor had she any thought of God.[*] She was cured by being made to eat and sleep well and to leave off some of her penances. Her recovery was owing to some one who understood her case; hitherto she had unintentionally deceived both her confessor and other people, as well as herself. I feel quite sure the devil had been at work here to serve his own ends and he was beginning to gain a great deal from it. It should be known that when God bestows such favours on the soul, although there may be languor both of mind and body, it is not shared by the soul, which feels great delight at seeing itself so near God, nor does this state ever continue for more than a very short time.[†] Although the soul may become absorbed again, yet, as I said,

---

* *Found.* ch. vi. 15.

† *Life,* ch. xviii. 16, 17.

unless already feeble, the body suffers neither exhaustion nor pain. I advise any of you who experience the latter to tell the Prioress, and to divert your thoughts as much as possible from such matters. The Superior should prevent such a nun from spending more than a very few hours in prayer, and should make her eat and sleep well until her usual strength is restored, if she has lost it in this way. If the nun's constitution is so delicate that this does not suffice, let her believe me when I tell her that God only calls her to the active life. There must be such people in monasteries: employ her in the various offices and be careful that she is never left very long alone, otherwise she will entirely lose her health. This treatment will be a great mortification to her: our Lord tests her love for Him by the way in which she bears His absence. He may be pleased, after a time, to restore her strength; if not, she will make as much progress, and earn as great a reward by vocal prayer and obedience, as she would have done by contemplation, and perhaps more.

13. (Risks of delusion in this mansion). There are people, some of whom I have known, whose minds and imaginations are so active as to fancy they see whatever they think about, which is very dangerous.* Perhaps I may treat of this later on, but cannot do so now. I have dwelt at length on this mansion, as I believe it to be the one most souls enter. As the natural is combined with the supernatural, the devil can do more harm here than later on, when God does not leave him so many opportunities. May God be for ever praised! Amen.

---

* *Found.* ch. viii. 7–8.

THE FIFTH MANSIONS

1

Prayer of Union

Begins to treat of the union of the soul with God in prayer.
How to be sure that we are not deceived in this matter.

1. (Graces of the fifth mansions). OH, my sisters, how shall I describe the riches, treasures, and joys contained in the fifth mansions! Would it not be better to say nothing about them? They are impossible to depict, nor can the mind conceive, nor any comparisons portray them, all earthly things being too vile to serve the purpose. Send me, O my Lord, light from heaven that I may give some to these Thy servants, some of whom by Thy good will often enjoy these delights, lest the devil in the guise of an angel of light should deceive those whose only desire is to please Thee.

2. (Contemplation to be striven for). I said "some," but in reality there are very *few** who never enter this mansion: some more and some less, but most of them may be said at least to gain admittance into these rooms. I think that certain graces I am

* *Found.* ch. iv. 8.

about to describe are bestowed on only a few of the nuns, but if the rest only arrive at the portal they receive a great boon from God, for "many are called, but few are chosen."* All we who wear the holy habit of the Carmelites are called to prayer and contemplation. This was the object of our Order,† to this lineage we belong. Our holy Fathers of Mount Carmel sought in perfect solitude and utter contempt of the world for this treasure, this precious pearl,‡ of which we speak, and we are their descendants. How little do most of us care to prepare our souls, that our Lord may reveal this jewel to us! Outwardly we may appear to practise the requisite virtues, but we have far more to do than this before it is possible to attain to contemplation, to gain which we should neglect no means, either small or great. Rouse yourselves, my sisters, and since some foretaste of heaven may be had on earth, beg our Lord to give us grace not to miss it through our own fault. Ask Him to show us where to find it—ask Him to give us strength of soul to dig until we find this hidden treasure, which lies buried within our hearts, as I wish to show you if it please God to enable me. I said "strength of *soul,*" that you might understand that strength of *body* is not indispensable when our Lord God chooses to withhold it. He makes it impossible for no one to gain these riches, but is content that each should do his best. Blessed be so just a God!

3. (Physical effects of the prayer of union). But, daughters, if you

---

* St. Matt. xx. 16: "Multi enim sunt vocati, pauci vero electi."

† "Maneant singuli in cellulis suis, vel juxta eas, die ac nocte in lege Domini meditantes et in orationibus vigilantes" (*Carmelite Rule*).

‡ St. Matt. xiii. 46.

would purchase this treasure of which we are speaking, God would have you keep back nothing from Him, little or great. He will have it all;* in proportion to what you know you have given will your reward be great or small. There is no more certain sign whether or not we have reached the prayer of union. Do not imagine that this state of prayer is, like the one preceding it, a sort of drowsiness (I call it "drowsiness" because the soul seems to slumber, being neither quite asleep nor wholly awake). In the prayer of union the soul is asleep, fast asleep, as regards the world and itself: in fact, during the short time this state lasts it is deprived of all feeling whatever, being unable to think on any subject, even if it wished. No effort is needed here to suspend the thoughts, if the soul can love—it knows not how, nor whom it loves, nor what it desires. In fact, it has died entirely to this world, to live more truly than ever in God. This is a delicious death, for the soul is deprived of the faculties it exercised while in the body:† delicious because, (although not really the case), it seems to have left its mortal covering, to abide more entirely in God. So completely does this take place, that I know not whether the body retains sufficient life to continue breathing; on consideration, I believe it does not; at any rate, if it still breathes, it does so unconsciously.

4. (Amazement of the intellect). The mind entirely concentrates itself on trying to understand what is happening, which is beyond its power; it is so astounded, that if consciousness

---

* "The reason why there are so few contemplatives is that there are so few persons who wholly withdraw themselves from transitory and created things" (*Imitation,* bk. iii. ch. xxxi. 1). See also *Way of Perf.* ch. xvi. 5. *Life,* ch. xi. 2–4; ch. xxii. 18, 19.

† *Way of Perf.* ch. xxv. 1. *Life,* ch. xvi. *Rel.* I. 1; viii. 7.

is not completely lost, at least no movement is possible: the person may be compared to one who falls into a dead faint with dismay.*

5. (The prayer of union and of quiet contrasted). Oh, mighty secrets of God! Never should I weary of trying to explain them if I thought it possible to succeed! I would write a thousand foolish things that one might be to the point, if only it might make us praise God more. I said this prayer produced no drowsiness in the mind; on the other hand, in the prayer (of quiet) described in the last mansion, until the soul has gained much experience it doubts what really happened to it. "Was it nothing but fancy, or was it a sleep? Did it come from God or from the devil, disguised as an angel of light?" The mind feels a thousand misgivings, and well for it that it should, because, as I said, nature may sometimes deceive us in this case. Although there is little chance of the poisonous reptiles entering here, yet agile little lizards will try to slip in, though they can do no harm, especially if they remain unnoticed. These, as I said, are trivial fancies of the imagination, which are often very troublesome. However active these small lizards may be, they cannot enter the fifth mansion, for neither the imagination, the understanding, nor the memory has power to hinder the graces bestowed in it.

6. (Divine and earthly union). I dare venture to assert that, if this is genuine union with God, the devil cannot interfere nor do any harm, for His Majesty is so joined and united with the essence of the soul, that the evil one dare not approach, nor can he even understand this mystery. This is certain, for it is

* *Life,* ch. xvii. 2.

said that the devil does not know our thoughts, much less can he penetrate a secret so profound, that God does not reveal it even to us.* Oh, blessed state, in which this cursed one cannot injure us! What riches we receive while God so works in us that neither we ourselves nor any one else can impede Him! What will He not bestow, Who is so eager to give, and Who can give us all He desires! You may perhaps have been puzzled at my saying "if this is genuine union with God," as if there might be other unions. There are indeed—not with God, but with vanities—when the devil transports the soul passionately addicted to them, but the union differs from that which is divine and the mind misses the delight and satisfaction, peace and happiness of divine union. These heavenly consolations are above all earthly joys, pleasure, and satisfaction. As great a difference exists between their origin and that of worldly pleasures as between their opposite effects, as you know by experience.

7. (Competent directors in these matters). I said somewhere†that the one seems only to touch the surface of the body, while the other penetrates to the very marrow: I believe this is correct, and I cannot express myself better. I fancy that you are not yet satisfied on this question, but are afraid of deception, for spiritual matters are very hard to explain. Enough, however, has been said for those who have received this grace, as the difference between divine union and any other is very striking. However, I will give you a clear proof which cannot

---

* According to St. Thomas, angels—whether good or bad—do not know the thoughts of man unless they become manifest by some exterior sign. S. Theol. I. q. lvii. art 4. See also St. John of the Cross, *Dark Night,* bk. ii. ch. xxiii. 2, 5.

† Mansion iv. ch. i. 5.

mislead you, nor leave any doubt whether the favour comes from God or no. His Majesty brought it back to my memory this very day; it appears to me to be an unmistakable sign. In difficult questions, although I think I understand them and am speaking the truth, I always say, "it appears to me"; for, in case my opinion is wrong, I am most willing to submit to the judgment of theologians. Although they may not have had personal experience in such matters, yet, in some way I do not understand, God Who sets them to give light to His Church, enables them to recognise the truth when it is put before them. If they are not thoughtless and indevout, but servants of God, they are never dismayed at His mighty works, knowing perfectly well that it is in His power to perform far greater wonders. If some of the marvels told are new to them, yet they have read of others of the same kind, showing the former to be possible. I have had great experience as to this and have also met with timid, half-instructed people, whose ignorance has cost me very dear.* I am convinced that those who refuse to believe that God can do far more than this, and that He is pleased now, as in the past, to communicate Himself to His creatures, shut fast their hearts against receiving such favours themselves. Do not imitate them, sisters: be convinced that it is possible for God to perform still greater wonders. Do not concern yourselves as to whether those who receive these graces are good or wicked; as I said, He knows best, and it is no business of yours: you should

---

* *Life,* ch. viii. 15.

serve Him with a single heart and with humility, and should praise Him for His works and wonders.*

8. (Proof of union). Let us now speak of the sign which proves the prayer of union to have been genuine. As you have seen, God then deprives the soul of all its senses that He may the better imprint in it true wisdom: it neither sees, hears, nor understands anything while this state lasts, which is never more than a very brief time;† it appears to the soul to be much shorter than it really is. God visits the soul in a manner which prevents its doubting, on returning to itself, that it dwelt in Him, and that He was within it, and so firmly is it convinced of this truth, that although years may pass before this favour recurs, the soul can never forget it nor doubt the fact,‡ setting aside the effects left by this prayer, to which I will refer later on. The conviction felt by the soul is the main point.

9. (Assurance left in the soul). But, you may ask, how can a person who is incapable of sight and hearing see§ or know these things? I do not say that she saw it at the time, but that she perceives it clearly afterwards, not by any vision, but by a certitude which remains in the heart, and which God alone could give. I know of some one who was unaware of God being in all things by presence, power and essence, yet was

---

* *Life,* ch. xviii. 16.

† *Life,* ch. xx. 13, 24.

‡ Philippus a SS. Trinitate, *l.c.,* pars iii. tr. i. disc. iv. art. 2, where he adds some further signs. Anton. a Sp. S., *l.c.,* tract. i. nn. 116 and 117.

§ "The soul does not see the good Master who teaches it, although clearly conscious of His presence" (*Concept.* ch. iv. 3).

firmly convinced of it by a divine favour of this sort.* She asked an ill-instructed priest of the kind I mentioned to tell her in what way God dwelt within us: he was as ignorant on the subject as she had been before our Lord revealed to her the truth, and answered that the Almighty was only present in us by grace.† Yet so strong was her conviction of the truth learnt during her prayer, that she did not believe him and questioned other spiritual persons on the subject, who confirmed her in the true doctrine, much to her joy. Do not mistake, and imagine that this certainty of God having visited the soul concerns any corporal presence, such as that of our Lord Jesus Christ Who dwells in the Blessed Sacrament, although we do not see Him: it relates solely to the Divinity. If we did not see it, how can we feel so sure of it? That I do not know: it is the work of the Almighty and I am certain that what I say is the fact. I maintain that a soul which does

---

* "There are three ways in which God is present in the soul. The first is His presence in essence, not in holy souls only, but in wretched and sinful souls as well, and also in all created things; for it is by this presence that He gives life and being, and were it withdrawn at once all things would return to nothing. This presence never fails in the soul. The second is His presence by grace, whereby He dwells in the soul, pleased and satisfied with it. This presence is not in all souls; for those who fall into mortal sin lose it, and no soul can know in a natural way whether it has it or not. The third is His presence by spiritual affection. God is wont to show His presence in many devout souls in divers ways, in refreshment, joy and gladness" (St. John of the Cross, *Spiritual Canticle,* stanza xi. 2)."In every soul, even that of the greatest sinner in the world, God dwells and is substantially present. This way of union or presence of God, in the order of nature, subsists between Him and all His creatures; by this He preserves them in being, and if He withdraws it they immediately perish and cease to be. And so, when I speak of the union of the soul with God, I do not mean this substantial presence which is in every creature, but that union and transformation of the soul in God by love which is only then accomplished when there subsists the likeness which love begets" (Saint John of the Cross, *Ascent,* bk. ii. ch. v. 3).Fr. Gracian, *Peregrinación de Anastasio* (Burgos, 1905), p. 171.

† *Life,* ch. xviii. 20. *Rel.* ix. 17; xi. 8. St. Teresa was so deeply impressed by the ignorance of this priest that she very frequently referred to it.

not feel this assurance has not been united to God entirely, but only by one of its powers, or has received one of the many other favours God is accustomed to bestow on men. In all such matters we must not seek to know how things happened: our understanding could not grasp them, therefore why trouble ourselves on the subject? It is enough to know that it is He, the all-powerful God, Who has performed the work. We can do nothing on our own part to gain this favour; it comes from God alone; therefore let us not strive to understand it.

10. (Divine union beyond our power to obtain). Concerning my words: "We can do nothing on our own part," I was struck by the words of the Bride in the Canticles, which you will remember to have heard: "The King brought me into the cellar of wine,"* (or "placed me" I think she says): she does not say she went of her own accord, although telling us how she wandered up and down seeking her Beloved.† I think the prayer of union is the "cellar" in which our Lord places us, when and how He chooses, but we cannot enter it through any effort of our own. His Majesty alone can bring us there and come into the centre of our souls. In order to declare His wondrous works more clearly, He will leave us no share in them except complete conformity of our wills to His, and abandonment of all things: He does not require the faculties or senses to open the door to Him; they are all asleep. He enters the innermost depths of our souls without a door, as He

---

* *Cant.* i. 3: "Introduxit me rex in cellaria sua." *Castle,* M. v. ch. ii. 11. *Way of Perf.* ch. xviii. I. *Concep.* ch. iv. 4–8; v. 5; vi. 7; vii. 2–5. *Life,* ch. xviii. 17.

† *Cant.* iii. 2: "Per vicos et plateas quæram quem diligit anima mea."

entered the room where the disciples sat, saying, "Pax vobis,"*
and as He emerged from the sepulchre without removing
the stone that closed the entrance. You will see farther on, in
the seventh mansions, far better than here, how God makes
the soul enjoy His presence in its very centre. O daughters,
what wonders shall we see, if we keep ever before our eyes
our own baseness and frailty and recognise how unworthy
we are to be the handmaids of so great a Lord, Whose marvels are beyond our comprehension! May He be for ever
praised! Amen.

---

* St. John xx. 19.

2

Effects of Union

Continues the same subject: explains the prayer of union by a delicate comparison and speaks of the effects it leaves upon the soul. This chapter should receive great attention.

1. (The soul compared to a butterfly). YOU may imagine that there is no more left to be described of the contents of this mansion, but a great deal remains to be told, for as I said, it contains favours of various degrees. I think there is nothing to add about the prayer of union, but when the soul on which God bestows this grace disposes itself for their reception, I could tell you much about the marvels our Lord works in it. I will describe some of them in my own way, and also the state in which they leave the soul, and will use a suitable comparison to elucidate the matter, showing that though we can take no active part in this work of God within us,* yet we may do much to prepare ourselves to receive this grace. You have heard how wonderfully silk is made—in a way such as God

---

* *Way of Perf.* ch. xxv. 3.

alone could plan—how it all comes from an egg resembling a tiny pepper-corn. Not having seen it myself, I only know of it by hearsay, so if the facts are inaccurate the fault will not be mine. When, in the warm weather, the mulberry trees come into leaf, the little egg, which was lifeless before its food was ready, begins to live. The caterpillar nourishes itself upon the mulberry leaves, until, when it has grown large, people place near it small twigs, upon which, of its own accord, it spins silk from its tiny mouth until it has made a narrow little cocoon in which it buries itself. Then this large and ugly worm leaves the cocoon as a lovely little white butterfly.

2. (The grandeurs of creation). If we had not seen this, but had only heard of it as an old legend, who could believe it? Could we persuade ourselves that insects so utterly without the use of reason as a silkworm or a bee would work with such industry and skill in our service that the poor little silkworm loses its life over the task? This would suffice for a short meditation, sisters, without my adding more, for you may learn from it the wonders and the wisdom of God. How if we knew the properties of all things? It is most profitable to ponder over the grandeurs of creation, and to exult in being the brides of such a wise and mighty King.

3. (Symbol of the soul and the silkworm). Let us return to our subject. The silkworm symbolises the soul which begins to live when, kindled by the Holy Spirit, it commences using the ordinary aids given by God to all, and applies the remedies left by Him in His Church, such as regular confession, religious books, and sermons; these are the cure for a soul dead in its negligence and sins and liable to fall into temp-

tation. Then it comes to life and continues nourishing itself on this food and on devout meditation until it has attained full vigour, which is the essential point, for I attach no importance to the rest. When the silkworm is full grown, as I told you in the first part of this chapter, it begins to spin silk and to build the house wherein it must die. By this house, when speaking of the soul, I mean Christ. I think I read or heard somewhere, either that our life is hid in Christ, or in God (which means the same thing), or that Christ is our life.* It makes little difference to my meaning which of these quotations is correct.

4. (Preparation of the soul for God's indwelling). This shows, my daughters, how much, by God's grace, we can do, by preparing this home for ourselves, towards making Him our dwelling-place, as He is in the prayer of union. You will suppose that I mean we can take away from or add something to God, when I say that He is our home, and that we can make this home and dwell in it by our own power. Indeed we can: though we can neither deprive God of anything nor add aught to Him, yet we can take away from and add to ourselves, like the silkworms. The little we can do will hardly have been accomplished when this insignificant work of ours, which amounts to nothing at all, will be united by God to His greatness and thus enhanced with such immense value that our Lord Himself will be the reward of our toil. Although He has had the greatest share in it, He will join our

---

* Col. iii. 3: "Vita vestra est abscondita cum Christo in Deo." Gal. ii. 20: "Vivo autem, jam non ego; vivit vero in me Christus."

trifling pains to the bitter sufferings He endured for us, and make them one.

5. (Mystic death of the silkworm). Forward, then, my daughters! hasten over your work and build the little cocoon. Let us renounce self-love and self-will,* care for nothing earthly, do penance, pray, mortify ourselves, be obedient, and perform all the other good works of which you know. Act up to your light; you have been taught your duties. Die! die! as the silkworm does when it has fulfilled the office of its creation, and you will see God and be immersed in His greatness, as the little silkworm is enveloped in its cocoon. Understand that when I say "you will see God," I mean in the manner described, in which He manifests Himself in this kind of union.

6. (Effects of divine union). Now let us see what becomes of "the silkworm," for all I have been saying leads to this. As soon as, by means of this prayer, the soul has become entirely dead to the world, it comes forth like a lovely little white butterfly! Oh, how great God is! How beautiful is the soul after having been immersed in God's grandeur and united closely to Him for but a short time! Indeed, I do not think it is ever as long as half an hour.† Truly, the spirit does not recognise itself, being as different from what it was as is the white butterfly from the repulsive caterpillar. It does not know how it can have merited so great a good, or rather, whence this grace came,‡ which it well knows it merits not.

---

* *Way of Perf.* ch. xxxi. 11.

† *Life,* ch. xviii. 16.

‡ *Life,* ch. xviii. 5–7.

The soul desires to praise our Lord God, and longs to sacrifice itself and die a thousand deaths for Him. It feels an unconquerable desire for great crosses, and would like to perform the most severe penances; it sighs for solitude, and would have all men know God, while it is bitterly grieved at seeing them offend Him. These matters will be described more fully in the next mansion; there they are of the same nature, yet in a more advanced state the effects are far stronger, because, as I told you, if, after the soul has received these favours, it strives to make still farther progress, it will experience great things. Oh, to see the restlessness of this charming little butterfly, although never in its life has it been more tranquil and at peace! May God be praised! It knows not where to stay nor take its rest; everything on earth disgusts it after what it has experienced, particularly when God has often given it this wine, which leaves fresh graces behind it at every draught.

7. (Increase of fervour and detachment). It despises the work it did while yet a caterpillar, the slow weaving of its cocoon thread by thread—its wings have grown and it can fly; could it be content to crawl? All that it can do for God seems nothing to the soul compared with its desire. It no longer wonders at what the saints bore for Him, knowing by experience how our Lord aids and transforms the soul, until it no longer seems the same in character and appearance. Formerly it feared penance, now it is strong: it wanted courage to forsake relations, friends, or possessions: neither its actions, its resolutions, nor separation from those it loved, could detach the soul, but rather seemed to increase its fondness. Now it finds even their rightful claims

a burden,* fearing contact with them, lest it should offend God. It wearies of everything, realising that no true rest can be found in creatures.

8. (Trials succeeding the prayer of union). I seem to have enlarged on this subject, yet far more might be said about it; those who have received this favour will think I have treated it too briefly. No wonder this pretty butterfly, estranged from earthly things, seeks repose elsewhere. Where can the poor little creature go? It cannot return to whence it came, for, as I told you, that is not in the soul's power, do what it will, but depends upon God's pleasure. Alas! what fresh trials begin to afflict the mind!† Who would expect this, after such a sublime grace? In fact, in one way or another we must carry the cross all our lives. If people told me that ever since attaining to the prayer of union they had enjoyed constant peace and consolation, I should reply that they could never have reached that state, but that, at the most, if they had arrived as far as the last mansion, their emotion must have been some spiritual satisfaction, joined to physical debility. It might even have been a false sweetness caused by the devil, who gives peace for a time, only to wage far fiercer war later on. I do not mean that those who reach this stage possess no peace; they do so in a very high degree, for their sorrows, though extremely severe, are so beneficial and proceed from so good a source as to procure both peace and happiness.

9. (Longing for death and zeal for God's honour). Discontent with this world gives such a painful longing to quit it, that

---

* *Rel.* ix. 11.

† *Way of Perf.* ch. xviii. 1–4. *Castle,* M. vi. ch. i. 3 *sqq.*: M. vii. ch. iv. 7.

if the heart finds comfort it is solely from the thought that God wishes it to remain here in banishment. Even this is not enough to reconcile it to fate, for, after all the gifts received, it is not yet so entirely surrendered to the will of God as it afterwards becomes. Here, although conformed to His will, the soul feels an unconquerable reluctance to submit, for our Lord has not given it higher grace. During prayer, this grief breaks forth into floods of tears, probably from the great pain felt at seeing God offended and at thinking how many souls, both heretics and heathens, are lost eternally, and, keenest grief of all, Christians also! The soul realises the greatness of God's mercy and knows that, however wicked men are, they may still repent and be saved, yet it fears that many precipitate themselves into hell.

10. (This zeal supernatural). Oh, infinite greatness of God! A few years ago—indeed, perhaps but a few days—this soul thought of nothing but itself. Who has made it feel such tormenting cares? If we tried for many years to obtain such sorrow by means of meditation, we could not succeed.

11. (God alone works this grace). God help me! If for long days and years I considered how great a wrong it is that God should be offended, and that lost souls are His children and my brethren; if I pondered over the dangers of this world, and how blessed it would be to leave this wretched life, would not that suffice? No, daughters, the pain would not be the same. For this, by the help of God, we can obtain by such meditation; but it does not seem to penetrate the very depths of our being like the other, which appears to cut the soul in pieces and grind it to powder, through no action—even sometimes with no wish—of its own. What is this sorrow, then? Whence

does it come? I will tell you. Have you not heard (I quoted the words to you just now, but did not apply to them this meaning)* how the Bride says that God "brought her into the cellar of wine and set in order charity in her."† This is what happens here. The soul has so entirely yielded itself into His hands and is so subdued by love for Him, that it knows or cares for nothing but that God should dispose of it according to His will. I believe that He only bestows this grace on those He takes entirely for His own. He desires that without knowing how, the spirit should come forth stamped with His seal, for indeed it does no more than does the wax when impressed with the signet. It does not mould itself, but need only be in a fit condition—soft and pliable; even then it does not soften itself, but must merely remain still and submit to the impression.

12. (The same zeal as that felt by Our Lord on earth). How good Thou art, O God! All is done for us by Thee, Who dost but ask us to give our wills to Thee, that we may be plastic as wax in Thy hands. You see, sisters, what God does to this soul, that it may know it is His. He gives it something of His own—that which His Son possessed when living on earth—He could bestow no greater gift on us. Who could ever have longed more eagerly to leave this life than did Christ? As He said at the Last Supper: "With desire have I desired" this.‡

---

* Fifth Mansions, ch. i, 10.

† *Cant.* ii. 4: "Introduxit me in cellam vinariam, ordinavit in me charitatem."

‡ St. Luke xxii. 15: "Desiderio desideravi hoc pascha manducare vobiscum antequam patiar."

O Lord! does not that bitter death Thou art to undergo present itself before Thine eyes in all its pain and horror? "No, for My ardent love and My desire to save souls are immeasurably stronger than the torments. This deeper sorrow I have suffered and still suffer, while living here on earth, makes other pain seem as nothing in comparison."

13. (Christ's keenest suffering). I have often meditated on this, and I know that the torture a friend of mine* has felt, and still feels, at seeing our Lord sinned against is so unbearable that she would far rather die than continue in such anguish. Then I thought that if a soul whose charity is so weak compared to that of Christ—indeed, in comparison with His this charity might be said not to exist—experiences this insufferable grief, what must have been the feelings of our Lord Jesus Christ, and what must His life have been? For all things were present before His eyes and He was the constant witness of the great offences committed against His Father. I believe, without doubt, that this pained Him far more than His most sacred Passion. There, at least, He found the end of all His trials, while His agony was allayed by the consolation of gaining our salvation through His death, and of proving how He loved His Father by suffering for Him. Thus, people who, urged by fervent love, perform great penances hardly feel them, but want to do still more, and count even that as little. What, then, must His Majesty have felt at thus publicly manifesting His perfect obedience to His Father and His love

* This friend is, of course, St. Teresa herself. See *Life,* ch. xiii. 14; ch. xxxii. 9. *Way of Perf.* ch. i. 3. *Castle,* M. vii. ch. i. 5, 6. *Excl.* x. 9.

for His brethren? What joy to suffer in doing God's will! Yet, I think, the constant sight of the many sins committed against God, and of the numberless souls on their way to hell, must have caused Him such anguish, that had He not been more than man, one day of such torment would have destroyed not only His life, but many more lives, had they been His.

3

Cause of Union

This chapter continues the same subject and speaks of another kind of union which the soul can obtain, with the help of God. The importance of love of our neighbour in this matter. This is very useful to read.

1. (Zeal for souls left by divine union). LET us now return to our little dove and see what graces God gives it in this state. This implies that the soul endeavours to advance in the service of our Lord and in self-knowledge. If it receives the grace of union and then does no more, thinking itself safe, and so leads a careless life, wandering off the road to heaven (that is, the keeping of the commandments), it will share the fate of the butterfly that comes from the silkworm, which lays some eggs that produce more of its kind, and then dies for ever. I say it leaves some eggs, for I believe God will not allow so great a favour to be lost, but that if the recipient does not profit by it, others will. For, whilst it keeps to the right path, this soul, with its ardent desires and great virtues, helps others and kindles their fervour with its own. Yet, even after having lost them, it may still long to benefit others and

delight to make known the mercies shown by God to those who love and serve Him.*

2. (The soul may fall from such a state). I knew a person to whom this happened. Although greatly erring, she longed that others should profit by the favours God had bestowed on her, and taught the way of prayer to people ignorant of it, thus helping them immensely.† God afterwards bestowed fresh light upon her; indeed the prayer of union had not hitherto produced the above effects in her. How many people there must be to whom our Lord communicates Himself who, like Judas, are called to the Apostleship, and made kings by Him, as was Saul, yet who afterwards lose everything by their own fault! We should learn from this, sisters, that if we would merit fresh favours and avoid losing those we already possess, our only safety lies in obedience and in following the law of God. This I say both to those who have received these graces and to those who have not.

3. (How divine union may always be attained to). In spite of all I have written, there still seems some difficulty in understanding this mansion. The advantage of entering is so great, that it is well that none should despair of doing so because God does not give them the supernatural gifts described above. With the help of divine grace true union can always be attained, by forcing ourselves to renounce our own will and by following the will of God in all things.‡

---

* *Life,* ch. vii. 18. *Way of Perf.* ch. xli. 8.

† *Life,* ch. vii. 21.

‡ *Found.* ch. v. 10. "These shall not attain to the true liberty of a pure heart, nor to the grace of a delightful familiarity with Me, unless they first resign themselves and offer

4. (Union with the will of God the basis of all supernatural union). Oh, how many of us affirm that we do this, and believe we seek nothing else—indeed we would die for the truth of what we say! If this be the case, I can only declare, as I fancy I did before, and shall again and again, that we have already obtained this grace from God. There is, then, no need to wish for that other delightful union described above, for its chief value lies in the resignation of our will to that of God, without which it could not be reached.* Oh, how desirable is this union! The happy soul which has attained it will live in this world and in the next without care of any sort. No earthly events can trouble it, unless it should see itself in danger of losing God or should witness any offence offered Him. Neither sickness, poverty, nor the loss of any one by death affect it, except it be that of persons useful to the Church of God, for the soul realises thoroughly that God's disposal is wiser than its own desires.

5. (Advantage of union gained by self-mortification). You must know that there are different kinds of sorrow: there are both griefs and joys rising from an impulse of nature or from a charity which makes us pity our neighbour, like that felt by our Saviour when He raised Lazarus from the dead.† These feelings do not destroy union with the will of God, nor do they disturb the soul by a restless, turbulent, and lasting passion.

---

themselves a daily sacrifice to Me: for without this, divine union neither is nor will be obtained" (*Imitation*, bk. iii. ch. xxxvii. 4).

* Philippus a SS. Trinitate, *l.c.,* p. iii. tr. i. disc. ii. art. 4.

† St. John xi. 35, 36: "Et lacrymatus est Jesus. Dixerunt ergo Judæi: Ecce quomodo amabat eum."

They soon pass away, for, as I said of sweetness in prayer,* they do not affect the depths of the soul, but only its senses and faculties. They are found in the former mansions, but do not enter the last of all. Is it necessary, in order to attain to this kind of divine union, for the powers of the soul to be suspended? No; God has many ways of enriching the soul and bringing it to these mansions besides what might be called a "short cut." But, be sure of this, my daughters, in any case the silkworm must die, and it will cost you more in this way. In the former manner this death is facilitated by finding ourselves introduced into a new life; here, on the contrary, we must give ourselves the death-blow. I own that the work will be much harder, but then it will be of higher value, so that your reward will be greater if you come forth victorious;† yet there is no doubt it is possible for you to attain this true union with the will of God.

6. (Defects which hinder this nation). This is the union I have longed for all my life and that I beg our Lord to grant me; it is the most certain and the safest. But alas, how few of us ever obtain it! Those who are careful not to offend God, and who enter the religious state, think there is nothing more to do. How many maggots remain in hiding until, like the worm which gnawed at Jonas's ivy,‡ they have destroyed our virtues. These pests are such evils as self-love, self-esteem, rash

---

* Fourth Mansions, ch. i. 5. Fifth Mansions, ch. i. 7.

† *Way of Perf.* ch. xvii. 2.

‡ Jonas iv. 6, 7: "And the Lord God prepared an ivy, and it came up over the head of Jonas, to be a shadow over his head, and to cover him, for he was fatigued: and Jonas was exceeding glad of the ivy. But God prepared a worm, when the morning arose on the following day: and it struck the ivy and it withered."

judgment of others even in small matters, and a want of charity in not loving our neighbour quite as much as ourselves. Although, perforce, we satisfy our obligations sufficiently to avoid sin, yet we fall far short of what must be done in order to obtain perfect union with the will of God.

7. (Divine union obtained by perfect love of God and our neighbour). What do you think, daughters, is His will? That we may become quite perfect and so be made one with Him and with His Father, as He prayed we might be.* Observe, then, what is wanting in us to obtain this. I assure you it is most painful for me to write on this subject, for I see how far I am, through my own fault, from having attained perfection. There is no need for us to receive special consolations from God in order to arrive at conformity with His will; He has done enough in giving us His Son to teach the way. This does not mean that we must so submit to the will of God as not to sorrow at such troubles as the death of a father or brother, or that we must bear crosses and sickness with joy.† This is well, but it sometimes comes from common sense which, as we cannot help ourselves, makes a virtue of necessity. How often the great wisdom of the heathen philosophers led them to act thus in trials of this kind! Our Lord asks but two things of us: love for Him and for our neighbour: these are what we must strive to obtain. If we practise both these virtues perfectly we shall be doing His will and so shall be united to Him. But, as I said, we are very far from obeying

---

* St. John xvii. 22, 23: "Ut sint unum, sicut et nos unum sumus. Ego in eis, et tu in me: ut sint consummati in unum." *Way of Perf.* ch. xxxii. 6.

† *Way of Perf.* ch. ix. 1, 2.

and serving our great Master perfectly in these two matters: may His Majesty give us the grace to merit union with Him; it is in our power to gain it if we will.

8. (Love for God and our neighbour are proportionate). I think the most certain sign that we keep these two commandments is that we have a genuine love for others. We cannot know whether we love God, although there may be strong reasons for thinking so, but there can be no doubt about whether we love our neighbour or no.* Be sure that in proportion as you advance in fraternal charity, you are increasing in your love of God,† for His Majesty bears so tender an affection for us, that I cannot doubt He will repay our love for others by augmenting, in a thousand different ways, that which we bear for Him. We should watch most carefully over ourselves in this matter, for if we are perfect on this point we have done all. I believe human nature is so evil that we could not feel a perfect charity for our neighbour unless it were rooted in the love of God.

9. (Real and imaginary virtues). In this most important matter, sisters, we should be most vigilant in little things, and take no notice of the great works we plan during prayer, which we imagine that we would perform for other people, even, perhaps, for the sake of saving a single soul. If our actions afterwards belie these grand schemes, there is no reason to imagine that we should do anything of the sort. I say the same of humility and the other virtues. The devil's wiles are

---

* 1 St. John iv. 20: "Qui enim non diligit fratrem suum quem videt, Deum quem non videt quomodo potest diligere?"

† *Way of Perf.* ch. xviii. 5.

many; he would turn hell upside down a thousand times to make us think ourselves better than we are. He has good reason for it, for such fancies are most injurious; sham virtues springing from this root are always accompanied by a vainglory never found in those of divine origin, which are free from pride.

10. (Illusionary good resolutions). It is amusing to see souls who, while they are at prayer, fancy they are willing to be despised and publicly insulted for the love of God, yet afterwards do all they can to hide their small defects; if any one unjustly accuses them of a fault, God deliver us from their outcries! Let those who cannot bear such things take no notice of the splendid plans they made when alone, which could have been no genuine determination of the will, but only some trick of the imagination, or the results would have been very different. The devil assaults and deceives people in this way, often doing great harm to women and others too ignorant to understand the difference between the powers of the soul and the imagination, and a thousand other matters of the sort. O sisters! how easy it is to know which of you have attained to a sincere love for your neighbour, and which of you are far from it. If you knew the importance of this virtue, your only care would be to gain it.

11. (Works, not feeling, procure union). When I see people very anxious to know what sort of prayer they practise, covering their faces and afraid to move or think, lest they should lose any slight tenderness and devotion they feel, I know how little they understand how to attain union with God, since they think it consists in such things as these. No, sisters, no; our Lord expects *works* from us! If you see a sick sister whom you

can relieve,* never fear losing your devotion; compassionate her; if she is in pain, feel for it as if it were your own, and, when there is need, fast so that she may eat, not so much for her sake as because you know your Lord asks it of you. This is the true union of our will with the will of God. If some one else is well spoken of, be more pleased than if it were yourself; this is easy enough, for if you were really humble it would vex you to be praised. It is a great good to rejoice at your sister's virtues being known, and to feel as sorry for the fault you see in her as if it were yours, hiding it from the sight of others.

12. (Fraternal charity will certainly gain this union). I have often spoken on this subject elsewhere,† because, my sisters, if we fail in this, I know that all is lost: please God this may never be our case. If you possess fraternal charity, I assure you that you will certainly attain the union I have described. If you are conscious that you are wanting in this charity, although you may feel devotion and sweetness, and a short absorption in the prayer of quiet (which makes you think you have attained to union with God), believe me, you have not yet reached it. Beg our Lord to grant you perfect love for your neighbour, and leave the rest to Him. He will give you more than you know how to desire if you constrain yourselves and strive with all your power to gain it, forcing your will as far as possible to comply in all things with your sisters' wishes, although you may sometimes forfeit your own rights by so doing. Forget your self-interests for theirs, however much

---

* *Way of Perf.* ch. vii. 4.

† *Way of Perf.* ch. iv. 3; vii. 4.

nature may rebel; when opportunity occurs take some burden upon yourself to ease your neighbour of it. Do not fancy that it will cost you nothing and that you will find it all done for you: think what the love He bore for us cost our Spouse, Who to free us from death Himself suffered the most painful death of all—the death of the Cross.

4

Spiritual Espousals

Further explanation of the same subject; explains this prayer. The importance of being on one's guard, as the devil eagerly desires to turn souls back from the right path.

1. (The spiritual espousals). YOU appear anxious to know what has become of the little dove and where she obtains rest, since obviously she can find it neither in spiritual consolations nor in earthly pleasures, but takes a higher flight. I cannot tell you until we come to the last mansion: God grant I may remember, or have leisure to write it. It is nearly five months since I began this work, and, as my head is too weak to read it again, no doubt it will be very disconnected and full of repetitions: however, as it is only for my sisters, that will matter little. Yet I should like to express myself more fully about the prayer of union, and will make use, to the best of my scanty wits, of a comparison. Later on we will speak of the little butterfly, which is never still, for it can find no true repose, yet always fertile, doing good both to itself and others.* You have often

---

* Compare: "habebit fructum in respectione animarum sanctarum" (*Breviar. Rom.*

heard that God spiritually espouses souls: may He be praised for His mercy in thus humbling Himself so utterly. Though but a homely comparison, yet I can find nothing better to express my meaning than the Sacrament of Matrimony, although the two things are very different. In divine union everything is spiritual and far removed from anything corporal, all the joys our Lord gives and the mutual delight felt in it being celestial and very unlike human marriage, which it excels a thousand times. Here all is love united to love; its operations are more pure, refined, and sweet than can be described, though our Lord knows how to make the soul sensible of them.

2. (The prayer of union resembles a betrothal). I think this union docs not attain as far as the spiritual espousals, but resembles the preliminaries that take place when two people are contemplating a betrothal. Their suitability and willingness for the alliance are first discussed; then they may be allowed to see one another sometimes, so as to come to a decision. Thus it is in the spiritual espousals: when the preliminary agreement has been made, and the soul thoroughly understands what great advantages she will gain, having resolved to fulfil the will of her Spouse in all things and to do all she can to please Him, His Majesty Who knows well whether this is so in reality, wishes in return to gratify His bride. He therefore bestows this favour upon her, visits her, and draws her into His presence, as He wishes her to know Him better. We might compare the prayer of union to a visit, for it lasts

---

Ant. ad Laudes de Com. Virg.); "quasi apis argumentosa Domino deservisti" (*Ibid.* Feast of St. Cæcilia).

but a very little while.* There is no longer any question of deliberation, but the soul in a secret manner sees to what a Bridegroom it is betrothed; the senses and faculties could not, in a thousand years, gain the knowledge thus imparted in a very short time. The Spouse, being Who He is, leaves the soul far more deserving of completing the espousals, as we may call them; the enamoured soul in its love for Him makes every effort to prevent their being frustrated. Should it grow neglectful, and set its affections on anything except our Lord, it will forfeit everything: this loss is as great as are the favours the soul has continually received, which are precious beyond description.†

3. (Before the spiritual nuptials temptation are dangerous). O Christian souls, you whom God has brought thus far, I implore you for His dear sake not to grow careless, but to avoid all occasions of sin; you are not strong enough yet to undergo temptation, as you will be after the espousals which take place in the next mansion. Here the betrothed are, as they say, only acquainted by sight,‡ and the devil will spare no pains to oppose and prevent their nuptials. Afterwards, when he sees the Bride is wholly given to her Bridegroom, he is afraid to interfere, having learnt by experience that if he molest her, while he loses much, she will gain greatly in merit.

4. (The great good done by souls faithful to these graces). I

---

* *Life,* ch. xviii. 16.

† *Way of Perf.* ch. xxxi. 10.

‡ Phil. a SS. Trinit. *l.c.* p. iii. tract. i. disc. ii. art. 2.

can assure you, my daughters,* that I have known people far advanced in the spiritual life who had reached this state of prayer, yet whom the devil reclaimed by his subtlety and wiles: as I have often said, all hell leagues together against such souls, because the loss of one of them entails the perdition of many more, as Satan is well aware. If we considered how many men God draws to Himself by means of one, we should praise Him fervently. Think of the multitudes converted by the martyrs, or by one young maiden like St. Ursula! Again, of how many victims the evil one was deprived by St. Dominic, St. Francis, and other founders of religious orders! How many more he loses, even now, through Father Ignatius [Loyola], who founded the Company [of Jesus]! As we read their lives, we learn that they received such graces from God. How was this great good done except by their efforts not to forfeit, through any fault of theirs, these divine espousals? Oh, my daughters, how willing our Lord is to grant us the same graces! In fact, there is even more urgent need now for persons to prepare for such favours, since there are fewer who care for His honour. We love ourselves too much and are too prudent to give up any of our rights. What a deception! May God in His mercy give us light, lest we sink into such darkness!

5. (Religious subject to the devil's deceptions). You may question or be in doubt on two points. First: "If the soul is entirely united with the will of God, as I have stated, how can it be deceived, since it ever seeks to follow His pleasure?

---

* Contrast with this paragraph what the Saint says in her *Life,* ch. xix. § 8.

Secondly, how can the devil enter and work such havoc as to destroy your soul while you are so utterly withdrawn from the world and constantly frequent the Sacraments?* At the same time you enjoy the society of angels (as we might call them) and by the mercy of God you desire nothing but to serve and please Him in all things?† It is not surprising that people in the world should run such risks." I admit you have the right to say this, for God has shown us signal mercy; but, as I said above, knowing as I do that Judas was amongst the Apostles, and that he held constant intercourse with God Himself, to Whose words he listened, I learn that the state of religion does not make us safe.

6. (Satan's stratagems). To your first question I reply, that doubtless if such a soul is always faithful to the will of God, it cannot be lost; the evil one, however, comes with his keen subtlety, and, under the pretext of good, leads it astray in some trivial matter and causes it to commit small defects, which he leads it to believe are harmless. Thus, little by little, the reason is obscured and the will is weakened, while the devil fosters his victim's self-love, until, by degrees, he succeeds in withdrawing it from union with the will of God and makes it follow his own will.

7. (Why they are permitted). The answer to your first inquiry will serve for the second. No enclosure can be too strict for Satan to enter, nor any desert too remote for him to visit. Besides, God may permit him to tempt the soul to prove its

---

* *Life,* ch. xxxvi. 26; ch. xxxix. 14. *Found.* ch. i. 1–4.

† *Way of Perf.* ch. i. 2; ch. xiii. 5. *Found.* ch. i. 3.

virtue; for as He intends it to enlighten others, it is better for it to fail in the beginning than when it might do them great harm.

8. (Prayer and watchfulness our safeguards). We must beg God constantly in our prayers to uphold us by His hand; we should keep ever in our minds the truth that if He leaves us, most certainly we shall fall at once into the abyss, for we must never be so foolish as to trust in ourselves. After this I think the greatest safeguard is to be very careful and to watch how we advance in virtue; we must notice whether we are making progress or falling back in it, especially as regards the love of our neighbour, the desire to be thought the least of all, and how we perform our ordinary, everyday duties. If we attend to this and beg Our Lord to enlighten us, we shall at once perceive our gain and loss.

9. (God's watchfulness over such souls). Do not suppose that after advancing the soul to such a state God abandons it so easily that it is light work for the devil to regain it. When His Majesty sees it leaving Him, He feels the loss so keenly that He gives it in many a way a thousand secret warnings which reveal to it the hidden danger.*

10. (Progress in virtue). In conclusion, let us strive to make constant progress: we ought to feel great alarm if we do not find ourselves advancing, for without doubt the evil one must be planning to injure us in some way; it is impossible for a soul that has come to this state not to go still farther, for love is never idle. Therefore it is a very bad sign when one comes to

---

* *Life,* ch. xix. 9.

a stand-still in virtue. She who aspires to become the spouse of God Himself, and has treated with His Majesty and come to such an understanding with Him, must not leave off and go to sleep.*

11. (Insignificance of our actions compared with their reward). To show you, my daughters, how Christ treats the souls He takes for His brides, I will now speak of the sixth mansions. You will then see how little, in comparison, is all that we can do or suffer in His service to prepare ourselves for the reception of such immense favours. Perhaps our Lord decreed that I should write this, in order that the knowledge of the great reward to come, and of His infinite mercy in seeking to give and to manifest Himself to such worms as we are, might make us forget our wretched, petty, earthly pleasures, and run on our way with eyes fixed on His grandeur, inflamed with love for Him.

12. (St. Teresa's motives for writing on prayer). May He enable me to explain some of these difficult matters; if our Lord and the Holy Ghost do not guide my pen, I know the task will prove impossible. I beg Him to prevent my saying anything unless it will profit you. His Majesty knows that, as far as I can judge, I have no other wish but that His Name may be glorified, and that we may strive to serve a Lord Who thus recompenses our efforts even in this world. What, then, will be our joy in heaven, where it will be continuous, without the interruptions, labours, and dangers of this tempestuous sea of life? Were it not for the fear of losing or offending

---

* *Life,* ch. xix. 7.

Him, we should wish to live until the end of the world,* that we might work for so great a God—our Lord and our Spouse. May His Majesty enable us to render Him some service free from the many faults we always commit, even in good works! Amen.

---

* *Rel.* ix. 19.

THE SIXTH MANSIONS

1

Preparation for Spiritual Matrimony

This chapter shows how, when God bestows greater favours on the soul, it suffers more severe afflictions. Some of the latter are described, and directions how to bear them given to the dwellers in this mansion. This chapter is useful for those suffering interior trials.

1. (Love kindled by divine favours). By the aid of the Holy Ghost, I am now about to treat of the sixth mansions, where the soul, wounded with love for its Spouse, sighs more than ever for solitude, withdrawing, as far as the duties of its state permit, from all that can interrupt it. The sight it has enjoyed of Him is so deeply imprinted on the spirit that its only desire is to behold Him again. I have already said that,* even by the imagination, nothing is seen in this prayer that can be called sight. I speak of it as "sight" because of the comparison I used.

---

* *Castle,* M. v. ch. i. 9. *Life,* ch. xxviii. 5.

2. (Our Lord excites the soul's longings). The soul is now determined to take no other Bridegroom than our Lord, but He disregards its desires for its speedy espousals, wishing that these longings should become still more vehement and that this good, which far excels all other benefits, should be purchased at some cost to itself. And although, for so great a gain, all that we must endure is but a poor price to pay, I assure you, daughters, that this pledge of what is in store for us is needed to inspire us with courage to bear our crosses.

3. (Courage needed to reach the last mansions). O my God, how many troubles both interior and exterior must one suffer before entering the seventh mansions! Sometimes, while pondering over this I fear that, were they known beforehand, human infirmity could scarcely bear the thought, nor resolve to encounter them, however great might appear the gain. If, however, the soul has already reached the seventh mansions, it fears nothing: boldly undertaking to suffer all things for God,* it gathers strength from its almost uninterrupted union with Him.

4. (Trials accompanying divine favours). I think it would be well to tell you of some of the trials certain to occur in this state. Possibly all souls may not be led in this way, but I think that those who sometimes enjoy such truly heavenly favours cannot be altogether free from some sort of earthly troubles. Therefore, although at first I did not intend to speak on this subject, yet afterwards I thought that it might greatly comfort a soul in this condition if it knew what usually happens to

---

* *Life,* ch. xl. 28 *sqq.*

those on whom God bestows graces of this kind, for at the time they really appear to have lost everything.

5. (Outcry raised against souls striving for perfection). I shall not enumerate these trials in their proper order, but describe them as they come to my memory, beginning with the least severe. This is an outcry raised against such a person by those amongst whom she lives, and even from others she has nothing to do with, but who fancy that at some time in her life they recollect having seen her. They say she wants to pass for a saint, that she goes to extremes in piety to deceive the world and to depreciate people who are better Christians than herself without making such a parade of it. But notice that she does nothing except endeavour to carry out the duties of her state more perfectly. Persons she thought were her friends desert her, making the most bitter remarks of all. They take it much to heart that her soul is ruined—she is manifestly deluded—it is all the devil's work—she will share the fate of so-and-so, who was lost through him, and she is leading virtue astray. They cry out that she is deceiving her confessors, and tell them so, citing examples of others who came to ruin in the same way, and make a thousand scoffing remarks of the same sort.*

6. (St. Teresa's personal experience of this). I know some one who feared she would be unable to find any priest who would hear her confession, to such a pass did things come; but, as it is a long story, I will not stop to tell it now. The

---

* The Saint went through all this herself; every detail is taken from her own experience. See *Life,* ch. xxv. 20; ch. xxviii. 20–24; ch. xxx. 6; ch. xxxiii. 2. Anton. a Sp. S. *l.c.* tract. ii. n. 268.

worst of it is, these troubles do not blow over, but last all her life, for one person warns the other to have nothing to do with people of her kind! You will say that, on the other hand, some speak in her favour. O my daughters, how few think well of her in comparison with the many who hate her!

7. (Praise distasteful to an enlightened soul). Besides this, praise pains such a soul more than blame, because it recognises clearly that any good it possesses is the gift of God and in no wise its own, seeing that but a short time ago it was weak in virtue and involved in grave sins.* Therefore commendation causes it intolerable suffering, at least at first, although later on, for many reasons, the soul is comparatively indifferent to either.

8. (This changes to indifference). The first is that experience has shown the mind that men are as ready to speak well as ill of others, so it attaches no more importance to the one than to the other. Secondly, our Lord having granted it greater light, it perceives that no good thing in it is its own, but is His gift, and becomes oblivious of self, praising God for His graces as if they were found in a third person.

9. (Humility of such souls). The third reason is that, realising the benefit reaped by others from witnessing graces given it by God, such a one thinks that it is for their profit He causes them to discover in her virtues that do not exist.

10. (Their zeal for God's glory). Fourthly, souls seeking God's honour and glory more than their own are cured of the temptation (which usually besets beginners) of thinking that human praise will cause them the injury they have seen it do

---

* *Life,* ch. xxviii. 19.

to others. Nor do these souls care much for men's contempt, if only, by their means, any one should praise God, at least for once—come what may afterwards.

11. (Perfect and final indifference to praise of blame). These and other reasons to a certain extent allay the great distress formerly given by human praise, which, however, still causes some discomfort, unless the soul has become utterly regardless of men's tongues. It is infinitely more grieved at being undeservedly esteemed by the world than by any calumny; and when at last it becomes almost indifferent to praise, it cares still less for censure, which even pleases it and sounds like harmonious music to the ears.

12. (Love of enemies). This is perfectly true; the soul is rather strengthened than depressed by its trials, experience having taught it the great advantages derived from them. It does not think men offend God by persecuting it, but that He permits them to do so for its greater gain.* So strong is this belief, that such a person bears a special affection for these people, holding them as truer friends and greater benefactors than those who speak well of her.†

13. (Bodily sufferings). Our Lord now usually sends severe bodily infirmity. This is a far heavier cross, especially if acute pain is felt; if this be violent, I think it is the hardest of earthly trials. I speak of exterior trials, but corporal pains, if of the worst kind, enter the interior of our being also, affecting both spirit and body, so that the soul, in its anguish, knows not what to

---

* *Rel.* ii. 4.

† Anton. a Sp. S. *l.c.* ii. n. 272. *Way of Perf.* ch. xv. 1; ch. xvii. 4. *Found.* ch. xxvii. 19, 20. *Life,* ch. xix. 12; ch. xxxi. 13–17, 25.

do with itself, and would far rather meet death at once by some quick martyrdom than suffer thus. However, these paroxysms do not last long, for God never sends us more than we can bear, and always gives us patience first.

14. (St. Teresa's physicall ills). Now to speak of other trials and illnesses of many kinds which generally occur to people in this state. I knew some one who, from the time when, forty years ago,[*] our Lord began to bestow on her the favour described, could not affirm, with any truth, that she had been a single day without pain and other kinds of suffering: I am speaking of physical infirmities besides heavy crosses sent her.[†] True, she had led a wicked life, and therefore held these troubles very light in comparison with the hell she had deserved.[‡] Our Lord leads those who have offended Him less by some other way, but I should always choose the way of suffering, were it only for the sake of imitating our Lord Jesus Christ; though, in fact, it profits us in many other manners. Yet, oh! the rest would seem trifling in comparison, could I relate the interior torments met with here, but they are impossible to describe!

15. (A timorous confessor). Let us first speak of the trial of meeting with so timorous and inexperienced a confessor that nothing seems safe to him; he dreads and suspects everything but the commonplace, especially in a soul wherein he detects any imperfection, for he thinks people on whom God be-

---

* "Forty years ago." The Saint seems to refer to her first experience in the mystical life, which took place during her illness in the winter of 1537–38. See *Life*, ch. iv. 9.

† *Life*, ch. iv. 6; ch. v.; vi.; vii. 18; xi. 23; xxx. 9.

‡ *Life*, ch. iii. 6, 7.

stows such favours must be angels, which is impossible while we live in our bodies.* He at once ascribes everything to the devil or melancholy. As to the latter, I am not surprised; there is so much of it in the world, and the evil one works such harm in this way that confessors have the strongest reason for anxiety and watchfulness about it.

16. (Anxiety on account of past sins). The poor soul, however, beset by the same fears, seeks its confessor as judge, and feels a torture and dismay at his condemnation that can only be realised by those who have experienced it themselves.† For one of the severe trials of these souls, especially if they have lived wicked lives, is their belief that God permits them to be deceived in punishment for their sins. While actually receiving these graces they feel secure, and cannot but suppose that these favours proceed from the Spirit of God; still, as this state lasts a very short time, while the remembrance of their misdeeds is ever before them, when, as is sure to happen, they discover any faults in themselves, these torturing thoughts return.‡

17. (Fears and aridity). The soul is quieted for a time when the confessor reassures it, although it returns later on to its former apprehensions, but when he augments its fears they become almost unbearable. Especially is this the case when such spiritual dryness ensues that the mind feels as if it never had thought of God, nor ever will be able to do so.

---

* *Life,* ch. xiii. 21–27. *Way of Perf.* ch. v. 1, 2.

† *Life,* ch. xxx. 15.

‡ *Life,* ch. xxxviii, 21. *Rel.* ii. 15.

When men speak of Him, they seem to be talking of some person heard of long ago.

18. (Scruples and fears raised by the devil). All this is nothing, without the further pain of thinking we cannot make our confessors understand the case and are deceiving them.* Although such a person may examine her conscience with the greatest care, and may know that she reveals even the first movement of her mind to her director, it does not help her. Her understanding being too obscured to discern the truth, she believes all that the imagination, which has now the upper hand, puts before her mind, besides crediting the falsehoods suggested to her by the devil, whom doubtless our Lord gives leave to tempt her. The evil spirit even tries to make her think God has rejected her. Many are the trials which assault this soul, causing an internal anguish so painful and so intolerable that I can compare it to nothing save that suffered by the lost in hell, for no comfort can be found in this tempest of trouble.†

19. (Bewilderment of the soul). If the soul seeks for consolation from its confessor, all the demons appear to help him to torment it more. A confessor who dealt with a person suffering in this manner thought that the state must be very dangerous, as so many things were troubling her; therefore, after she had recovered from her trials, he bade her tell him whenever they recurred: however, he found this made matters worse than

---

* *Life,* ch. xxviii. 20 *sqq.*

† Antonius a Sp. S. *l.c.* tr. ii. n. 313. On this subject, which is commonly called the passive purgation of the intellect, it would be advisable to consult some good author such as Philippus a SS. Trinitate, *l.c.* part. i. tr. iii. disc. iii.–v., especially disc. iv. art. 5, 6.

ever. She lost all control over herself: although she had learnt to read, yet she could no more understand a book in the vulgar tongue than if she had not known the alphabet, for her mind was incapable of acting.*

20. (God alone relieves these troubles). In short, there is no other remedy in such a tempest except to wait for the mercy of God, Who unexpectedly, by some casual word or unforeseen circumstance, suddenly dispels all these sorrows; then every cloud of trouble disappears and the mind is left full of light and far happier than before.† It praises our Lord God like one who has come out victorious from a dangerous battle, for it was He Who won the victory. The soul is fully conscious that the conquest was not its own, as all weapons of self-defence appeared to be in the enemies' hands. Thus it realises its weakness, and how little man can help himself if God forsake him.

21. (Human weakness). This truth now needs no demonstration, for past experience has taught the soul its utter incapacity; it realises the nothingness of human nature and what miserable creatures we are. Although in a state of grace from which it has not fallen—for, in spite of these torments, it has not offended God, nor would it do so for any earthly thing‡—yet so hidden is this grace, that the sufferer believes that neither now, nor in the past, has she ever possessed the faintest spark of love for God.§ If at any time she has done good, or if His

---

* *Life,* ch. xxv. 21.

† *Life,* ch. xxv. 23.

‡ *Life,* ch. xxiv. 3. *Way of Perf.* ch. xli. 5. *Castle,* M. vii. ch. iv. 1.

§ *Excl.* xvi. 4.

Majesty bestowed any favours on her, they seem to have been but a dream or a fancy, while her sins stand clearly before her.

22. (Earthly consolations are of no avail). O Jesus! how sad it is to see a soul thus forsaken, and how little, as I said, can any earthly comfort avail! Do not imagine, sisters, if you are ever brought to such a state, that rich and independent people have more resources than yourselves in these troubles. No, no! to offer such consolations would be like setting all the joys of the world before people condemned to death: far from mitigating, it would increase their torture. So with the souls I spoke of: their comfort must come from above—nothing earthly can help them. This great God wishes us to acknowledge His sovereignty and our own misery—an important point for those who are to advance still farther.

23. (Prayer gives no comfort at such a time). What can the poor soul do if such a trial lasts for many days? Prayer makes no difference as far as comforting the heart, which no consolation can enter, nor can the mind even grasp the meaning of the words of vocal prayer: mental prayer is out of the question at such a time, since the faculties are unequal to it. Solitude harms the soul, yet society or conversation is a fresh torment. Strive as the sufferer may to hide it, she is so wearied and out of sorts with all around that she cannot but manifest her condition.

24. (Remedies for these interior trials). How can the soul possibly tell what ails it? Its pains are indescribable; it is wrung with nameless anguish and spiritual suffering. The best remedy for these crosses (I do not mean for gaining deliverance from them, for I know of nothing that will do that, but for enabling one to bear them) is to perform external works of

charity and to trust in the mercy of God, which never fails those who hope in Him.* May He be for ever blessed! Amen.

25. (Trials caused by the devil). The devils also bring about exterior trials, which are more unusual, therefore need not be mentioned. They are far less painful, for whatever the demons may do, I believe they never succeed in paralysing the faculties or disturbing the soul in the former manner. In fact, the reason is able to discern that the evil spirits can do no more harm than God permits; and while the mind has not lost its powers, all sufferings are comparatively small.

26. (And other afflictions). I shall treat of other internal afflictions met with in this mansion, when describing the different kinds of prayer and favours bestowed here by our Lord. Although some of these latter pains are harder to endure, as appears by their bodily effects, yet they do not deserve the name of crosses, nor have we the right to call them so. Indeed, they are great graces from God, as the soul recognises amidst its pangs, realising how far it is from meriting such graces.

27. (Preparatory to entering the seventh mansions). This severe torture felt by souls just at the entrance of the seventh mansion is accompanied by many other sufferings, some of which I will mention: to speak of them all would be impossible, nor could I portray them, because they come from another and far higher source than the rest. If I have succeeded so ill in writing of trials of a lower kind, much less could I treat of the others. May God assist me in all things, through the merits of His Son! Amen.

---

* *Life,* ch. xxxi. 27.

2

The Wound of Love

*Treats of several ways whereby our Lord quickens the soul;
there appears no cause for alarm in them, although they are
signal favours of a very exalted nature.*

1. (Our Lord excites the love of His Spouse). It seems as if we
   had deserted the little dove for a long time, but this is not
   the case, for these past trials cause her to take a far higher
   flight. I will now describe the way in which the Spouse treats
   her before uniting her entirely to Himself. He increases her
   longing for Him by devices so delicate that the soul itself
   cannot discern them; nor do I think I could explain them,
   except to those who have personal experience. These desires
   are delicate and subtle impulses, springing from the inmost
   depths of the soul; I know of nothing to which they can be
   compared.

2. (The wound of love). These graces differ entirely from anything we ourselves can gain, and even from the spiritual consolation before described.* In the present case, even when the

---

* Mansion iv. ch. i. *Life,* ch. xxix. 10–15. *Rel.* viii. 15.

mind is not recollected or even thinking of God, although no sound is heard, His Majesty arouses it suddenly, as if by a swiftly flashing comet, or by a clap of thunder.* Yet the soul thus called by God hears Him well enough—so well, indeed, that sometimes, especially at first, it trembles and even cries out, although it feels no pain. It is conscious of having received a delicious wound, but cannot discover how, nor who gave it, yet recognises it as a most precious grace, and hopes the hurt will never heal.

3. (The pain it causes). The soul makes amorous complaints to its Bridegroom, even uttering them aloud; nor can it control itself, for it knows that, though He is present, He will not manifest Himself so that it may enjoy Him. This causes a pain, keen although sweet and delicious, from which the soul could not escape even if it wished; this, however, it never desires.† This favour is more delightful than the pleasing absorption of the faculties in the prayer of quiet, which is unaccompanied by suffering.‡

4. (The call of the Bridegroom). I am at my wit's end, sisters, as to how to make you understand this operation of love; I know not how to do so. It seems contradictory to say that the Beloved clearly shows He dwells in the soul and calls by so unmistakable a sign, and a summons so penetrating, that the spirit cannot choose but hear it, while yet He appears to reside in the seventh mansion. He speaks in this manner, which is not

---

* The saint first wrote "relampago," flash of lightning, but afterwards altered it to "trueno," clap of thunder.

† *Rel.* viii. 16. St. John of the Cross, *Spiritual Cant.* st. i. 22 *sqq.*

‡ *Life,* ch. xxix. 18.

a set form of speech, and the inhabitants of the other mansions, the senses, the imagination and the faculties, dare not stir.*

5. (The effect on the soul). O Almighty God! how profound are Thy secrets, and how different are spiritual matters from anything that can be seen or heard in this world! I can find nothing to which to liken these graces, insignificant as they are compared with many others Thou dost bestow on souls. This favour acts so strongly upon the spirit that it is consumed by desires, yet knows not what to ask, for it realises clearly that its God is with it. You may inquire, if it realises this so clearly, what more does it desire, and why is it pained? What greater good can it seek? I cannot tell: I know that this suffering seems to pierce the very heart, and when He Who wounded it draws out the dart He seems to draw the heart out too, so deep is the love it feels.†

6. (A spark of the fire of love). I have been thinking that God might be likened to a burning furnace,‡ from which a small spark flies into the soul which feels the heat of this great fire, which, however, is insufficient to consume it. The sensation is so delightful that the spirit lingers in the pain produced by its contact. This seems to me the best comparison I could find, for the pain is delicious and is not really pain at all, nor does it always continue in the same degree; sometimes it lasts for a long time, and on other occasions passes quickly. This is as God chooses, for no human means can obtain it; and though felt at times for a long while, yet it is intermittent.

---

* *Life,* ch. xv. 1.

† *Life,* ch. xxix. 17–18.

‡ *Life,* ch. xv. 6; xviii. 4; xxi. 9.

7. (The spark dies out). In fact, it is never permanent and therefore does not wholly inflame the spirit; but when the soul is ready to take fire, the little spark suddenly dies out, leaving the heart longing to suffer anew its loving pangs. No grounds exist for thinking this comes from any natural cause, or from melancholy, or that it is an illusion of the devil or the imagination. Undoubtedly this movement of the heart comes from God, Who is unchangeable; nor do its effects resemble those of other devotions, in which the strong absorption of delight makes us doubt their reality.

8. (This grace evidently divine). There is no suspension here of the senses or other faculties: they wonder at what is happening, without impeding it. Nor do I think that they can either increase or dispel this delightful pain. Any one who has received this favour from our Lord will understand my meaning on reading this; let her thank Him fervently: there is no need to fear deception, but far more fear of not being sufficiently grateful for so signal a grace. Let her endeavour to serve Him and to amend her life in every respect, and she will see what will follow, and how she will obtain still higher and higher gifts.

9. (One such wound repays many trials). A person on whom this grace was bestowed passed several years without receiving any other favour, was yet perfectly satisfied, for even had she served God for very many years in the midst of severe trials, she would have felt abundantly repaid. May He be for ever blessed, Amen!

10. (First reason of immunity from deception). Perhaps you wonder why we may feel more secure against deception concerning this favour than in other cases. I think it is for

these reasons. Firstly, because the devil cannot give such delicious pain: he may cause pleasure or delight which appears spiritual, but is unable to add suffering, especially suffering of so keen a sort, united to peace and joy of soul. His power is limited to what is external; suffering produced by him is never accompanied with peace, but with anxieties and struggles.

11. (Second and third reasons). Secondly, because this welcome storm comes from no region over which Satan has control. Thirdly, because of the great benefits left in the soul, which, as a rule, is resolute to suffer for God, and longs to bear many crosses. It is also far more determined than before to withdraw from worldly pleasures and intercourse and other things of the same sort.

12. (The imagination not concerned in it). It is very clear that this is no fiction: the imagination may counterfeit some favours, but not this, which is too manifest to leave room for doubt. Should any one still remain uncertain, let her know that hers were not genuine impulses,* that is, if she is dubious as to whether or no she experienced them, for they are as certainly perceived by the soul as is a loud voice by the ears. It is impossible for these experiences to proceed from melancholy, whose whims arise and exist only in the imagination, whereas this emotion comes from the interior of the soul.

13. (St. Teresa never alarmed at this prayer). I may be mistaken, but I shall not change my opinion until I hear reasons to the contrary from those who understand these matters. I know some one who has always greatly dreaded such deceptions,

---

* *Life,* ch. xv. 15, 16.

yet could never bring herself to feel any alarm about this state of prayer.*

14. ("The odour of Thine ointment"). Our Lord also uses other means of rousing the soul; for instance—when reciting vocal prayer, without seeking to penetrate the sense, a person may be seized with a delightful fervour,† as if suddenly encompassed with a fragrance powerful enough to diffuse itself through all the senses. I do not assert that there really is any perfume, but use this comparison because it somewhat resembles the manner by which the Spouse makes His presence understood, moving the soul to a delicious desire of enjoying Him, and thus disposing it to heroic acts, and causing it to render Him fervent praise.

15. (No reason to fear deception here). This favour springs from the same source as the former, but causes no suffering here, nor are the soul's longings to enjoy God painful: this is what is more usually experienced by the soul. For the reasons already given, there appears no cause here for fear, but rather for receiving it with thanksgiving.

---

* *Life,* ch. xxix. 6–10.

† *Life,* ch. xv. 12. On the matter treated by St. Teresa in this chapter, compare St. John of the Cross, *Spiritual Canticle,* stanza i. (*circa finem*), stanza ix.; *The Living Flame of Love,* stanza ii.

Introductory Note
to Chapter 3

THE readers, especially those not well acquainted with Scholastic philosophy, will, perhaps, be glad to find here a short explanation of the various kinds of Vision and Locution, Corporal, Imaginary, and Intellectual. The senses of Taste, Touch, and Smell are not so often affected by mystical phenomena, but what we are about to say in respect of Sight and Hearing applies, *mutatis mutandis,* to these also.

1. A CORPORAL VISION is when one sees a bodily object. A Corporal Locution is when one hears words uttered by a human tongue. In both cases the respective senses are exercising their normal function, and the phenomenon differs from ordinary seeing or hearing merely by the fact that in the latter the object seen is a real body, the words perceived come from a real tongue, whereas in the Vision or Locution the object is either only apparent or at any rate is not such as it seems to be. Thus, when young Tobias set out on a journey, his companion, Azarias, was not a real human being, but an archangel in human

form. Tobias did really see and hear him, and felt the grip of his hand; Sarah and her parents, as well as Tobias's parents, saw and heard him too, but all the time the archangel made himself visible and audible by means of an assumed body, or perhaps of an apparent body. It would be more correct to describe such a phenomenon as an APPARITION than as a Vision, and in fact the apparitions of our Risen Lord to the holy women and the Apostles belong to this category. For, though His was a real body, it was glorified and therefore no longer subject to the same laws which govern purely human things. (St. Thomas, *Summa theol. III.,* qu. 54, art. 1–3.)

St. Teresa tells us more than once that she never beheld a Corporal Vision, nor heard a Corporal Locution.

2. An IMAGINARY VISION OR LOCUTION is one where nothing is seen or heard by the senses of seeing or hearing, but where the same impression is received that would be produced upon the imagination by the senses if some real object were perceived by them. For, according to the Scholastics, the Imagination stands half-way between the senses and the intellect, receiving impressions from the former and transmitting them to the latter. This is the reason why imaginary Visons and Locutions are so dangerous that, according to St. Teresa, St. John of the Cross, and other spiritual writers, they should not only never be sought for, but as much as possible shunned, and, under all circumstances, discountenanced. For the Imagination is closely connected with the Memory, so that it is frequently impossible to ascertain whether a Vision, etc., is not perhaps a semiconscious or unconscious reproduction of scenes witnessed. It is here also that deception, wilful or unwilful, self-deception or deception by a higher agency, is to be feared. Hence the general rule

that such Visions or Locutions should only be trusted upon the strongest grounds. According to St. Thomas Aquinas (*Summa theol. 2a 2æ,* qu. 175, art. 3 ad 4ᵐ), the visions of Isaias, St. John in the Apocalypse, etc., were Imaginary.

As an example of Imaginary Visions we may mention St. Stephen, who saw "the heavens opened, and the Son of Man standing on the right hand of God"; or St. Peter, who saw "the heavens opened, and a certain vessel descending, as it were of a great linen sheet, let down by the four corners from heaven to the earth . . . and there came a voice to him: Arise, Peter, kill and eat" (Acts vii. 55; x. 11–13).

These Visions, Locutions, etc., are not hallucinations. The latter are due to physical disorder which affects the memory and causes it to represent impressions formerly received by it, in a disorderly and often grotesque manner. The Imaginary Vision takes place independently of a morbid state, is caused by an extraneous power, good or evil, and has for its object things of which the memory neither has nor ever has had cognisance.

3. AN INTELLECTUAL VISION OR LOCUTION is one where nothing is seen or heard by the eyes and ears, and where no sensation is received by the imagination. But the impression which would be delivered by the imagination to the intellect, had it come through the senses and been handed on to the imagination, is directly imprinted upon the intellect. To understand this it is necessary to bear in mind that the impressions we receive through the senses must undergo a transformation—must be spiritualised—before they reach the intellect. This is one of the most difficult problems of psychology; none of the solutions offered by various schools of philosophy seem to render it entirely free from obscurity. According to St. Thomas Aquinas,

the impression received by the eye (*Species sensibilis*) is spiritualised by a faculty called *Intellectus agens* by means of abstraction (*Species impressa*), and is treasured up in the memory, like lantern slides, available at demand. The mind, identifying itself with the *Species impressa,* produces the "Word of the Mind" (*Verbum mentis*), wherein consists the act of Understanding or Mental Conception. In the Intellectual Vision or Locution, God, without co-operation on the part of the senses, the imagination, or the memory, produces directly on the mind the *Species impressa.* As this is supernatural with regard to its origin, and often also with respect to its object, it stands to reason that it is too exalted for the memory to receive it, so that such Visions and Locutions are frequently only imperfectly remembered and sometimes altogether forgotten, as St. Teresa tells us. On the other hand, they are far less dangerous than Corporal or Imaginary Visions and Locutions, because the senses and the imagination have nothing to do with them, whilst evil spirits are unable to act directly upon the mind, and self-deception is altogether excluded for the reasons stated by St. Teresa.

An instance of such a vision is mentioned by St. Paul: "I know a man in Christ above fourteen years ago (whether in the body I know not, or out of the body I know not: God knoweth), such an one rapt even to the third heaven. And I know such a man (whether in the body or out of the body, I know not: God knoweth): that he was caught up into paradise, and heard secret words, which it is not granted to man to utter" (2 Cor. xii. 2–4).

3

Locutions

*Treats of the same subject and of the way God is sometimes
pleased to speak to the soul. How we should behave in such
a case, in which we must not follow our own opinion. Gives
signs to show how to discover whether this favour is a deception
or not: this is very noteworthy.*

1. (Locutions). GOD arouses the soul in another manner which,
   though in some ways apparently a greater favour than the
   above mentioned, yet may prove more dangerous, therefore
   I will give some particulars about it. He does this by means
   of words addressed to the soul in many different ways; sometimes they appear to come from without, at other times from
   the inner depths of the soul, or again, from its superior part,
   while other speeches are so exterior as to be heard by the ears
   like a real voice.

2. (Sometimes caused by melancholia). At times, indeed very
   often, this may be only a fancy; especially with persons of a
   lively imagination or who are afflicted with melancholy to
   any marked extent. I think that no attention should be paid

to either class of people when they say they see, hear, or learn anything supernaturally. Do not disturb them by saying that it comes from the devil,* but listen to them as if they were sick persons. Let the prioress or confessor to whom they tell their story bid them think no more of it, as such matters are not essential in the service of God: the devil has deceived many Christians thus, although perhaps it is not so in their case; therefore they need not trouble themselves about it. Thus we must accommodate ourselves to their humour: if we tell them their fancies proceed from melancholia, there will be no end to the matter, for they will persist in maintaining they have seen and heard these things, for so it seems to them.

3. (Caution needed at first). The truth is, care should be taken to keep such people from too much prayer, and to persuade them, as far as possible, to take no notice of their fancies: the devil makes use of these weak souls to injure others, even if they themselves escape unhurt. There is need for caution, both with feeble and strong souls at first, until it is certain from what spirit these things proceed. I maintain that, in the beginning, it is always wiser to resist these communications; if they come from God this is the best way to receive more, for they increase when discouraged. At the same time the soul should not be too strictly controlled or disquieted, for it cannot help itself in the matter.

4. (Locutions frequently occur during prayer). To return to discuss the words addressed to the soul: any kind I mentioned may come either from God, the devil, or the imagination. By the help of God, I will endeavour to describe the signs

---

* *Life,* ch. xxiii. 14.

distinguishing the one from the other, and when these locutions are dangerous, for they occur to many persons who practise prayer. I do not wish you to think, sisters, that there is any harm either in believing or in disregarding them. When they only console you, or warn you of your faults, it matters not whence they come, or whether they are only fancies.

5. (Resist those containing false doctrine). I caution you on one point—although they may come from God, you must not esteem yourself more highly, for He often spoke to the Pharisees*—all the good consists in profiting by His words. Take no more notice of any speeches you hear which disagree with the Holy Scriptures, than if you heard them from Satan himself. Though they may only rise from your vivid imagination, look upon them as a temptation against the faith. Always resist them; then they will leave you, and cease, for they have little strength of their own.†

6. (First sign of genuine locutions). Now let us return to the first point—whether these communications come from the inferior or the superior part of the soul, or from without, does not affect their originating from God. In my opinion these are the most certain signs of their being divine.

7. (Effect of the words: "Be not troubled"). The first and truest is the power and authority they carry with them, for these words are operative.‡

---

* Antonius a Sp. S. *l.c.* tr. iii. n. 323. St. John of the Cross, *Ascent of Mount Carmel,* bk. ii. ch. xxvii.

† *Life,* ch. xxv. 13, 18.

‡ Ps. cxlviii. 5: "Ipse dixit et facta sunt." *Life,* ch. xxv. 5. Ant. a Sp. S. *l.c.* tr. iii. n. 353. St. John of the Cross, *Ascent of Mount Carmel,* bk. ii. ch. xxxi, calls these "substantial words."

8. For example: a soul is suffering all the sorrow and disquiet I have described: the mind is darkened and dry; but it is set at peace, freed from all trouble and filled with light, merely by hearing the words, "Be not troubled." These deliver it from all its pains, although it felt as though, if the whole world and all its theologians had united in trying to persuade it there was no cause for grief, it could not, in spite of all their efforts, have been delivered from its affliction.*

9. ("It is I, be not afraid"). Again, a person is troubled and greatly terrified at being told by her confessor and other people that her soul is under the influence of the evil one: she hears a single sentence which says, "It is I, be not afraid,"† and is at once freed from all fears and filled with consolation; indeed, she believes it would be impossible for any one to disturb her confidence.‡

10. ("Be at peace"). Again, when exceedingly anxious about a certain important business, not knowing whether or not it will be successful, on hearing words bidding her, "Be at peace, all will go well," she feels reassured and free from all care in the matter.§ Many other instances of the same sort could be mentioned.

11. (Second sign). The second sign is a great calm and a devout and peaceful recollection which dwell in the soul, together with a desire to praise God. They say that communications,

---

* *Life*, ch. xxvi. 6; ch. xxx. 17. *Rel.* i. 26.

† St. Luke xxiv. 36.

‡ *Life,* ch. xxv. 22; ch. xxxiii. 10. *Rel.* vii. 22. St. John of the Cross, *Ascent of Mount Carmel,* bk. ii. ch. xxxi. 1.

§ *Life,* ch. xxxv. 7. *Rel.* ix. 6. St. John of the Cross, *Ascent of Mount Carmel,* bk. iii. ch. ii. 7.

at any rate in this mansion, are not uttered directly by God, but are transmitted by an angel.* Then, O my God, if a word sent to us by Thee through Thy messenger has such force, what effects wilt Thou not leave in the soul united to Thee in a mutual bond of love?†

12. (Third sign). The third proof is that these words do not pass from the memory, but remain there for a very long time; sometimes they are never forgotten. This is not the case with what *men* may utter, which, however grave and learned they may be, is not thus impressed on our memory. Neither, if they prophesy of things to come, do we believe them as we do these divine locutions, which leave us so convinced of their truth, that, although their fulfilment sometimes seems utterly impossible, and we vacillate and doubt about them, there still remains in the soul a certainty of their verity which cannot be destroyed. Perhaps everything may seem to militate against what was heard, and years pass by, yet the spirit never loses its belief that God will make use of means unknown to men for the purpose, and that, finally, what was foretold must surely happen; as indeed it does.‡

13. (The devil suggests doubts about true locutions). Still, as I said, the soul is troubled at seeing many obstacles in the way

------

* *Rel.* v. 14.

† *Life,* ch. xxv. 23–25. See also Schram, *Instit. theol. myst.* 528 schol.; 529 schol. ii. and iii.; 531 schol. ii.; 532 schol. ii. Exterior locutions may proceed direct from God, but generally are due to the ministry of angels; the same holds good with regard to the imaginary ones. Intellectual locutions, in which the words are merely impressed upon the substance of the soul without intervention of the imagination, can only proceed from God, Who alone is able to act upon the substance of the soul. See also *Life,* ch. xxvii. 7 (end), 8, 9, and 10, and the corresponding chapters in St. John's *Ascent of Mount Carmel.*

‡ *Life,* ch. xxv. 3, 10. *Rel.* ii. 17.

of the accomplishment of the prophecy. The words, their effects, and the assurance they carried with them, convinced the soul at the moment that they came from God. Afterwards, however, doubts arise as to whether the locutions came from the devil or from the imagination, although while hearing them the person would have died to defend their truth.* But, as I said, these misgivings must be suggested by the evil one to afflict and intimidate her, especially if by carrying out a command thus given great good will result to souls, and some work be done conducing notably to the honour and service of God, concerning which great difficulties have to be overcome. In such cases, where will Satan stop short? At least, he weakens faith, and it is a terrible evil to doubt that God has power to work in a way far beyond our understanding.

14. (Confidence of the soul rewarded). Despite all these difficulties, and although the confessors consulted on these matters say the words were but fancies, while events take such an unfavourable turn as to make the realisation of these predictions seem impossible, there yet remains so lively a spark of certainty in the mind (I know not whence it comes) that, although all other hopes die out, it cannot, if it would, quench this ardent spark of confidence. At last, as I said, our Lord's words are accomplished, at which the soul is so satisfied and joyful that it can do nothing but praise His Majesty—more because it sees His words prove true than on account of the thing itself, even though it may be of consequence to the person concerned.

---

* *Life,* ch. xxv. 10.

15. (Its joy at seeing God's words verified). I know not why the soul attaches such importance to these communications being verified. I think that if the person herself were detected in telling falsehoods, she would not be so grieved as at these locutions proving untrue—as if she could do anything in the matter beyond repeating what has been said to her! A certain person was frequently reminded, in such a case, of the Prophet Jonas, when he found Nineveh was not to be destroyed.*

16. (Its zeal for God's honour). In fact, as these words come from the Spirit of God, it is right thus to trust them and to desire that He, Who is supreme truth, should not be thought a deceiver. Justly, therefore, does their hearer rejoice, when, after a thousand delays and enormous difficulties, they are accomplished. Although this success may entail great suffering on herself, yet she prefers it to the nonfulfilment of what she knows our Lord most certainly foretold. Possibly every one is not so weak as this, if indeed it is a weakness, though I cannot myself condemn it as an evil.

17. (Locutions coming from the fancy). If these locutions proceed from the imagination,† they show no such signs, bringing neither conviction, peace, nor interior joy with them. However, in some cases I have come across, on account of a very weak constitution or vivid imagination, or of other causes I do not know, persons while absorbed in the prayer of quiet and in spiritual slumber are so entirely carried out

---

* Jonas iv. 1: "Et afflictus est Jonas afflictione magna et iratus est; et oravit ad Dominum et dixit: Obsecro, Domine, numquid non hoc est verbum meum cum adhuc essem in terra mea?"

† *Life,* ch. xxv. 4 (end) and 5 (beginning).

of themselves by their deep state of recollection as to be unconscious of anything external. All their senses being thus dormant, as if asleep—as indeed, at times, they really are—they thus, in a sort of dream, fancy they are spoken to, or see things they imagine come from God, but which leave no more effect than dreams.

18. (Imaginary answers given to prayer). Again, one who very lovingly asks something of our Lord may fancy that an answer comes from Him.* This often occurs, but I think that no one accustomed to receive divine communications could be deceived on this point by the imagination.

19. (A confessor should be consulted about locutions). The devil's deceptions are more dangerous; but if the foregoing signs are present, we may feel fairly confident that these locutions are from God, though not so certain but that, if they refer to some weighty matter in which we are called upon to act, or if they concern a third person, we should consult some confessor who is both learned and a servant of God, before he attempt or think of acting on them, although we may have heard them repeated several times and are convinced of their truth and divine origin.† His Majesty wishes us to take this course; it is not disobedience to His commands, for He has bidden us hold our confessor as His representative, even where there is no doubt that the communications come from Him: thus we shall gain courage, if the matter is a very difficult one. Our Lord will reassure our confessor, whom,

---

* *Life*, ch. xxv. 4 (beginning).

† *Way of Perf.* ch. xxxix. 6. *Life,* ch. xxvi. 4, 5. St. John of the Cross, *Ascent of Mount Carmel,* bk. ii. ch. xxii. 14–18.

when He so chooses, He will inspire with faith that these locutions are from the Holy Ghost.* If not, we are freed from all further obligations in the matter. I think it would be very dangerous to act against our confessor's advice, and to prefer our own opinions in such a matter. Therefore, sisters, I admonish you, in the name of our Lord, never to do anything of the sort.

20. (Interior locutions). God speaks to the soul in another way, by a certain intellectual vision, which I think undoubtedly proceeds from Him, and will be described later on.† It takes place far within the innermost depths of the soul, which appears to hear distinctly, in a most mysterious manner, with its spiritual hearing, the words spoken to it by our Lord Himself. The way in which the spirit perceives these words, and the results produced by them, convince us that they cannot in any way come from the devil. Their powerful after-effects force us to admit this, and also clearly show they do not spring from the imagination.‡ Careful consideration will assure us of this for the following reasons:—

21. (First sign of genuine locutions). Firstly, the clearness of the language varies in the different kinds of locutions. Those that are divine are so distinct that the hearer remembers if there were a syllable missing, and also what special words were made use of, although a whole sentence may have been spoken. If, however, the speech is only a freak of fancy, it

---

* *Rel.* vii. 15.

† *Infra.* ch. viii.

‡ *Life,* ch. xxvii. 8.

would not be so audible, nor the words be so distinct, but would be only half articulated.*

22. (Second sign). The second reason is, that often the person was not thinking of what is heard; sometimes it even comes unexpectedly during conversation, although at times it refers to some thought that passed quickly through the mind, or to a subject it was before engaged upon. Frequently, however, it concerns things of whose existence the hearer knew nothing, nor even imagined such events could ever come to pass; therefore it is impossible for the imagination to have framed such speeches and deceived the mind by fancies about what it had never wished, nor sought for, nor even thought about.†

23. (Third sign). The third reason is, that in a genuine case the soul seems to listen to the words, whereas when the imagination is at work, little by little it goes on composing what the person wishes to hear.‡

24. (Fourth sign). The fourth reason is, because divine locutions differ immensely from others, a single word comprising a depth of meaning which our understanding could not thus quickly condense into one phrase.§

25. (Fifth sign). Fifthly, because, in a manner I cannot explain, these communications, without any further explanations, frequently give us to understand far more than is implied by the words themselves. I shall speak farther on of this way

---

* *Life*, ch. xxv. 6 and 10 (end).

† *Life*, ch. xxv. 9, 16.

‡ *Life*, ch. xxv. 4, 6.

§ *Life*, ch. xxv. 12 (beginning).

of understanding hidden things, which is very subtle, and a favour for which we should thank God. Some people are exceedingly suspicious about these and other communications of the same kind. I speak particularly of some one* who experienced them herself, though there may be others who cannot understand them. I know that she has considered the subject very carefully, God often having bestowed this grace on her. Her principal difficulty was to discover whether they were merely fancied. It is easier to know when they come from the devil, although, being so wily, he can with facility imitate the spirit of light. However, he would do this in a form of words pronounced distinctly, so that there would be no more doubt as to their reality than if they came from the spirit of truth, while those coming from the imagination leave us uncertain whether we heard the words or not. But Satan could never counterfeit the effects I spoke of;† he leaves neither peace nor light in the soul, only anxiety and confusion. In any case, he can do little or no harm to one who is humble and who, as I advised, does not act on what is heard.

26. (Results of true locutions). If the soul receives favours and caresses from our Lord, let it examine carefully whether it rates itself more highly in consequence; unless self-abasement increases with God's expressions of love, they do not come from the Holy Spirit. Inevitably, when they are divine, the greater the favours, the less the soul esteems itself, and the more keenly

---

* The whole of this chapter as well as chapter xxv. of the *Life* prove clearly that the Saint speaks about herself and that she investigated the subject with the greatest care.

† *Life,* ch. xxv. 15.

it remembers its sins.* It becomes more oblivious of self-interest: the will and memory grow more fervent in seeking solely God's honour with no thought of self. It also becomes more careful not to deviate deliberately from the will of God, and feels a keener conviction that, instead of meriting such favours, it deserves hell.

27. (They should remove alarm). When these results follow, no graces or gifts received during prayer need alarm the soul which should rather trust in the mercy of God, Who is faithful and will not allow the devil to deceive it; however, it is always well to be on one's guard.

28. (Answer to an objection). Those our Lord does not lead by this path may suppose that the soul can avoid listening to these locutions, and that even if they are interior it is at least possible to distract the attention from them so as not to hear them and thus escape danger. This cannot be done: I am not speaking of those that are freaks of the fancy, which may be prevented by ceasing to desire certain things, or by paying no attention to its inventions. This is not feasible when these communications come from the Holy Ghost; Who, when He speaks, stops all other thoughts and compels the mind to listen.† Notice this, that I believe it would be easier for a person with very keen ears to avoid hearing a loud voice, for he could occupy his thoughts and mind in other things. Not so here; the soul can do nothing, nor has it ears to stop, nor power to think of aught but what is said to it. For He

---

* *Life,* ch. xii. 5, "the nearer we draw unto God the more this virtue (humility) should grow"; ch. xv. 16; ch. xix. 2; ch. xx. 38. *Rel.* ii. 15; vii. 17; viii. 7, 9. *Way of Perf.* ch. xvii. 3.

† *Life,* ch. xxv. 21.

Who could stay the sun on its course (at the prayer of Josue,[*] I believe) can so quiet the faculties and the interior of the spirit as to make it perceive that another and a stronger Lord than itself governs this castle; it is thus affected with profound devotion and humility, seeing that it cannot but listen. May the divine Majesty vouchsafe that, forgetting ourselves, our only aim may be to please Him, as I said. Amen. God grant I have succeeded in explaining what I wished, and that it may be some guide to those who may experience such favours.

---

[*] Josue x. 12, 13: "Tunc locutus est Josue . . . : sol contra Gabaon ne movearis; steteruntque sol et luna."

4

Raptures

Treats of how God suspends the soul in prayer by a trance, ecstasy, or rapture, which I believe are all the same thing. Great courage required to receive extraordinary favours from His Majesty.

1. (Courage required by the soul for the divine espousals). WHAT rest can the poor little butterfly find, with all the trials I have told you of, and many more? All serve to make her desire the Bridegroom more ardently. His Majesty, well aware of our weakness, fortifies her by these and other means, that she may obtain courage for union with a Lord so great and may take Him for her Spouse. Perhaps you will laugh, and think I am talking foolishly: there can be no call for courage here; there is no woman, however low her class, who would not dare to wed a king. So I think, were he an earthly monarch, but there is need of more fortitude than you suppose in order to espouse the King of heaven.* Our nature appears too timid and

---

* *Life*, ch. xxxix. 30.

base for anything so high; without doubt, unless God gave us the grace, it would be impossible for us, however much we might appreciate its benefits. You will learn how His Majesty ratifies these espousals; probably this is done when He ravishes the soul by ecstasies, so depriving it of its faculties; if the use of these were retained, I think the sight of its close vicinity to so mighty a Sovereign would probably deprive the body of life. I am speaking of genuine raptures, not fancies that come from women's weakness—which so often occur nowadays, making them imagine everything to be a rapture or an ecstasy. As I think I said, some are so feebly constituted as to die of a single prayer of quiet.*

2. (Raptures). I should like to describe here several kinds of raptures of which I have learnt from spiritual persons with whom I have discussed the subject, but I am not sure whether I shall succeed in explaining them, as I did elsewhere.† It has been decided that it will not be amiss to repeat what was said about these and other things that happen in this state, were it only so as to treat of all that the mansions contain in proper order.

3. (Rapture caused by the spark of love). In one sort of rapture, the soul, although perhaps not engaged in prayer at the time, is struck by some word of God which it either remembers or hears.‡ His Majesty, touched with pity by what He has seen it suffer for so long past in its longing for Him, appears to increase the spark I described in the interior of the spirit until it entirely inflames the soul, which rises with new life like

---

* *Castle,* M. iv. ch. iii. 11.

† *Life,* ch. xx. *passim.*

‡ Philippus a SS. Trinitate, *l.c.* p. iii. tr. i. disc. iii. art. 3.

a phoenix from the flames. Such a one may piously believe her sins are now forgiven,* that is, if she be in the disposition and have made use of the means required by the Church. The soul being thus purified, God unites it to Himself in a way known only to Him and the spirit, nor does even the latter so understand what happens as to be able to explain it to others afterwards. The mind, however, had not lost the use of its faculties, for this ecstasy does not resemble a swoon or a fit, in which nothing either interior or exterior is felt.

4. (The powers and senses absorbed). What I do understand is that the soul has never been more alive to spiritual things, nor so full of light and of knowledge of His Majesty as it is now. This might seem impossible; if the powers and senses were so absorbed that we might call them dead, how does the soul understand this mystery? I cannot tell; perhaps no one but the Creator Himself can say what passes in these places—I mean this and the following mansions, which may be treated as one, the door leading from one to the other being wide open. However, as there are some things in the last rooms, only shown to those who get thus far, I thought it better to divide them.

5. (Mysteries revealed during ecstasies). While the soul is in this suspension, our Lord favours it by discovering to it secrets, such as heavenly mysteries and imaginary visions, which admit of description afterwards, because they remain so imprinted on the memory that it never forgets them. But when the visions are intellectual they are not thus easily related, some of those received at such a time being so sublime that it is not fitting for man, while living in this world, to understand

---

* *Rel.* ix. 4. *Way of Perf.* ch. xix. 8.

them in a way that can be told, although, when the use of the faculties returns, much can be described of what was seen in intellectual vision. Possibly you do not know what a vision is, especially an intellectual one. Since I have been bidden by one who has authority, I will tell you at the proper time. Although seemingly superfluous, it may prove useful to certain people.

6. (These mysteries are unspeakable). "But," you will ask me, "if the very sublime favours our Lord bestows in this mansion cannot afterwards be remembered, what profit do they bring?"* Oh, daughters! their value cannot be overrated; for though the recipient is incapable of describing them, they are deeply imprinted in the centre of the soul and are never forgotten. "How can they be remembered if no image is seen and the powers of the soul do not comprehend them?" I, too, do not understand this, but I know that certain truths of the greatness of God remain so impressed on the spirit by this favour, that, did not faith teach Who He is and that it is bound to believe He is God, it would henceforth worship Him as such, as did Jacob, when he saw the ladder.† Doubtless the Patriarch learnt other secrets he was unable to reveal, for, unless he had received more interior light, he could never have discovered such sublime mysteries merely by watching angels ascending and descending the steps. I am not certain whether this quotation is correct; although I have heard the passage, I cannot feel sure of recalling it exactly.

7. (Moses and the burning bush). Neither was Moses able to

---

* Philippus a SS. Trin. *l.c.*

† Gen. xxviii. 12.

relate more than God willed of what he had seen in the burning bush;* but unless the Almighty had clearly revealed certain mysteries to his soul, causing it to see and know its God was present, the lawgiver could never have undertaken so many and such great labours. Such mighty revelations were shown him amidst the thorns of the bush, as to give him the needful courage for his great deeds on behalf of the Children of Israel. We must not, sisters, search out reasons for understanding the hidden things of God, but, believing Him to be Almighty, we should be convinced that such worms as ourselves, with our limited power of intelligence, are unable to comprehend His wonders. Let us praise Him fervently for allowing us to understand something of them.

8. (Simile of the museum). I wish I could find some simile for my subject: none seem to suit the purpose, but I will make use of the following. Imagine that you are in an apartment—I fancy it is termed a *camarin* (or private museum)—belonging to a king or a great nobleman, in which are placed number-less kinds of articles of glass, porcelain, and other things, so arranged that most of them are at once seen on entering the room.

9. (St. Teresa's visit to the Duchess of Alva). While on a visit to the house of the Duchess of Alva (where at her request I was bidden by obedience to stay during a journey),† I was taken into such a room. I stood amazed on entering it, and wondered what could be the use of such a jumble of

---

* Exod. iii. 2.

† Doña Maria Enriquez, wife of Ferdinand de Toledo, Duke of Alva. This visit took place in February 1574, and lasted two days, the Saint being then on her journey from Salamanca to Alva de Tormes.

knick-knacks; then I thought that the sight of so many different things should lead one to praise God. It is fortunate I saw them, for they offer me a suitable comparison in this case. Although I was in the room some time, there were so many objects in it that I forgot what I had seen and could no more remember each object, nor of what it was made, than if I had never seen it, although I recalled the sight of the whole collection.

10. (Joy of the soul during raptures). Something of this sort occurs when the spirit is very closely united to God. It is introduced into this mansion of the empyrean heaven, which must be in the centre of our souls—for since God resides in them, He must own one of the mansions. While the soul is in ecstasy, our Lord does not appear to wish it to apprehend these mysteries, and its inebriation of joy in Him suffices it. Sometimes, however, He is pleased to withdraw it from this rapture, and it at once perceives what the mansion contains. On returning to itself, the mind can recall what has been seen, but is unable to describe it, nor can it, by its natural abilities, attain to see more of the supernatural than God has chosen to show it.

11. (No imaginary vision). Do I seem to own that the soul really sees something and that this is an imaginary vision? I mean nothing of the sort: I am speaking of an intellectual vision, but being so ignorant and dull I can explain nothing, and am well aware that if anything is rightly stated, it does not come from myself.

12. (True and false raptures). I think that if the soul learns no mysteries at any time during raptures, they are no true raptures, but some natural weakness that may occur to people of delicate constitutions, such as women, when by its strenuous

efforts the spirit overpowers physical nature, and produces stupor, as I think I said in connection with the prayer of quiet.*

13. (Revelations of future bliss). This is not so in genuine raptures, for then, I believe, God ravishes the soul wholly to Himself, as one who is His very own and His bride, and shows her some small part of the kingdom she has thus won. However little this may be, all is great that is in this great God. He will allow of no obstacle from the powers or the senses, but bids that the doors of all the mansions should be closed at once, only leaving open the one He is in, that we may enter it. Blessed be such mercy—well may men be accursed who do not seek to profit by it, but who forfeit it!

14. (The soul's preparation). Oh, my sisters, what nothingness is all we have given up, or that we do, or ever could do, for a God who thus wills to communicate Himself to a worm! If we hope to enjoy this favour even during our mortal life, what are we doing? Why do we delay? What can repay the loss of the time of a "Memento"† in searching for this Lord, like the bride, through the streets and the squares?‡ Oh, what a mockery is everything in this world that does not lead towards, and help us to attain to this state! Even though all the earthly pleasures, riches, and happiness that can be imagined could last for eternity, they would be disappointing and base contrasted with

---

* *Castle,* M. iv. ch. iii. 2.

† The Saint wrote here and elsewhere *Memento,* and not *momento* as is commonly printed. It refers, of course, to that short interruption at Mass when the priest makes a Memento of those for whom he intends to pray. Likewise St. Teresa often speaks of the "space of a Credo or an Ave Maria" always implying a very short duration.

‡ Cant. iii. 2: "Per vicos et plateas quæram quem diligit anima mea."

the treasures which are to be enjoyed for ever—and yet even *these* are nothing compared with the possession for our own of the Lord of all treasures in heaven and earth.

15. (The soul blinded by its faults). Oh, human blindness! When, oh when shall this dust be taken from our eyes? Although we think it insufficient to blind us, yet I see some little motes or grains of dust, which, if left to spread, will suffice to harm us greatly. At least, for the love of God, my sisters, let these faults convince us of our misery, that they may serve to clear our sight as did the clay the eyes of the blind man who was cured by our Spouse.* Thus, realising our imperfections, we shall beg Him more fervently to let us benefit by our defects that we may please Him in all things.

16. (God ready to give these graces to all). I have unconsciously wandered far from my subject: forgive me, sisters. Believe me, when I come to these wonders of God's greatness (I mean when I come to speak of them), I cannot but feel keenly grieved at seeing what we lose by our own fault. It is true that His Majesty grants such favours to whom He chooses; yet if we sought Him as He seeks us, He would give them to us all. He only longs for souls on whom He may bestow them, for His gifts diminish not His riches.

17. (Faculties lost during ecstasy). To return to what I was describing. By the commands of the Bridegroom, the doors of the mansions, and even those of the keep and of the whole castle, are closed; for when He intends ravishing the soul He takes away the power of speech, and although occasionally the other faculties are retained rather longer, no word can be

---

* St. John ix. 6.

uttered.* Sometimes the person is at once deprived of all the senses, the hands and body become as cold as if the soul had fled; occasionally no breathing can be detected.† This condition lasts but a short while; I mean in the same degree,‡ for when this profound suspension diminishes the body seems to come to itself and gain strength to return again to this *death* which gives more vigorous *life* to the soul.

18. (Spiritual inebriation). This supreme state of ecstasy never lasts long, but, although it ceases, it leaves the will so inebriated,§ and the mind so transported out of itself, that for a day, or sometimes for several days, such a person is incapable of attending to anything but what excites the will to the love of God; although wide awake enough to this, she seems asleep as regards all earthly matters.

19. (Fervour and love of suffering left in the soul). Oh, when the soul wholly returns to itself, how abashed does it feel at having received this favour, and how passionate are its desires of serving God in any way He asks of it! If the former states of prayer caused the powerful effects described, what will not such a signal grace as this do? Such a person wishes she had a

---

* *Life,* ch. xx. 18. "Like a person who, having a rope around his neck, and being strangled, tries to breathe."

† *Life,* ch. xx. 23, 29. *Way of Perf.* ch. xxxii. *Rel.* viii. 8, 11. "The first effect of ecstatic prayer concerns the body, which remains as if the soul had departed; it grows cold from a deficiency of natural heat, the eyes close gently, and the other senses are suspended; and yet a weak body recovers health in this prayer" (Anton. a Spiritu Sancto, *Direct, Mystic.* tr. iv. d. 2 § 4, n. 150).

‡ "Digo para estar in un ser."

§ Christusque nobis sit cibus, Potusque noster sit fides, Læti bibamus sobriam Ebrietatem spiritus (Hymn for Lauds, Feria secunda, old version. Compare Anton, a Sp. S. *l.c.* tr. iv. n. 30.)

thousand lives* to spend for God; she would have all earthly creatures changed into as many tongues to praise Him on her account. She longs to perform most severe penances,† nor do they cost her much, for the power of her love almost prevents their being felt. She realises how little the martyrs suffered during their tortures, for pain is easy when our Lord thus aids us: therefore such a soul complains to His Majesty when He gives her no suffering.‡

20. (Scandal caused to spectators by such favours). She considers it a great favour when God sends her this rapture in secret, for when others see it the shame and confusion she feels are so great as somewhat to diminish her transport. Knowing the malice of the world, she fears her ecstasy will not be attributed to its proper cause, but may give rise to rash judgment instead of the praise due for it to God. Although this pain and distress are unavoidable, they seem to me to show a certain want of humility, for if she wished to be despised, what would she care?§

21. (Our Lord's predilection for such a soul). Our Lord once said to some one who was troubled by such thoughts: "Do not be disturbed; people will either praise Me or condemn thee; in either case thou wilt be the gainer."¶ I learnt afterwards that

* *Life,* ch. xx. 30.

† *Castle,* M. vii. ch. iii. 4. *Way of Perf.* ch. xxxviii. 1. *Excl.* xiv. 3. *Life,* ch. xl. 27.

‡ *Life,* ch. xvi. 6. *Rel.* i. 4.

§ *Life,* ch. xx. 5, 6.

¶ *Life,* ch. xxxi. 15. St. John of the Cross in stanza xiii. 8 of the *Spiritual Canticle,* refers to this and the following chapters. "This," he says, "is an appropriate opportunity for discussing the difference between raptures, ecstasies, and other elevations and subtle flights of the spirit, to which spiritual persons are liable; but as my object is she was greatly encouraged and comforted by this speech; I speak of it in case others may suffer in the same way. Apparently our Lord would have all men know that this soul is His own, and that none may molest it, for it is all His. Men are welcome to attack, if they will, the body, the honour, and the possessions of such a person, for glory will accrue to His Majesty from all they do; but the soul they may not assail: unless by a most culpable presumption it withdraws from the protection of its Spouse, He will defend it against the whole world and against all hell besides.

22. (Illusionary raptures). I do not know whether I have succeeded in teaching you what a rapture is; to explain it fully, would, as I said, be impossible. Still I do not think time has been lost in describing a genuine rapture. The effects in false raptures are very different. I do not call them "false" because people who experience them intentionally deceive others, but because they are themselves unwittingly deceived. As the signs and effects do not correspond with this great grace, the favour itself becomes so discredited that naturally, when our Lord afterwards bestows it on any soul, nobody believes in it. May He be for ever blessed and praised! Amen, Amen!

---

to do nothing more than explain this canticle, I leave the subject for those who are better qualified than I am. I do this the more readily because our mother, the blessed Teresa of Jesus, has written admirably on this matter, whose writings I hope to see soon published."

5

The Flight of the Spirit

Treats of the same subject as the last chapter, and describes the flight of the spirit, which is another way by which God elevates the soul: this requires great courage in one experiencing it. This favour, by which God greatly delights the soul, is explained. This chapter is very profitable.

1. (The flight of the spirit). THERE is another form of rapture, which, though essentially the same as the last, yet produces very different feelings in the soul. I call it the "flight of the spirit,"* for the soul suddenly feels so rapid a sense of motion that the spirit appears to hurry it away with a speed which is very alarming, especially at first. Therefore I said that the soul on whom God bestows this favour requires strong courage, besides great faith, trust, and resignation, so that God may do what He chooses with it.

2. (Self-control completely lost). Do you suppose a person in perfect possession of her senses feels but little dismay at her soul being drawn above her, while sometimes, as we read,

---

* *Rel.* viii. 10, 11. *Life*, ch. xviii. 8; ch. xx. 3;

even the body rises with it?* She does not know where the spirit is going, who is raising her, nor how it happens; for at the first instant of this sudden movement one does not feel sure it is caused by God. Can it possibly be resisted? No; resistance only accelerates the motion, as some one told me. God now appears to be teaching the soul, which has so often placed itself absolutely in His hands and offered itself entirely to Him, that it no longer belongs to itself; thus it is snatched away more vehemently in consequence of its opposition. This person, therefore, resolved to resist no more than does a straw when attracted by amber (a thing you may have seen); she therefore yielded herself into the hands of Him who is Almighty, seeing it is best to make a virtue of necessity. Speaking of straw, doubtless it is as easy for a stalwart, strapping fellow to lift a straw as for our mighty and powerful Giant to elevate our spirit.[†]

3. (Symbol of the two cisterns). It seems that the cistern of water of which I spoke (but I cannot quite remember where) in the fourth mansion,[‡] was formerly filled gently and quietly, without any movement; now, however, this great God, who

---

* *Life*, ch. xx. 9. St. John of the Cross, *Spiritual Canticle*, stanzas xiv.–xv. 23 sqq. Philippus a SS. Trinit. *l.c.* p. iii. tr. i. disc. iii. art. 3. "This prayer of rapture is superior to the preceding grades of prayer, as also to the ordinary prayer of union, and leaves much more excellent effects and operations in many other ways." St. Catherine of Siena (*Dialogue*, ch. lxxix. 1) says: "Wherefore, oftentimes, through the perfect union which the soul has made with Me, she is raised from the earth almost as if the heavy body became light. But this does not mean that the heaviness of the body is taken away, but that the union of the soul with Me is more perfect than the union of the body with the soul; wherefore the strength of the spirit, united with Me, raises the body from the earth." (Transl. by Algar Thorold.)

† *Life*, ch. xxii. 20.

‡ *Castle*, M. iv. ch. ii. 3.

restrains the springs and the waters, and will not permit the ocean to transgress its bounds,* lets loose the streams, which with a powerful rush flow into the cistern and a mighty wave rises, strong enough to raise on high the little vessel of our soul. Neither the ship herself, nor her pilot and sailors, can at their choice control the fury of the sea and stop it from carrying the boat where it will: far less can the interior of the soul now stay where it chooses, or force its senses or faculties to act more than He Who holds them in His dominion decrees; as for the exterior powers, they are here quite useless.

4. (Obligations following these favours). Indeed I am amazed, sisters, while merely writing of this manifestation of the immense power of this great King and Monarch. What, then, must be felt by those who actually experience it? I am convinced that if His Majesty were to reveal Himself thus to the greatest sinners on earth, they would never dare to offend Him again—if not through love, at least through fear of Him. What obligations bind those taught in so sublime a manner to strive with all their might not to displease such a Master! In His Name, I beg of you, sisters, who have received these or the like favours, not to rest content with merely receiving them, but to remember that she who owes much has much to pay!†

5. (Humility produced by them). This thought terrifies the soul exceedingly: unless the great courage needed was given it by our Lord, it would suffer great and constant

---

* Prov. viii. 29.

† St. Luke xii. 48: "Cui multum datum est, multum quæretur ab eo, et cui commendaverunt multum, plus petent ab eo."

grief; for, looking first at what His Majesty has done for it and then upon itself, it sees how little good it has performed compared with what it was bound to do, and that the paltry service it has rendered was full of faults, failures, and tepidity. To efface the remembrance of the many imperfections of all its good deeds (if indeed it has ever performed any), it thinks best to forget them altogether and to be ever mindful of its sins, casting itself on the mercy of God, since it cannot repay its debt to Him, and begging for the pity and compassion He ever shows to sinners.

6. (How our crucified Lord comforted such a soul). Perhaps He will answer as He did to some one who was kneeling before a crucifix in great affliction on this account, for she felt she had never had anything to offer God, nor to sacrifice for His sake. The Crucified One consoled her by saying that He gave her for herself all the pains and labours He had borne in His passion, that she might offer them as her own to His Father.* I learnt from her that she at once felt comforted and enriched by these words, which she never forgets, but recalls whenever she realises her own wretchedness, and feels encouraged and consoled. I could relate several other incidents of the same kind learnt in conversation with many holy people much given to prayer, but I will not recount them lest you might imagine they relate to myself.

7. (A humble soul fears these favours). I think this example is very instructive; it shows that we please our Lord by self-knowledge, by the constant recollection of our poverty and miseries, and by realising that we possess nothing but what we

---

* *Rel.* ix. 8. This happened at Seville in 1575 or 1576.

have received from Him.* Therefore there is need of courage, sisters, in order to receive this and many other favours which come to a soul elevated to this state by our Lord; I think that if the soul is humble it requires more valour than ever for this last mercy. May God grant us humility for His Name's sake.

8. (Mysteries learnt during the flight of the spirit). To return to this sudden rapture of the spirit. The soul really appears to have quitted the body, which, however, is not lifeless, and though, on the other hand, the person is certainly not dead, yet she herself cannot, for a few seconds, tell whether her spirit remains within her body or not.† She feels that she has been wholly transported into another and a very different region from that in which we live, where a light so unearthly is shown‡ that, if during her whole lifetime she had been trying to picture it, and the wonders seen, she could not possibly have succeeded. In an instant her mind learns so many things at once that if the imagination and intellect spent years in striving to enumerate them, it could not recall a thousandth part of them.

9. (Imaginary visions sometimes accompany intellectuals ones). This vision is not intellectual but imaginary and is seen by the eyes of the soul more clearly than earthly things are seen by our bodily eyes. Although no words are pronounced, the spirit is taught many truths; if, for instance, it beholds any of the saints, it knows them at once as well as if intimately

---

* 1 Cor. iv. 7: "Quid autem habes quod non accepisti?"

† 2 Cor. xii. 2: "Sive in corpore nescio, sive extra corpus nescio, Deus scit."

‡ This is called "lumen prophetiæ" and is a transient form of the "lumen gloriæ." See St. Thomas Aquinas, *Sum. theol.* 2a 2æ, q. 175, art. 3 ad 2.

acquainted with them for years.* Occasionally, besides what the eyes of the soul perceive in intellectual vision, other things are shown it. In an imaginary vision it usually sees our Lord, accompanied by a host of angels; neither the bodily eyes, however, nor the eyes of the soul† see anything, for these visions, and many other things impossible to describe, are revealed by some wonderful intuition that I cannot explain. Perhaps those who have experienced this favour and possess more ability than myself may be able to describe it, although it seems to me a most difficult task.

10. (How the flight of the spirit takes place). I cannot tell whether the soul dwells in the body meanwhile or not: I would neither affirm that it does, nor that the body is deprived of it. I have often thought that as, though the sun does not leave his place in the heavens, yet his rays have power to reach the earth instantaneously, so the soul and the spirit, which make one and the same thing (like the sun and his rays) may, while remaining in its own place, through the strength of the ardour coming to it from the true Sun of Justice, send up some higher part of it above itself. In fact, I do not understand what I am talking about, but the truth is that, with the swiftness of a bullet fired from a gun, an upward flight takes place in the interior of the soul. (I know no other name for it but "flight.") Although noiseless, it is too manifest a movement to be any

---

* The same thing is related of some Saints while on earth, *e.g.* St. Paul the first hermit and St. Anthony, who greeted each other by name though neither knew nor had heard of the other.

† These words, though necessary for the context, were only begun, but not completed by St. Teresa.

illusion,* and the soul is quite outside itself; at least that is the impression made upon it. Great mysteries are revealed to it meanwhile, and when the person returns to consciousness she is so greatly benefited that she holds all this world's goods as filth, compared with what she has seen. Henceforth earthly life is grievous to her, and what used to please her now remains uncared for and unnoticed.†

11. (The soul fortified by it). Those children of Israel who were sent on first to the Land of Promise brought back tokens from it;‡ so here our Lord seems to seek to show the soul something of the land to which it is travelling, to give it courage to pass through the trials of its painful journey, now that it knows where it must go to find rest. You may fancy that such profit could not thus quickly be obtained, yet only those who have experienced what signal benefits this favour leaves in the soul can realise its value.

12. (Three great graces left in the soul). This clearly shows it to be no work of the devil; neither the imagination nor the evil one could represent what leaves such peace, calm, and good fruits in the soul, and particularly the following three graces

---

* *Life*, ch. xx. 32. *Castle*, M. iv. ch. i. 10.

† Compare §§ 8–10 with Philippus a SS. Trinit. *l.c.* p. iii. tr. i. disc. iii. art. 3. "Muchas veces he pensado, si como el sol estándose en el cielo, que sus rayos tienen tanta fuerza, que no mudándose él de allí, de presto llegan acá; si el alma y el espíritu (que son una misma cosa, como le es el sol y sus rayos) puede, quedándose ella en su puesto, con la fuerza de calor que le viene del verdadero Sol de justicia, alguna parte superior salir sobre sí misma. En fin, yo no sé lo que digo, lo que es verdad es, que con la presteza que sale la pelota de un arcabuz, cuando le ponen el fuego, se levanta en lo interior un vuelo (que yo no sé otro nombre que le poner) que aunque no hace ruido, hace movimento tan claro, que no puede ser antojo en ninguna manera; y muy fuera de si misma, á todo lo que puede entender, se le muestran grandes cosas."

‡ Num. xiii. 24.

of a very high order.* The first of these is a perception of the greatness of God, which becomes clearer to us as we witness more of it. Secondly, we gain self-knowledge and humility as we see how creatures so base as ourselves in comparison with the Creator of such wonders, have dared to offend Him in the past or venture to gaze on Him now.

13. (The third grace). The third grace is a contempt for all earthly things unless they are consecrated to the service of so great a God. With such jewels the Bridegroom begins to deck His Bride; they are too valuable for her to keep them carelessly.† These visions are so deeply engraved in her memory that I believe she can never forget them until she enjoys them for evermore, for to do so would be the greatest misfortune.‡ But the Spouse Who gave her these gifts has power to give her grace not to lose them.

14. (Fear caused by this power). I told you that courage was required by the soul, for do you think it is a trifling matter for the spirit to feel literally separated from the body, as it does when perceiving that it is losing its senses without understanding the reason? There is need that He Who gives all the rest should include fortitude. You will say this fright is well rewarded, and so say I. May He Who can bestow such graces be for ever praised, and may His Majesty vouchsafe that we may be worthy to serve Him. Amen.

---

* *Life*, ch. xx. 31. The same distinctions with respect to divine and diabolical locutions may be found in *Life*, ch. xxv. 5.

† "Dexteram meam et collum meum cinxit lapidibus pretiosis, tradidit auribus meis inæstimabiles margaritas" (from the Office of St. Agnes).

‡ This is undoubtedly the correct rendering of this difficult and obscure passage.

6

Spiritual Jubilation

Describes an effect which proves the prayer spoken of in the last chapter to be genuine and no deception. Treats of another favour our Lord bestows on the soul, to make it praise Him fervently.

1. (The soul longs for death). THESE sublime favours leave the soul so desirous of fully enjoying Him Who has bestowed them, that life becomes a painful, though delicious torture, and death is ardently longed for. Often, with tears, such a one implores God to take her from this exile where everything she sees wearies her.* Solitude alone brings great alleviation for a time, but soon her grief returns, and yet she cannot bear to be without it. In short, this poor little butterfly can find no lasting rest. So tender is her love, that at the slightest provocation it flames forth and the soul takes flight. Thus, in this mansion raptures occur very frequently, nor can they be resisted, even in public. Persecutions and

---

* *Excl.* ii. See poems, "Cuan triste es, Dios mio," and the two versions of "Vivir sin vivir en mi."

slanders ensue;* however she may try, she cannot keep free from the fears suggested to her by so many people, especially by her confessors.

2. (The soul cannot help desiring these favours). Although in one way she feels great confidence within her soul, especially when alone with God, yet, on the other hand, she is greatly troubled by misgivings lest she is deceived by the devil, and so should offend Him Whom she deeply loves. She cares little for blame, except when her confessor finds fault with her, as if she could help what happens! She asks every one to pray for her,† since she has been told to do so, and begs His Majesty to direct her by some other way than this, which is so full of danger. Nevertheless, so great are the benefits left by these favours that she cannot but see that they lead her on the way to heaven,‡ of which she has read and heard and learnt in the law of God. As, strive how she may, she cannot resist desiring to receive these graces, she resigns herself into God's hands. Yet she is grieved at finding herself forced to wish for these favours, which appears to be disobedience to her confessor, for she believes that in obedience, and in avoiding any offence against God, lies her safeguard against deception. Thus she feels she would prefer to be cut in pieces rather than wilfully commit a venial sin, yet is greatly grieved at seeing that she cannot avoid unwittingly falling into a great number. God bestows on such people so intense a desire neither ever to displease Him, in however small a matter,

---

* *Life*, ch. xxv. 18.

† *Life*, ch. xxv. 20. *Rel.* vii. 7.

‡ *Life*, ch. xxvii. 1, 2.

nor to commit any avoidable imperfection, that, were there no other reason, they would try to avoid society, and they greatly envy those who live in deserts.* On the other hand, they seek to live amidst men in the hopes of helping if but one soul to praise God better.† In the case of a woman, she grieves over the impediment offered by her sex,‡ and envies those who are free to proclaim aloud to all Who is this mighty God of hosts.§

3. (St. Teresa bewails her inability to serve God). Oh poor little butterfly! chained by so many fetters, that stop thee from flying where thou wouldst! Have pity on her, O my God, and so dispose her ways that she may be able to accomplish some of her desires for Thy honour and glory! Take no account of the poverty of her merits, nor of the vileness of her nature, O Lord, Thou Who hast the power to compel the vast ocean to retire, and didst force the wide river Jordan to draw back, that the Children of Israel might pass through!¶ Yet spare her not, for aided by Thy strength she can endure many trials. She is resolved to do so—she desires to suffer them. Stretch forth Thine arm, O Lord, to help her, lest she waste her life on trifles! Let Thy greatness appear in this Thy creature, womanish and weak as she is, that men, seeing the good in her is not her own, may praise Thee for it! Let it cost her what it may, and as dear as she desires, for she longs to lose a thousand lives to

---

* Rel. i. 6.

† Life, ch. xxxii. 14; ch. xxxv. 13. Castle, M. vii. ch. iv. 21. Found. ch. i. 6, 7.

‡ Way of Perf. ch. i.

§ III Reg. xix. 10.

¶ Ps. cxiii. 3, Exod. xiv., and Jos. iii.

lead one soul to praise Thee but a little better! If as many lives were hers to give, she would count them well spent in such a cause, knowing, as a truth most certain, that she is unworthy to bear the lightest cross, much less to die, for Thee.

4. (Fervour resulting from ecstasies). I cannot tell why I have said this, sisters, nor what made me do so; indeed I never intended it. You must know that these effects are bound to follow from such trances or ecstasies: they are not transient, but permanent desires; when opportunity occurs of acting on them, they prove genuine. How can I say that they are permanent, when at times the soul feels cowardly in the most trivial matters and too timorous to undertake any work for God?

5. (Excessive desires to see God should be restrained). I believe it is because our Lord, for its greater good, then leaves the soul to its natural weakness, which at once convinces it so thoroughly that any strength it possessed came from His Majesty, as to destroy self-love and to endue it with a greater knowledge of the mercy and greatness of God, which He deigned to show forth in one so vile. However, the soul is usually in the former state. Beware of one thing, sisters; these ardent desires to behold our Lord are sometimes so distressing as to need rather to be checked than to be encouraged—that is, if feasible, for in another kind of prayer, of which I shall speak later, it is not possible, as you will see.

6. (They endanger health). In the state I speak of, these longings can sometimes be arrested, for the reason is at liberty to conform to the will of God and can quote the words of St. Martin,* while, if these desires become very oppressive,

---

* "When St. Martin was dying, his brethren said to him: 'Why, dear Father, will you

the thoughts may be turned to some other matter. As such desires are generally found in persons far advanced in perfection, the devil may excite them in order to make us think we are of their number—in any case, it is well to be cautious. For my part, I do not believe he could cause the calm and peace given by this pain to the soul, but would disturb it by such uneasiness as we feel when afflicted concerning any worldly matter. However, a person inexperienced in both kinds of sorrow cannot understand the difference, but thinking such grief an excellent thing, will excite it as much as possible, which greatly injures the health, as these longings are incessant, or at least very frequent.

7. (Tears often come from physical causes).You must also notice that bodily weakness may cause such pain, especially with people of sensitive characters, who cry over every trifling trouble.* Times without number do they imagine they are mourning for God's sake, when they are doing no such thing. If for a considerable space of time, whenever such a person hears the least mention of God or thinks of Him at all, these fits of uncontrollable weeping occur,† the cause may be an accumulation of humour round the heart, which has a great deal more to do with such tears than has the love of

---

leave us? Or to whom can you commit us in our desolation? We know, indeed, that you desire to be with Christ, but your reward above is safe and will not be diminished by delay; rather have pity on us whom you are leaving desolate.' Then Martin, always pitiful, moved by these lamentations, is said to have burst into tears. Turning to God, he replied to the mourners around him only by crying: 'O Lord, if I am still necessary to Thy people, I do not shrink from toil; Thy will be done'" (Sulpitius Severus, *Life of St. Martin*, letter 3).

* *Way of Perf.* ch. xvii. 4; ch. xix. 6.

† *Life*, ch. xxix. 12.

God. Such persons seem as if they would never stop crying: believing that tears are beneficial, they do not try to check them nor to distract their minds from the subject, but encourage them as much as possible. The devil seizes this opportunity of weakening nuns, so that they become unable to pray, or to keep their Rule.

8. (St. Teresa's own experience). I think you must be puzzling over this, and would like to ask what I would have you do, as I see danger in everything. If I am afraid of delusions in so good a thing as tears, perhaps I myself am deluded, and may be I am! But, believe me, I do not say this without having witnessed it in other people, although not in my own case, for there is nothing tender about me, and my heart is so hard as often to grieve me.* However, when the fire burns fiercely within, stony as my heart may be, it distils like an alembic.† It is easy to know when tears come from this source, for they are soothing and gentle rather than stormy, and rarely do any harm. This delusion, when it is one, has the advantage, with a humble person, of only injuring the body and not the soul. But if one is not humble, it is well to be ever on one's guard.

9. (Works, not tears, are asked by God). Let us not fancy that if we cry a great deal we have done all that is needed—rather we must work hard and practise the virtues: that is the essential—leaving tears to fall when God sends them, without trying to force ourselves to shed them. Then, if we do not take too much notice of them, they will leave the parched soil of our

---

* Compare with this what we have said in note 1 to the second chapter of the Fourth Mansions. *Rel.* ii. 12.

† *Life*, ch. xix. 1–3.

souls well watered, making it fertile in good fruit, for this is the water which falls from heaven.* However we may tire ourselves in digging to reach it, we shall never get any water like this; indeed, we may often work and search until we are exhausted, without finding as much as a pool, much less a springing well!

10. (Confide entirely in God). Therefore, sisters, I think it best for us to place ourselves in the presence of God, to contemplate His mercy and grandeur and our own vileness, and to leave Him to give us what He will, be it water or drought, for He knows best what is good for us; thus we enjoy peace, and the devil will have less chance to deceive us.

11. (The jubilee of the soul). Amongst these favours, at once painful and pleasant, Our Lord sometimes causes in the soul a certain jubilation,† and a strange and mysterious kind of prayer. If He bestows this grace on you, praise Him fervently for it; I describe it so that you may know that it is something real. I believe that the faculties of the soul are closely united to God, but that He leaves them at liberty to rejoice in their happiness, together with the senses, although they do not know what they are enjoying nor how they do so. This may sound gibberish, yet it really happens. So excessive is its jubilee, that the soul will not enjoy it alone, but speaks of it to all around it, that they may help it to praise God, which is its one desire.‡

12. (Impossibility of concealing this joy). Oh, what rejoicings

---

* Way of Perf. ch. xix. 6. Life. ch. xviii. 12 sqq.

† Philippus a SS. Trinit. l.c. p. iii. tr. i. disc. iv. art. 5. Antonius a Sp. S. l.c. tr. iv. n. 156.

‡ Rel. ii. 12.

would this person utter, and what demonstrations would she make, if possible, so that all might know her happiness! She seems to have found herself again, and wishes, like the father of the prodigal son, to invite all her friends to feast with her,* and to see her soul in its rightful place, because (at least for the time being) she cannot doubt its security. I believe she is right, for the devil could not possibly infuse a joy and peace into the very centre of her being which make her whole delight consist in urging others to praise God. It requires a painful effort to keep silent and to dissemble such impulsive happiness. St. Francis must have experienced this when, as the robbers met him rushing through the fields, crying aloud, he told them, in answer to their questions, that he was the "herald of the great King."† So felt other saints who retired into the deserts, that, like St. Francis, they might proclaim the praises of their God.

13. (The world's judgment of this jubilee). I knew Fray Peter of Alcantara, who used to do this. I believe he was a saint, on account of the life he led, yet people often took him for a fool

---

* St. Luke xv. 23.

† "He plunged into a vast forest, and there in a loud voice and in French, he made the echoes resound with the praises of God. Some robbers, attracted by his singing, rushed out upon him. But the sight of so poor a man destroyed their hopes of booty. They questioned him, and Francis gave them no answer beyond saying in allegorical language: 'I am the herald of the great King!' The robbers considered themselves insulted by these words. They threw themselves upon him, beat him severely, and went off, after having thrown him into a ditch full of snow. This treatment only added fire to the zeal of Francis. He sang his holy canticles with greater love than before" (Rev. Father Léon, *Lives of the Saints and Blessed of the Order of St. Francis*, vol. i. ch. i.).

when they heard him.* Oh happy folly, sisters! Would that God might let us all share it! What mercy He has shown you in placing you where, if He gave you this grace and it were perceived by others, it would rather turn to your advantage than bring on you contempt, as it would do in the world, where men so rarely hear God praised that it is no wonder they take scandal at it.

14. (Which is often felt by the nuns of St. Joseph's). Oh, miserable times and wretched life spent in the world! How blest are those whose happy lot it is to be freed from them!† It often delights me, when in my sisters' company, to see how the joy of their hearts is so great that they vie with one another in praising our Lord for placing them in this convent: it is evident that their praises come from the very depths of their souls. I should like you to do this often, sisters, for when one begins she incites the rest to imitate her. How can your tongues be better employed, when you are together, than in praising God, Who has given us so much cause for it?

15. (The Saint's delight in this jubilee). May His Majesty often grant us this kind of prayer, which is most safe and beneficial; we cannot acquire it for ourselves, as it is quite supernatural. Sometimes it lasts for a whole day and the soul is like one

---

* "St. Peter of Alcantara, in the jubilation of his soul through the impetuosity of divine love, was sometimes unable to refrain from singing the divine praises aloud in a wonderful manner. To do this more freely, he sometimes went into the woods, where the peasants who heard him sing took him for one who was beside himself" (Rev. Alban Butler, *Lives of the Saints*).

† *Way of Perf.* ch. ii. 8; ch. iii. 1; ch. viii. 1.

inebriated, although not deprived of the senses;* nor like a person afflicted with melancholia,† in which, though the reason is not entirely lost, the imagination continually dwells on some subject which possesses it and from which it cannot be freed. These are coarse comparisons to make in connection with such a precious gift, yet nothing else occurs to my mind. In this state of prayer, a person is rendered by this jubilee so forgetful of self and everything else, that she can neither think nor speak of anything but praising God, to which her joy prompts her. Let us all of us join her, my daughters, for why should we wish to be wiser than she? What can make us happier? And may all creatures unite their praises with ours for ever and ever! Amen, amen, amen!

---

* Compare with this what has been said in the fourth chapter of this Mansion, § 17 (note 17).

† Melancholia here as elsewhere means hysteria.

7

The Humanity of Our Lord

Describes the grief felt on account of their sins by souls on whom God has bestowed the before-mentioned favours. Shows that, however spiritual a person may be, it is a great error not to keep before our mind the Humanity of our Lord and Saviour Jesus Christ and His sacred Passion and Life, as also the glorious Mother of God and the saints. The benefits gained by such meditation. This chapter is most profitable.

1. (Sorrow for sin felt by souls in the sixth Mansion). IT may seem to you, sisters, that souls to whom God has communicated Himself in such a special manner may feel so sure of enjoying Him for ever as no longer to require to fear or to mourn over their past sins. Those of you will be most apt to hold this opinion who have never received the like favours; souls to whom God has granted these graces will understand what I say. This is a great mistake, for sorrow for sin increases in proportion to the divine grace received, and I believe will never quit us until we come to the land where nothing can grieve us any more. Doubtless we feel this pain more at one time than another, and it is of a different kind. A soul so

advanced as that we speak of does not think of the punishment threatening its offences, but of its great ingratitude towards Him to Whom it owes so much,* and Who so justly deserves that it should serve Him, for the sublime mysteries revealed have taught it much about the greatness of God.

2. (How this sorrow is felt). This soul wonders at its former temerity and weeps over its irreverence; its foolishness in the past seems a madness which it never ceases to lament as it remembers for what vile things it forsook so great a Sovereign. The thoughts dwell on this more than on the favours received, which, like those I am about to describe, are so powerful that they seem to rush through the soul at times like a strong, swift river. The sins, however, remain like the mire in the river bed, and dwell constantly in the memory, making a heavy cross to bear.

3. (St. Teresa's grief for her past sins). I know some one who, though she had ceased to wish for death in order to see God,† yet desired it that she might be freed from her continual regret for her past ingratitude towards Him to Whom she owed, and always would owe, so much. She thought no one's guilt could be compared to her own, for she felt there could be none with whom God had borne so patiently, nor on whom He had bestowed such graces.

4. (Such souls, centred in God, forget self-interest). Souls which have reached the state I speak of have ceased to fear hell. At times, though very rarely, they grieve keenly over the possibility of their losing God; their sole dread is lest He should

---

* *Life,* ch. vi. 7.

† *Excl.* vi. 4, 5. *Supra,* M. v. ch. 2, 5. *Poems* (those mentioned ch. vi. note 1).

withdraw His hand, leaving them to offend Him, and so they might return to their former miserable condition. They care nothing for their own pain or glory; if they are anxious not to stay long in purgatory, it is more on account of its keeping them from the Presence of God than because of its torments. Whatever favours God may have shown a soul, I think it is dangerous for it to forget the unhappy state it was once in: painful as the remembrance may be, it is most beneficial.

5. (The remembrance of divine benefits increases contrition). Perhaps *I* think so because I have been so wicked, and that may be the reason why I never forget my sins; people who have led good lives have no cause for grief, although we always fall at times whilst living in this mortal body. This pain is not lessened by reflecting that our Lord has already forgiven and forgotten our faults; our grief is rather increased at seeing such kindness and favours bestowed on one who deserves nothing but hell. I think St. Paul and the Magdalen must thus have suffered a cruel martyrdom;* their love was intense, they had received many mercies and realised the greatness and the majesty of God: they must have found it, therefore, very hard to bear the remembrance of their sins, which they must have regretted with a most tender sorrow.

6. (Meditation on our Lord's Humanity). You may fancy that one who has enjoyed such high favours need not meditate on the mysteries of the most sacred Humanity of our Lord Jesus Christ, but will be wholly absorbed in love. I have written

---

* *Life,* ch. xxi. 9. All editions have *Peter.* St. Teresa only wrote P°, but the parallel passage proves she meant Pablo, and not Pedro. See also M. i. ch. i. 5.

fully about this elsewhere.* I have been contradicted, and told that I was wrong and did not understand the matter; that our Lord guides souls in such a way that after having made progress it is best to exercise oneself in matters concerning the Godhead and to avoid what is corporeal; yet nothing will make me admit that this latter is a good way.

7. (Warning against discontinuing it). I may be mistaken; we may all really mean the same thing, but I found the devil was trying to lead me astray in this manner. Having been warned by experience in this respect, I have decided to speak again about it here, although I have very often done so elsewhere.† Be most cautious on the subject; attend to what I venture to say about it, and do not believe any one who tells you the contrary. I will endeavour to explain myself more clearly than I did before. If the person who undertook to write on the matter had treated it more explicitly he would have done well, for it may do much harm to speak of it in general terms to us women, who have scanty wits.

8. (Christ and the saints our models). Some souls imagine they cannot meditate even on the Passion, still less on the most blessed Virgin, or on the saints, the memory of whose lives greatly benefits and strengthens us.‡ I cannot think what such

---

* *Life,* ch. xxii. 9–11.

† *Life,* ch. xxii. 1; ch. xxiii. 18; ch. xxiv. 2.

‡ "Deliberate forgetfulness and rejection of all knowledge and of form must never be extended to Christ and His sacred Humanity. Sometimes, indeed, in the height of contemplation and pure intuition of the divinity the soul does not remember the Sacred Humanity, because God raises the mind to this, as it were, confused and most supernatural knowledge; but for all this, studiously to forget it is by no means right, for the contemplation of the sacred Humanity and loving meditation upon it will

persons are to meditate upon, for to withdraw the thoughts from all corporeal things, like the angelic spirits who are always inflamed with love, is not possible for us while in this mortal flesh; we need to study, to meditate upon and to imitate those who, mortals like ourselves, performed such heroic deeds for God. How much less should we wilfully endeavour to abstain from thinking of our only good and remedy, the most sacred Humanity of our Lord Jesus Christ? I cannot believe that any one really does this; they misunderstand their own minds, and so harm both themselves and others. Of this, at least, I can assure them: they will never thus enter the two last mansions of the castle. If they lose their Guide, our good Jesus, they cannot find the way, and it will be much if they have stayed safely in the former mansions. Our Lord Himself tells us that He is "the Way": He also says that He is "the Light," that "No man cometh to the Father but by Him," and that "He that seeth Me, seeth the Father also."*

9. (Meditation of contemplatives). Such persons tell us that these words have some other meaning; I know of no other meaning but this, which my soul has ever recognised as the true one, and which has always suited me right well. Some people (many of whom have spoken to me on the subject), after our Lord has once raised them to perfect contemplation, wish to enjoy it continually. This is impossible; still, the

---

help us up to all good, and it is by it we shall ascend most easily to the highest state of union. It is evident at once that, while all visible and bodily things ought to be forgotten, for they are a hindrance in our way, He, Who for our salvation became man, is not to be accounted among them, for He is the truth, the door, and the way, and our guide to all good" (St. John of the Cross, *Ascent of Mount Carmel,* bk. iii. ch. i. 12–14).

* St. John viii. 12; xiv. 6, 9.

grace of this state remains in their souls in such a way that they cannot reason as before on the mysteries of the Passion and the Life of Christ. I cannot account for this, but it is very usual for the mind thus to remain less apt for meditation. I think it must be because, as the one end of meditation is to seek God, after He has once been found, and the soul is accustomed to seek Him again by means of the will, it no longer wearies itself by searching for Him with the intellect.

10. (Meditation during aridity). It also appears to me that as the will is already inflamed with love, this generous faculty would, if it could, cease to make use of the reason. This would be well, were it not impossible, especially before the soul has reached the two last mansions.* Time spent in prayer would thus be lost, as the will often needs the use of the understanding to rekindle its love. Notice this point, sisters, which is important, therefore I will explain it more fully. Such a soul desires to spend all its time in loving God, and wishes to do nothing else; but it cannot succeed, for, though the will is not dead, yet the flame which kindled it is dying out, and the spark needs fanning into a glow. Ought the soul to remain quiescent in this aridity, waiting, as did our father Elias, for fire to descend from heaven† to consume the sacrifice which it makes of itself to God? Certainly not; it is not right to expect miracles; God will work them for this soul when He chooses. As I have told

---

* *Life,* ch. xv. 20. St. John of the Cross treats the subject most carefully. He shows how and when meditation becomes impossible: *Ascent of Mount Carmel,* bk. ii. ch. xii (*circa finem*); ch. xiii. (*per totum*). *Living Flame of Love,* stanza iii. line iii. *Obscure Night,* bk. i. ch. x. and bk. ii. ch. viii. That it should be procured whenever possible: *Obscure Night,* bk. i. ch. x. (*in fine*); that it should be resumed: *Ascent of Mount Carmel,* bk. ii. ch. xv.

† *III Reg.* xviii. 30–39.

you already, and shall do again, His Majesty wishes us to hold ourselves unworthy of their being wrought on our account, and desires us to help ourselves to the best of our abilities.

11. (We must search for God when we do not feel His presence). In my opinion, we ought, during our whole life, to act in this manner, however sublime our prayer may be. True, those whom our Lord admits into the seventh mansion rarely or never need thus to help their fervour, for the reason I will tell you of, if I recollect it, when I come to write of this room where; in a wonderful manner, souls are constantly in the company of Christ our Lord, both in His Humanity and His Divinity.* Thus, when the fire in our hearts, which I spoke of, does not burn in the will, nor do we feel the presence of God, we must search for Him as He would have us do, like the Bride in the Canticles,† and must ask all creatures "who it was that made them"; as St. Augustine (either in his *Soliloquies* or his *Confessions*) tells us that he did.‡ Thus we shall not stand like blockheads, wasting our time in waiting for what

---

* Continual sense of the presence of God: *Life,* ch. xxvii. 6; *Rel.* xi. 3: "the intellectual vision of the Three Persons and of the Sacred Humanity seems ever present." *Castle*, M. vii. ch. iv. 15.

† Cant. iii. 3: "Num quem diligit anima mea vidistis?"

‡ "I asked the earth, and it answered me: 'I am not He'; and whatsoever it contains confessed the same. I asked the sea and the depths, and the living, creeping things, and they answered: 'We are not thy God, seek above us.' I asked the heavens, I asked the moving air; and the whole air with its inhabitants answered: 'Anaximenes was deceived, I am not God.' I asked the heavens, sun, moon, stars. 'Nor,' say they, 'are we the God Whom thou seekest.' And I replied unto all things which encompass the door of my flesh: 'Ye have told me of my God, that ye are not He; tell me something of Him.' And they cried out with a loud voice: 'He made us.' By my thought of them I questioned them, and their beauty gave their answer" (*St. Augustine's Confessions,* bk. x. ch. 6). St. Teresa may have read this in *St. Augustine's Confessions* (see above, p. 108), or in the *Soliloquies,* a collection of extracts from St. Augustine, St. Bernard, St. Anselm, etc., which was printed in Latin at Venice in 1512, translated into Spanish and brought

we before enjoyed. At first, it may be that our Lord will not renew His gift again for a year, or even for many years; His Majesty knows the reason, which we should not try to discover, for there is no need for us to understand it.

12. (Reasoning and mental prayer). As most certainly the way to please God is to keep the commandments and counsels, let us do so diligently, while meditating on His life and death and all we owe Him; then let the rest be as God chooses. Some may answer that their mind refuses to dwell on these subjects; and for the above causes, this to a certain extent is true. You know that it is one thing to reason, and another thing for the memory to bring certain truths before the mind. Perhaps you may not understand me; possibly I fail to express myself rightly, but I will do my best. Using the understanding much, in this manner, is what I call meditation.

13. (A form of meditation on our Lord's Life and Passion). Let us begin by considering the mercy God showed us by giving us His only Son; let us not stop here, but go on to reflect upon all the mysteries of His glorious life; or let us first turn our thoughts to His prayer in the garden, then allow them to continue the subject until they reach the crucifixion. Or we may take some part of the Passion, such as Christ's apprehension, and dwell on this mystery, considering in detail the points to be pondered and thought over, such as the treachery of Judas, the flight of the Apostles, and all that followed. This is an admirable and very meritorious kind of prayer.*

---

out at Valladolid in 1515, and again at Medina del Campo in 1553, and at Toledo in 1565. The words quoted by St. Teresa occur in chapter xxxi. See *Life,* ch. xl. 10.

* *Life,* ch. xiii. 17–23.

14. (Simplicity of contemplatives' meditation). Souls led by God in supernatural ways and raised to perfect contemplation are right in declaring they cannot practise this kind of meditation. As I said, I know not why, but as a rule they are unable to do so. Yet they would be wrong in saying that they cannot dwell on these mysteries, nor frequently think about them, especially when these events are being celebrated by the Catholic Church. Nor is it possible for the soul which has received so much from God to forget these precious proofs of His love, which are living sparks to inflame the heart with greater love for our Lord, nor can the mind fail to understand them. Such a soul comprehends these mysteries, which are brought before the mind and stamped on the memory, in a more perfect way than do other people, so that the mere sight of our Lord prostrate in the garden, covered with His terrible sweat, suffices to engross the thoughts, not merely for an hour, but for several days. The soul looks with a simple gaze upon Who He is, and how ungratefully we treat Him in return for such terrible sufferings. Then the will, although perhaps without sensible tenderness, desires to render Him some service for such sublime mercies, and longs to suffer something for Him Who bore so much for us; and employs itself in similar considerations in which the memory and understanding also take their part.

15. (Souls in every state of prayer should think of the Passion). I think this is why such souls cannot reason connectedly about the Passion, and fancy they are unable to meditate on it. Those who do not meditate on this subject had better begin to do so; for I know that it will not impede the most sublime prayer, nor is it well to omit practising this often. If God then

sees fit to enrapture them, well and good; even if they are reluctant, He will make them cease to meditate. I am certain that this way of acting is most helpful to the soul, and not the hindrance it would become were great efforts made to use the intellect. This, as I said, I believe, cannot be done when a higher state of prayer is attained. It may be otherwise in some cases, for God leads souls in many different ways. Let not those be blamed, however, who are unable to discourse much in prayer, nor should they be judged incapable of enjoying the great graces contained in the mysteries of Jesus Christ, our only Good, which no one, however spiritual he may be, can persuade me it is well to omit contemplating.

16. (Need of the example of Christ and the saints). There are souls who, having made a beginning, or advanced half-way, when they begin to experience the prayer of quiet, and to taste the sweetness and consolations God gives, think it is a great thing to enjoy these spiritual pleasures continually. Let them, as I advised elsewhere, cease to give themselves up so much to this absorption. Life is long and full of crosses, and we have need to look on Christ, our pattern, to see how He bore His trials, and even to take example by His Apostles and saints, if we would bear our own trials perfectly. Our good Jesus and His most blessed Mother are too good company to be left, and He is well pleased if we grieve at His pains, even though sometimes at the cost of our own consolations and joys.* Besides, daughters, consolations are not so frequent in prayer that we have no time for this as well. If any one should tell me she continually enjoys them, and that she is

---

* *Way of Perf.* ch. xxv. 7.

one of those who can never meditate on the divine mysteries, I should feel very doubtful about her state. Be convinced of this, keep free from this deception, and to the utmost of your power stop yourselves from being constantly immersed in this intoxication. If you cannot do so, tell the Prioress, so that she may employ you too busily for you to think of the matter; thus you will be free from this danger, which, if it does no more, when it lasts long, greatly injures the health and brain. I have said enough to prove, to those who require it, that however spiritual their state, it is an error so to avoid thinking of corporeal things as to imagine that meditation on the most sacred Humanity can injure the soul.

17. (Faith shows us our Lord as both God and Man). People allege, in defence, that our Lord told His disciples it was expedient for them that He should go from them.[*] This I cannot admit. He did not say so to His blessed Mother, for her faith was firm. She knew He was both God and man; and although she loved Him more dearly than did His disciples, it was in so perfect a way that His bodily presence rather helped her. The faith of the Apostles must have been weaker than it was later on, and than ours has reason to be. I assure you, daughters, that I consider this a most dangerous idea, whereby the devil might end by robbing us of our devotion to the most blessed Sacrament.

18. (St. Teresa's experience on meditation on the sacred Humanity). The mistake I formerly made[†] did not lead me as far as

---

[*] St. John xvi. 7: "Expedit vobis ut ego vadam; si enim non abiero, Paracletus non veniet ad vos." *Life,* ch. xxii. 1, 2 and note.

[†] *Life,* ch. xxii. 11. Although the Saint defends herself against the charge of self-

this, but I did not care so much about meditating on our Lord Jesus Christ, but preferred to remain absorbed, awaiting spiritual consolations. I recognised clearly that I was going wrong, for as I could not always keep in this state, my thoughts wandered hither and thither and my soul seemed like a bird, ever flying about and finding no place for rest. Thus I lost much time and did not advance in virtue, nor make progress in prayer.

19. (Evil of giving up such meditation). I did not understand the reason, and as I believed that I was acting wisely I think I should never have learnt it but for the advice of a servant of God whom I consulted about my mode of prayer. Then I perceived plainly how mistaken I had been, and I have never ceased regretting that there was a time when I did not realise how difficult it would be to gain by so great a loss. Even if I could, I would seek for nothing save by Him through Whom comes all the good we possess. May He be for ever praised! Amen.

---

contradiction, there can be no doubt from this avowal that she too was at one time mistaken on this point.

8

Intellectual Visions

*Speaks of the manner in which God communicates with the
soul by intellectual vision; and gives advice upon the subject.
Of the effects produced by this vision, when genuine. Secrecy
about these favours is enjoined.*

1. (The Lord's presence accompanying the soul). To prove to
   you more clearly, sisters, the truth of what I have been saying,
   and to show that the more the soul advances, the closer does
   this good Jesus bear it company, it would be well for me to
   tell you how, when He so chooses, it cannot withdraw from
   His presence. This is clearly shown by the manners and ways
   in which His Majesty communicates Himself to us, manifesting His love by wonderful apparitions and visions which,
   if He is pleased to aid me, I will describe to you, so that you
   may not be alarmed if any of these favours are granted you.
   We ought, even if we do not receive them ourselves, to praise
   Him fervently for thus communing with creatures, seeing
   how sovereign are His majesty and power.
2. (St. Teresa's experience of this). For example, a person who
   is in no way expecting such a favour, nor has ever imagined

herself worthy of receiving it, is conscious that Jesus Christ stands by her side, although she sees Him neither with the eyes of the body nor of the soul.* This is called an intellectual vision; I cannot tell why. I knew a person to whom God granted both this grace and others I shall describe later on. At first it distressed her, for she could not understand it; she could see nothing, yet so convinced did she feel that Jesus Christ was thus in some way manifesting Himself, that she could not doubt that it was some kind of vision, whether it came from God or no. Its powerful effects were a strong argument that it was from Him; still she was alarmed, never having heard of an intellectual vision, nor was she aware that such a thing could be. She, however, felt certain of our Lord's presence,† and He spoke to her several times in the way that I described. Before she had received this favour, she had heard words spoken, but had never known who uttered them.

3. (Confidence and graces resulting from this vision). She was frightened by this vision, which, unlike an imaginary one, does not pass away quickly, but lasts for several days and even sometimes for more than a year. She went, in a state of great anxiety, to her confessor,‡ who asked her how, if she saw nothing, did she know that our Lord was near her, and bade her describe His appearance. She said she was unable to do so, nor could she see His face, nor tell more than she had already done, but that she was sure it was the fact, that it was He Who spoke to her, and it was no trick of her imagination.

---

* *Life*, ch. xxvii. 3, 5. *Rel.* vii. 26.

† *Life*, ch. xxvii. 7.

‡ *Life, l.c.* 4. Father Juan de Pradanos was then the Saint's confessor.

Although people constantly cautioned her against this vision, she, as a rule, found it impossible to disbelieve in it, especially when she heard the words: "It is I, be not afraid."*

4. (Effects of this vision). The effect of this speech was so powerful that, for the time being, she could not doubt its truth. She felt much encouraged, and rejoiced at being in such good company, seeing that this favour greatly helped her to a constant recollection of God and an extreme care not to displease in any way Him Who seemed ever by her side, watching her. Whenever she desired to speak to His Majesty in prayer, or even at other times, He seemed so close that He could not fail to hear her. He did not, however, speak to her whenever she wished, but unexpectedly, when necessity arose. She was conscious of His being at her right hand, although not in the way we know an ordinary person to be beside us, but in a more subtle manner, which cannot be described. This Presence is, however, quite as evident and certain, and indeed far more so, than the ordinary presence of other people about which we may be deceived; not so in this, for it brings with it graces and spiritual effects which could not come from melancholia. Nor could the devil thus fill the soul with peace, with a constant desire to please God, and such utter contempt of all that does not lead to Him. As time went on, my friend recognised that this was no work of the evil one, as our Lord showed her more and more clearly.

5. (It produces humility). I know, however, that she often felt great alarm and was at times overcome with confusion, being

---

* *Life*, ch. xxv. 22; ch. xxx. 17. *Supra*, M. vi. ch. iii. 5. *Rel*. vii. 22. St. John of the Cross, *Ascent of Mount Carmel*, bk. ii. ch. xxxi. 1.

unable to account for so high a favour having been granted her. She and I were so very intimate,* that I knew all that passed in her soul, hence my account is thoroughly true and reliable. This favour brings with it an overwhelming sense of self-abasement and humility; the reverse would be the case, did it come from Satan.† It is evidently divine; no human effort could produce such feelings, nor could any one suppose that such profit came from herself, but must needs recognise it as a gift from the hand of God.

6. (And prepares the soul for other graces). Although I believe some of the former favours are more sublime, yet this brings with it a special knowledge of God; a most tender love for Him results from being constantly in His company, while the desires of devoting one's whole being to His service are more fervent than any hitherto described. The conscience is greatly purified by the knowledge of His perpetual and near presence, for, although we know that God sees all we do, yet nature inclines us to grow careless and forgetful of it. This is impossible here, for our Lord makes the soul conscious that He is close at hand. The soul is thus prepared to receive the other graces mentioned, by constantly making acts of love to Him Whom it sees or feels at its side. In short, the benefits caused by this grace prove how great and how valuable it is. The soul thanks our Lord for bestowing it on one unworthy of it, but who would refuse to exchange it for any earthly riches or delight.

7. (Consciousness of the presence of the saints). When our Lord

---

* In fact, one and the same person.

† *Life*, ch. xix. 2; ch. xx. 38. *Way of Perf.* ch. xxxvi. 10.

chooses to withdraw His presence, the soul in its loneliness makes every possible effort to induce Him to return. This, however, avails but little, for this grace comes at His will, and not by our endeavours. At times we may enjoy the company of some saint,* which also brings us great profit. You will ask me, if we see no one, how can we know whether it is Christ, or His most glorious Mother, or a saint? Such a person cannot answer this question, or know how she distinguishes them, but the fact remains undoubted. It seems easy to recognise our Lord when He speaks, but it is surprising how the soul can, without hearing a word from him, recognise which saint has been sent by God to be its companion and helper.

8. (Obligations resulting from this grace). There are other spiritual matters which cannot be explained. Our inability to grasp them should teach us how incapable is our nature of understanding the sublime mysteries of God. Those on whom these favours are bestowed should marvel at and praise God's mercy for them. As these particular graces are not granted to everybody, any one who receives them should esteem them highly, and strive to serve God more zealously, since He has given her such special aid. Therefore such a person does not rate herself more highly on this account, but rather thinks she serves Him less than any one else in the world; feeling herself to be under greater obligations to Him than others, any fault she commits pierces her to the heart, as indeed it ought under the circumstances.

9. (Signs that this favour is genuine). When the effects described are felt, any of you whom our Lord leads by this way may

---

* *Life*, ch. xxix. 6.

be certain that it is neither deception nor fancy in her case. I believe it to be impossible for the devil to produce an illusion lasting so long, nor could he benefit the soul so remarkably, nor cause such interior peace. It is not his custom, nor, if he would, could such an evil creature bring about so much good; the soul would soon be clouded by self-esteem and the idea that it was better than others. The mind's continual keeping in the presence of God,* and the concentration of its thoughts on Him, would so enrage the fiend, that, although he might try the experiment once, he would not often repeat it. God is too faithful to permit him so much power over one whose sole endeavour is to please His Majesty and to lay down her life for His honour and glory; He would soon unmask the demon's artifices.

10. (A confessor should be consulted). I contend, and always shall do, that if the soul reaps the effects described from these divine graces, although God may withdraw these special favours, His Majesty will turn all things to its advantage; even if He permit the devil to deceive it at any time, the evil spirit will only reap his own confusion. Therefore, as I told you, daughters, none of you who are led by this way need feel alarm. Fear is good, and we should be cautious and not over-confident, for if such favours made you careless, it would prove they were not from God, as they did not leave the results I described. It would be well at first to tell your case, under the seal of confession, to a thoroughly qualified theologian (for that is the source whence we must obtain light) or to some highly spiritual person. If your confessor is not

* Gen. xvii. 1: "Ambula coram Me et esto perfectus."

very spiritual, a good theologian would be preferable;* best of all, one who unites both qualities.† Do not be disturbed if he calls it mere fancy; if it is, it can neither harm nor benefit your soul much. Recommend yourself to the divine Majesty and beg Him not to allow you to be misled.

11. (Our Lord will enlighten our advisors). It would be worse should he tell you the devil is deceiving you, although no learned man would say so if he sees in you the effects described. Even should your adviser say this, I know that the same Lord Who is beside you will comfort and reassure you, and will go to your counsellor and give him light that he may impart it to you.‡ If the director, though given to prayer, has not been led by God in this way, he will at once take fright and condemn it. Therefore I advise you to choose a qualified theologian, and, if possible, one who is also spiritual. The Prioress ought to allow you this, for, although she may feel sure that you are safe from delusion, because you lead a good life, yet she is bound to allow you to consult some one for your mutual security. When you have conferred with these persons, be at peace; trouble yourself no more about the matter, for sometimes, when there is no cause for fear, the demon gives rise to such immoderate scruples that the person cannot be satisfied with consulting her confessor only once on the

---

* "Magni doctores scholastici, si non sint spirituales, vel omni rerum spiritualium experientia careant, non solent esse magistri spirituales idonei—nam theologia scholastica est perfectio intellectus; mystica, perfectio intellectus et voluntatis: unde bonus theologus scholasticus potest esse malus theologus mysticus. In rebus tamen difficilibus, dubiis, spiritualibus, praestat mediocriter spiritualem theologum consulere quam spiritualem idiotam" (Schram, *Theolog. Mystic,* § 483).

† *Life,* ch. v. 6.

‡ *Life,* ch. xxv. 18 *sqq. Way of Perf.* ch. iv. 11; ch. v. 3.

subject, especially if he is inexperienced and timid, or if he bids her consult him again.

12. (Cautions about this vision). Thus, that which should have been kept strictly private becomes public;* such a person is persecuted and tormented, and finds that what she believed to be her own secret has become public property. Hence she suffers many troubles, which may even devolve upon the Order in such times as these. I warn all Prioresses that great caution, therefore, is required in such matters; also that they must not think a nun more virtuous than the rest because such favours are shown her. Our Lord guides every one in the way He knows to be best. This grace, if made good use of, prepares one receiving it to become a great servant of God, but sometimes our Lord bestows it on the weakest souls; therefore, in itself, it is neither to be esteemed nor condemned. We must look to the virtues; she who is most mortified, humble, and single-minded in serving God is the most holy. However, we can never feel very certain about such matters, until the true Judge rewards each one according to his merits. Then we shall be surprised to find how very different is His judgment from that of this world. May He be for ever praised. Amen!

---

* *Life*, ch. xxiii. 14–15. *Rel.* vii. 17.

9

Imaginary Visions

This chapter speaks of the manner in which God communicates with the soul by imaginary visions. Strong reasons are given for not desiring to be led in this way; this is very profitable reading.

1. (The jewel in the locket). Now we come to treat of imaginary visions, whereby it is held that the devil is more liable to deceive people than by the other visions I have already described. This is probably true. When, however, imaginary visions are divine, they seem, in a certain manner, more profitable for us than the others, as being more suited to our nature—with the exception of the visions sent by our Lord in the seventh mansion, which far surpass all others. The presence of our Lord described in the last chapter may thus be symbolised. Let us suppose that we have in our possession a gold locket, containing a precious stone of the highest value and powers, which, although we have not seen it, we are certain is in the case, and its virtues benefit us when we wear the pendant. Although we have never gazed on it, we value it

highly, knowing by experience that it has cured us of maladies for which it is remedial. However, we dare not look at it, nor open the locket, nor could we do so even if we wished, for the owner of the jewel alone knows the secret of unfastening its casket. Although he lent it us for our use, yet he kept the key for himself; he will open the trinket when he chooses to show us its contents, and close it again when he sees fit to do so.

2. (The simile explained). Our Lord treats us here in this way. Now, suppose the owner of this locket suddenly opened it at times for the benefit of the person to whom he has entrusted it; doubtless the latter would value the diamond more highly through remembering its wonderful lustre. This may be compared to what happens when our Lord is pleased to caress the soul. He shows it in vision His most sacred Humanity, under whatever form He chooses; either as He was during His life on earth,* or after His resurrection.† The vision passes as quickly as a flash of lightning, yet this most glorious picture makes an impression on the imagination that I believe can never be effaced until the soul at last sees Christ to enjoy Him for ever. Although I call it a "picture," you must not imagine that it looks like a painting; Christ appears as a living Person, Who sometimes speaks and reveals deep mysteries. You must understand that though the soul sees this for a certain space of time, it is no more possible to continue looking at it than to gaze for a long time on the sun, therefore this vision passes very quickly, although its brightness

---

* *Life*, ch. vii. 11.

† *Life*, ch. xxix. 4.

does not pain the interior sight in the same way as the sun's glare injures our bodily eyes.

3. (The apparition of Christ). The image is seen by the interior sight alone; but of bodily apparitions I can say nothing, for the person I know so intimately never experienced anything of the kind herself, and therefore could not speak about them with certainty.* The splendour of Him Who is revealed in the vision resembles an infused light, as of the sun, covered with a veil as transparent as a diamond, if such a texture could be woven, while His raiment looks like fine linen. The soul to whom God grants this vision almost always falls into an ecstasy, nature being too weak to bear so dread a sight. I say "dread," though this apparition is more lovely and delightful than anything that could be imagined, even though any one should live a thousand years, and spend all that time in trying to picture it, for it far surpasses our limited imagination and understanding; yet the presence of such surpassing majesty inspires the soul with great fear.

4. (Awe produced by this vision). There is no need to ask how the soul knew Who He was or who declared with absolute certainty that He was the Lord of heaven and earth. This is not so with earthly kings; unless we were told their names or saw their attendant courtiers, they would attract little notice. O Lord! how little do we Christians know Thee! What will that day be in which Thou comest as our Judge, since now, when Thou comest as a Friend to Thy spouse, the sight of Thee strikes us with such awe? O daughters! what will it be

---

* *Life*, ch. vii. 11, 12.

when He says in wrath: "Go, accursed of My Father?"* Let this impression be the result of this favour granted by God to the soul and we shall reap no little benefit from it, since St. Jerome, saint as he was, ever kept the thought of the last judgment before his eyes.† Thus we shall care nothing what sufferings we endure from the austerities of our Rule, for, long as they may last, the time is but a moment compared to this eternity of pain. I sincerely assure you that, wicked as I am, I have never feared the torments of hell,‡ for they have seemed to me as nothing when I remembered that the lost would see the beautiful, meek, and pitiful eyes of our Lord turned on them in wrath.§ I have thought, all my life, that this would be more than my heart could bear.

5. (False and genuine visions). How much more must any one fear this to whom our Lord so revealed Himself in vision here as to overcome her feelings and produce unconsciousness! This must be the reason that the soul remains in a rapture: our Lord strengthens its weakness so as to unite it to His greatness in this sublime communion with God. When any one can contemplate this sight of our Lord for a long time, I do not believe it is a vision, but rather some overmastering

---

* St. Matt. xxv. 41: "Discedite a me, maledicti, in ignem æternum."

† "Whenever I ponder on the Day of Judgment I am overwhelmed by the thought and tremble from head to foot" (St. Jerome). The following saying is by some attributed to St. Jerome, though not to be found in his works: "Whether I eat or drink, or whatever else I do, the dreadful trumpet of the last day seems always sounding in my ears: Arise, ye dead, and come to judgment" (Alban Butler, Life of St. Jerome). The Life of Christ by Ludolf of Saxony gives this quotation with the word vox instead of tuba (part ii. ch. lxxxvii. 9).

‡ Life, ch. iii. 7.

§ Excl. xiii. 3.

idea which causes the imagination to fancy it sees something; this illusion, however, is but as a dead image in comparison with the living reality of the other case.

6. (Illusive visions). Not only three or four, but a large number of people have spoken to me on the subject, therefore I know by experience that there are souls which, either because they possess vivid imaginations or active minds, or for some other reason of which I am ignorant, are so absorbed in their own ideas as to feel certain they see whatever their fancy imagines. If they had ever beheld a genuine vision, they would recognise the deception unmistakably. They themselves fabricate, piece by piece, what they fancy they see: no after effects are produced on the mind, which is less moved to devotion than by the sight of a sacred picture. It is clear that no attention should be paid to such fancies, which pass more quickly than dreams from the memory.

7. (Effects of a genuine vision). In the favour I am speaking about, the case is very different. A person is far from thinking of seeing anything, no idea of which has crossed the mind, when suddenly the vision is revealed in its entirety, causing within the powers and senses of the soul a fright and confusion soon changed into a blissful peace. Thus, after St. Paul was thrown prostrate on the ground, a great tempest and noise followed from heaven;* so, in the interior world of the soul, there is a violent tumult, followed instantly, as I said, by perfect calm. Meanwhile, certain sublime truths have been so impressed on the mind that it needs no other master, for,

_____

* Acts ix. 3, 4.

with no effort of its own, Wisdom Himself has enlightened its former ignorance.

8. (Conviction left by a genuine vision). The soul for some time afterwards possesses such certainty that this grace comes from God, that whatever people may say to the contrary it cannot fear delusion. Later on, when her confessor suggests doubts to her, God may allow such a person to waver in her belief for a time, and to feel misgivings lest, in punishment for her sins, she may possibly have been left to go astray. However, she does not give way to these apprehensions, but (as I said in speaking of other matters)* they only affect her in the same way as the temptations of the devil against faith, which may disturb the mind, but do not shake the firmness of belief. In fact, the more severe the assault,† the more certain is she that the evil one could never have produced the great benefits she is conscious of having received, because he exercises no such power over the interior of the soul. He may present a false apparition, but it does not possess such truth, majesty, and efficacy.

9. (Its effects upon after conduct). As confessors cannot see these effects, which perhaps the person to whom God has shown the vision is unable to explain, they are afraid of deception, as, indeed, they have good reason to be. Therefore caution is necessary, and time should be allowed to see what effects follow. Day by day, the progress of the soul in humility and in the virtues should be watched: if the devil is concerned in the matter, he will soon show signs of himself and will be

---

* *Castle,* M. vi. ch. iii. 12.

† *Way of Perf.* ch. xl. 4.

detected in a thousand lies. If the confessor is experienced and has received such favours himself, he will not take long in discovering the truth. In fact, he will know immediately, on being told of the vision, whether it is divine or comes from the imagination or the demon: more especially if he has received the gift of discerning spirits—then, if he is learned, he will understand the matter at once, even though he has not personally experienced the like.

10. (A confessor should be consulted). The great point is, sisters, that you should be perfectly candid and straightforward with your confessor: I do not mean in declaring your sins—that is evident enough—but in giving him an account of your prayer.* Unless you do this, I cannot assure you of your safety, nor that you are led by God. Our Lord desires that we should be as truthful and open with those who stand in His place as we should be with Himself; that we should wish them to know not only our thoughts but especially all relating to our actions, however insignificant. Then you need feel no trouble nor anxiety,† because even were your vision not from God, it could do you no harm if you are humble and possess a good conscience; for His Majesty knows how to glean good from evil. What the devil intended to injure you will benefit you instead: believing that God has granted you such signal favours, you will strive to please Him better, and will keep His image ever before your memory.

11. (How to treat visions). A great theologian‡ once said that he

---

* *Life*, ch. xxvi. 5; ch. xxviii. 21.

† *Way of Perf.* ch. xl. 3.

‡ This was Father Dominic Bañez. *Found.* ch. viii. 3–*Life*, ch. xxix. 6, 7 and note.

should not trouble himself though the devil, who is a clever painter, should present before his eyes the living image of Christ, which would only kindle his devotion and defeat the evil one with his own weapons. However wicked an artist may be, we should reverence his picture if it represents Him Who is our only Good. This great scholar held that it was very wrong to advise any one who saw a vision of our Lord to offer it signs of scorn,* because we are bound to show respect to the portrait of our King wherever we see it. I am sure that he was right, for even in the world, any one who was on friendly terms with a person would take it as an of-fence were his portrait treated with contempt. How much more, then, should we always show respect to a crucifix or a picture of our heavenly Sovereign, wherever it meets our gaze! Although I have written about this elsewhere, I am glad of the opportunity of saying it now, for I know some one who was deeply pained at being bidden to behave in this way. I know not who can have invented such a torture for one who felt bound to obey the counsel given by her confessor, for she would have thought her soul was at stake had she disobeyed him. My advice is, if you are given such an order, that, humbly alleging the reasons I have set before you to your confessor, you should not carry it out. I am perfectly satisfied with the motives given for doing so by him who counselled me on this subject.

12. (Effects of seeing the face of Christ). One great advantage gained by the soul from this favour shown by our Lord is that, when thinking on Him or on His life and Passion, the

---

* *Letters of Blessed John of Avila* (translated by the Benedictines of Stanbrook), i. 5, p. 19.

remembrance of His most meek and beautiful face brings with it the greatest consolation. In the same way, we feel happier after having seen a benefactor than if we had never known him personally. I can assure you that the remembrance of the joy caused by this vision gives us the greatest comfort and assistance.

13. (Reasons why visions are not to be sought). Many other advantages result; but as I have written elsewhere* at length about the effects these visions produce, and must do so again later on, I will say no more now, lest I weary us both. However, I most earnestly advise you, when you know or hear of God bestowing these graces on others, that you never pray nor desire to be led by this way yourself, though it may appear to you to be very good; indeed, it ought to be highly esteemed and reverenced, yet no one should seek to go by it, for several reasons. Firstly, it is a want of humility to desire what you have never deserved, therefore I do not think any one who longs for these graces can be really humble: a common labourer never dreams of wishing to be made a king—the thing seems impossible, and he is unfit for it; a lowly mind has the same feeling about these divine favours. I do not believe God will ever bestow these gifts on such a person, as before doing so He always gives thorough self-knowledge. How can that soul, while filled with such lofty aspirations, realise the truth that He has shown it great mercy in not casting it into hell?

14. (The second reason). The second reason is that such a one is certain to be deceived, or at least is in great danger of delu-

---

* *Life*, ch. xxviii. 13, 14.

sion, for an entrance is thus left open to the devil, who only needs to see the door left ajar to slip in at once and play us a thousand tricks.

15. (The third reason). Thirdly: when people strongly desire a thing, the imagination makes them fancy they see or hear it, just as when a man's mind is set upon a thing all day he dreams of it at night.

16. (Fourth reason). Fourthly: it would be very presumptuous of me to choose a way for myself without knowing what is good for me.* I should leave our Lord, Who knows my soul, to guide me as is best for me, that His will may be done in all things.

17. (Fifth reason). Fifthly: do you think people on whom our Lord bestows these favours have little to suffer? No, indeed! their trials are most severe and of many kinds. How can you tell whether you would be able to bear them?

18. (Sixth reason). Sixthly: perhaps what you think would be your gain might prove your loss, as happened to Saul when he was made king.† In short, sisters, there are other reasons besides these; believe me, it is safer to wish only what God wishes, Who knows us better than we know ourselves, and Who loves us. Let us place ourselves, entirely in His hands, that His will may be done in us; we can never go astray if our will is ever firmly fixed on this.

19. (Additional reasons). Know that for having received many favours of this kind, you will not merit more glory, but will

---

* St. Teresa, when led in this way, always asked to be delivered from favours so dangerous as visions, etc. See *Life,* ch. xxv. 20; ch. xxvii. 3.

† I. Reg. xv. 26–28.

be the more stringently obliged to serve, since you have received more. God does not deprive us of anything by which we merit more, for this remains in our own control. There are many saints who never knew what it was to receive one such favour, while others, who have received them, are not saints at all. Do not imagine that these gifts are continually bestowed; indeed, for one that is granted, the soul bears many a cross, so that, instead of longing to receive more favours, it only strives to use them better.

20. (The virtues more meritorious than consolations). True, such a grace is a most powerful aid towards practising the virtues in their highest perfection, but it is far more meritorious to gain them at the cost of one's own toil. I was acquainted with some one,* indeed with two people (of whom one was a man), on whom our Lord had bestowed some of these gifts. They were both so desirous of serving His Majesty at their own cost without these great consolations, and so longed to suffer for His sake, that they remonstrated with Him for giving them these favours, and, if it had been possible, would have refused to receive them. When I say "consolations," I do not mean these visions, which greatly benefit the soul and are highly to be esteemed, but the delights given by God during contemplation.

21. (Fervent souls desire to serve God for Himself alone). I believe that these desires are supernatural, and proper to very fervent souls who wish to prove to God that they do not serve Him for pay; so, as I said, such people do not urge

---

* *Life*, ch. xl. 27. She herself was one, and the other, no doubt, was St. John of the Cross.

themselves to work harder for Him by the thought of the glory they will gain, but rather labour to satisfy their love, of which the nature is to toil for the Beloved in a thousand ways. Such souls would fain find a way to consume themselves in Him, and were there need that, for the sake of God's greater glory, they should be annihilated for ever, they would count it great gain. May He be for ever praised Who, in abasing Himself to hold converse with us miserable creatures, vouchsafes to manifest His greatness! Amen.

10

Intellectual Visions Continued

*Speaks of various other graces God bestows on the soul in
different ways, and of the great benefits conferred by them.*

1. (Reasons for speaking of these supernatural favours). OUR
Lord communicates with the soul by means of these apparitions on many occasions—sometimes when it is afflicted,
at other times when it is about to receive some heavy cross,
and again for the sake of the mutual delight of Himself and
His beloved. There is no need for me to specify each different case, nor do I intend to do so. I only wish to teach you
(as far as I am acquainted with them myself) what are the
different favours God shows a soul in this state, that you may
understand their characteristics and the effects they produce.
Thus you will not mistake every idle fancy for a vision, and if
you really see one, knowing that such a thing is possible, you
will not be disturbed nor unhappy. As the devil gains greatly
by this, he is delighted to see a soul troubled and distressed,
knowing how this hinders it from employing itself wholly in
loving and praising God.

2. (An intellectual vision). His Majesty has far higher ways of communicating Himself to the soul, which are less dangerous, for I do not think the evil spirit can imitate them. They are more difficult to explain, being more abstruse; therefore imaginary visions are easier to describe. God is sometimes pleased, while a person is engaged in prayer, and is in perfect possession of her senses, to suspend them and to discover sublime mysteries to her, which she appears to see within God Himself. This is no vision of the most sacred Humanity, nor can I rightly say the soul "sees," for it sees nothing; this is no imaginary vision, but a highly intellectual one, wherein is manifested how all things are beheld in God, and how He contains them within Himself.* It is of great value, for, although passing in an instant, it remains deeply engraved in the memory, producing a feeling of great shame in the mind, which perceives more clearly the malice of offences against God, since these most heinous sins are committed within His very being, seeing that we dwell within Him. I will try to explain this truth to you by a comparison, for, although it is obvious, and has been often told us, we either never reflect upon it or do not wish to understand it. If we realised it, we could not possibly behave with such audacity.

3. (God compared to a palace in which His creatures dwell). Let us compare God to a very spacious and magnificent mansion or palace, and remember that this edifice is God Himself. Can the sinner withdraw from it in order to carry out his crimes? No, certainly not, for within this very palace, that is,

---

* *Life,* ch. xl. 13–16.

within God Himself, are perpetrated all the abominations, impurities, and evil deeds that sinners commit. Oh awful thought, well worthy to be pondered over! What profit it would bring to us, who know so little and understand these truths but partially, or how could we possibly be so reckless in our daring? Let us, sisters, meditate on the infinite mercy and patience of God in not casting us down to hell at once, and let us render Him hearty thanks. Surely we should be ashamed of resenting anything done or said against us—*we,* who are the scum of the earth, when we see what outrages are offered to *God* our *Creator,* within His very being, by us His creatures; yet we are wounded whenever we hear of an unkind word having been spoken of us in our absence, although perhaps with no evil intention.

4. (Forgive as we are forgiven). Oh misery of mankind! When, daughters, shall we imitate Almighty God in any way? Oh, let us not think we are doing great things if we suffer injuries *patiently,* rather let us bear them with *alacrity*; let us love our enemies, since this great God has not ceased to love us, in spite of our many sins! This is indeed the chief reason that all should forgive any harm done them. I assure you, daughters, that though this vision passes very quickly, our Lord has bestowed signal grace on her to whom He grants it, if she seeks to profit by keeping it constantly in mind.

5. (The vision shows God to be Truth itself). Short as the time lasts, yet, in a manner impossible to describe, God also manifests that in Him there is a verity which makes all truth in creatures seem obscure. He convinces the soul that He alone is that Truth which cannot lie, thus demonstrating the meaning of David's words in the psalm: "Every man

is a liar,"* which could never be thus realised by any other means, however often we might hear that God is truth infallible. As I recall Pilate and how he besought our Lord in His Passion to tell him: "What is truth?"† I realise how little mortals know of that sublime veracity.

6. (We should imitate God by truthfulness). I wish I could explain this better, but am unable to do so. Let us learn from it, sisters, that if we would bear any resemblance to our God and our Spouse, we must strive to walk ever in the truth. I do not merely mean that we should not tell falsehoods,— thank God, I see that in these convents you are most careful never to do so on any account, but I desire that, as far as possible, we should act with perfect truth before God and man, and above all that we should not wish to be thought better than we are; that in all our deeds we should ascribe to God what is His, and attribute what is ours to ourselves, and that we should seek for verity in all things. Thus we shall care little for this world, which is but deception and falsehood, and therefore cannot last. Once, while I was wondering why our Lord so dearly loves the virtue of humility, the thought suddenly struck me, without previous reflection, that it is because God is the supreme Truth, and humility is the *truth*, for it is most true that we have nothing good of ourselves, but only misery and nothingness: whoever ignores this, lives a life of falsehood. They that realise this fact most deeply are the most pleasing to God, the supreme Truth, for they walk

---

* Ps. cxv. 11: "Omnis homo mendax."

† St. John xviii. 38: "Quid est veritas?"

in the truth. God grant, sisters, that we may have the grace never to lose this self-knowledge! Amen.

7. (Why God reveals these truths). Our Lord shows the soul these favours because she is now indeed His bride, resolute to do His will in all things; therefore He wishes to give her some idea how to accomplish it, and to manifest to her some of His divine attributes. I need say no more about it, but I believe the two points above mentioned will prove very useful. These favours should cause no fear, but lead us to praise God for bestowing these graces. I think neither the devil nor our own imaginations can have much to do with them, therefore the soul may rest in perfect peace.

11

The Dart of Love

*Treats of how God inspires the soul with such vehement and
impetuous desires of seeing Him as to endanger life. The benefits resulting from this divine grace.*

1. (Favours increase the soul's desire for God). WILL all these
graces bestowed by the Spouse upon the soul suffice to content this little dove or butterfly (you see I have not forgotten
her after all!) so that she may settle down and rest in the place
where she is to die? No, indeed, her state is far worse than
ever; although she has been receiving these favours for many
years past, she still sighs and weeps, because each grace augments her pain. She sees herself still far away from God, yet
with her increased knowledge of His attributes her longing
and her love for Him grow ever stronger as she learns more
fully how this great God and Sovereign deserves to be loved.
As, year by year her yearning after Him gradually becomes
keener, she experiences the bitter suffering I am about to describe. I speak of "years," because relating what happened to
the person I mentioned, though I know well that with God

time has no limits and in a single moment He can raise a soul to the most sublime state I have described. His Majesty has the power to do all He wishes, and He wishes to do much for us. These longings, tears, sighs, and violent and impetuous desires and strong feelings, which seem to proceed from our vehement love, are yet as nothing compared with what I am about to describe, and seem but a smouldering fire, the heat of which, though painful, is yet tolerable.

2. (The dart of love). While the soul is thus inflamed with love, it often happens that from a passing thought or spoken word of how death delays its coming, the heart receives, it knows not how or whence, a blow as from a fiery dart.* I do not say that this actually is a "dart," but, whatever it may be, decidedly it does not come from any part of our being.† Neither is it really a "blow," though I call it one, but it wounds us severely—not, I think, in that part of our nature subject to physical pain, but in the very depths and centre of the soul, where this thunderbolt, in its rapid course, reduces all the earthly part of our nature to powder. At the time we cannot even remember our own existence, for, in an instant, the faculties of the soul are so fettered as to be incapable of any action, except the power they retain of increasing our torture. Do not think I am exaggerating; indeed I fall short of explaining what happens, which cannot be described.

3. (Spiritual sufferings produced). This is a trance of the senses and faculties, except as regarding what helps to make the agony more intense. The understanding realises acutely what

---

* *Life,* ch. xxix. 17 (Transverberation).

† *Life,* ch. xxix. 13, 14. *Rel.* viii. 16–19.

cause there is for grief in separation from God, and His Majesty now augments this sorrow by a vivid manifestation of Himself. This increases the anguish to such a degree that the sufferer gives vent to loud cries, which she cannot stifle, however patient and accustomed to pain she may be, because this torture is not corporal, but attacks the innermost recesses of the soul. The person I speak of learnt from this how much more acutely the spirit is capable of suffering than is the body; she understood that this resembled the pains of purgatory, where the absence of the flesh does not prevent the torture from being far worse than any we can feel in this world.

4. (Its physical effects). I saw some one in this condition who, I really thought, would have died, nor would it have been surprising, for there is great danger of death in this state. Short as is the time it lasts, it leaves the limbs all disjointed and the pulse as feeble as if the soul were on the point of departure, which is indeed the case, for the natural heat fails, while that which is supernatural so burns the frame that were it increased ever so little God would satisfy the soul's desire for death. Not that any pain is felt by the body at the moment, although, as I said, all the joints are dislocated, so that for two or three days afterwards the suffering is too severe for the person to have even the strength to hold a pen;* indeed I believe that the health becomes permanently enfeebled in consequence. At the time this is not felt, probably because the spiritual torments are so far more keen that the bodily ones remain unnoticed; just as when there is very severe pain in

---

* St. John of the Cross, *Obscure Night*, bk. ii. ch. i. (*in fine*); *Spiritual Canticle*, stanza xiii.; stanza xiv.-xv. (*in fine*). When this happened to St. Teresa she was unable to write for twelve days. Ribera, *Acta SS*. p. 555 (*in fine*). *Rel.* viii. 13. *Life*, ch. xx. 16.

one part, slighter aches elsewhere are hardly perceived, as I know by experience. During this favour, there is no physical suffering either great or small, nor do I think the person would feel it were she torn to pieces.

5. (Torture of the desire for God). Perhaps you will say this is an imperfection, and you may ask why she does not conform herself to the will of God, since she has so completely surrendered herself to it. Hitherto she has been able to do so, and she consecrated her life to it; but now she cannot, because her reason is reduced to such a state that she is no longer mistress of herself, nor can she think of anything but what tends to increase her torment—for why should she seek to live apart from her only Good? She feels a strange loneliness, finding no companionship in any earthly creature; nor could she, I think, among those who dwell in heaven, since they are not her Beloved: meanwhile, all society is a torture to her. She is like one suspended in mid-air, who cannot touch the earth nor mount to heaven; she is unable to reach the water while parched with thirst, and this not a thirst that can be borne, but one which nothing will quench—nor would she have it quenched, save with that water of which our Lord spoke to the Samaritan woman, but this is not given her.*

6. (These sufferings are a purgatory). Alas, O Lord, to what a state dost Thou bring those who love Thee! Yet these sufferings are as nothing compared with the reward Thou wilt give for them. It is right that great riches should be dearly bought. Moreover, her pains purify her soul so that it may enter the

---

* St. John iv. 15. *Life,* ch. xxx. 24. *Way of Perf.* ch. xix. 4 *sqq. Excl.* ix. *Found.* ch. xxxi. 42. See note, *Life,* ch. i. 6.

seventh mansion, as purgatory cleanses spirits which are to enter heaven:* then indeed these trials will appear like a drop of water compared to the sea. Though this torment and grief could not, I think, be surpassed by any earthly cross (so at least this person said, and she had endured much both in body and mind), yet they appeared to her as nothing in comparison with their recompense. The soul realises that it has not merited anguish which is of such measureless value. This conviction, although bringing no relief, enables the sufferer to bear her trials willingly—for her entire lifetime, if God so wills,—although instead of dying once for all, this would be but a living death, for truly it is nothing else.

7. (The torments of hell). Let us remember, sisters, how those who are in hell lack this submission to the divine will and the resignation and consolation God gives such a soul, and the solace of knowing that their pains benefit them, but the damned will continually suffer more and more; (*more and more,* I mean in regard to accidental pains†). The soul feels far more keenly than the body, and the torments I have just described are incomparably less severe than those endured by the lost, who also know that their anguish will last for ever; what, then, will become of these miserable souls? What can

---

* St. John of the Cross, *Obscure Night*, bk. ii. ch. xii.

† Marginal note in the Saint's handwriting. The "substantial" pain of hell consists in the irrevocable loss of God, our last end and supreme Good; this is incurred from the first moment in its fullest intensity and therefore cannot increase. The physical pain with which the bodies will be afflicted when united to the souls after the general resurrection may vary, but will neither increase nor abate. The "accidental" pain of the damned arises from various causes, for instance from the ever-increasing effects of evil actions, and therefore increases in the same proportion. Thus a heresiarch will suffer keener accidental pain as more and more souls are lost through his false teaching.

we do, or suffer, in our short lives which is worth reckoning if it will free us from such terrible and endless torments? I assure you that, unless you have learnt by experience, it would be impossible to make you realise how acute are spiritual pangs and how different from physical pain. Our Lord wishes us to understand this, so that we may realise what gratitude we owe Him for having called us to a state where we may hope, by His mercy, to be freed from and forgiven our sins.

8. (St. Teresa's painful desire after God). Let us return to the soul we left in such cruel torment. This agony does not continue for long in its full violence—never, I think, longer than three or four hours; were it prolonged, the weakness of our nature could not endure it except by a miracle. In one case, where it lasted only a quarter of an hour, the sufferer was left utterly exhausted; indeed, so violent was the attack that she completely lost consciousness. This occurred when she unexpectedly heard some one remark that life seemed unending; she was engaged in conversation at the time, which was on the last day of Easter. All Eastertide she had suffered such aridity as hardly to realise what mystery was being celebrated.*

9. (This suffering irresistible). It is as impossible to resist this suffering as it would be to prevent the flames having heat enough to burn us if we were thrown into a fire. These feelings cannot

---

* *Rel.* iv. 1. *Concep.* ch. vii. 2. Isabel of Jesus, in her deposition in the Acts of Canonisation (Fuente, *Obras,* vol. vi. 316) declares that she was the singer. The words were: Véante mis ojos, Dulce Jesús bueno: Véante mis ojos, Y muérame yo luégo. (Fuente, *l.c.* vol. v. 143, note 1. *Œuvres,* ii. 231 (Poem 36, English version).) There is a slight difference in the two relations of this occurrence. In *Rel.* iv. St. Teresa seems to imply that it happened on Easter Sunday evening, but here she says distinctly "Pascua de Resurreccion, el postrer dia," that is, on Easter Tuesday, April 17, 1571, at Salamanca.

be concealed: all who are present recognise the dangerous condition of such a person, although they are unable to see what is passing within her. True, she knows her friends are near, but they, and all earthly things seem to her but shadows. To show you that, should you ever be in this state, it is possible for your weakness and human nature to be of help to you, I may tell you that at times, when a person seems dying from her desire for death,* which so oppresses her soul with grief that it appears on the point of leaving her body, yet her mind, terrified at the thought, tries to still its pain so as to keep death at bay. Evidently this fear arises from human infirmity, for the soul's longings for death do not abate meanwhile, nor can its sorrow be stilled or allayed until God brings it comfort.† This He usually does by a deep trance, or by some vision, whereby the true Comforter consoles and strengthens the heart, which thus becomes resigned to live as long as He wills.‡

10. (Effects of the dart of love). This favour entails great suffering, but leaves most precious graces within the soul which loses all fear of any crosses it may henceforth meet with, for in comparison with the acute anguish it has gone through all else seems nothing. Seeing what she has gained, the sufferer

---

* Compare the words "Que muero porque no muero," in the *Glosa* of St. Teresa. *Way of Perf.* ch. xlii. 2. *Castle,* M. vii. ch. iii. 14.

† *Way of Perf.* ch. xix. 10. *Excl.* vi.; xii. 2; xiv.

‡ See the two versions of the poems written by the Saint on her recovery from the trance into which she was thrown, beginning "Vivir sin vivir in me" and the poem, "Cuan triste es, Dios mio" (Poems 2, 3, and 4, English version). See also St. Teresa's poem, "Ya toda me entregué y dí" (Poem 7, English version). Struck by the gentle Hunter And overthrown, Within the arms of Love My soul lay prone. Raised to new life at last, This contract 'tween us passed, That the Beloved should be mine own, I His alone.

would gladly endure frequently the same pains,* but can do nothing to help herself in the matter. There are no means of reaching that state again until God chooses to decree it, when neither resistance nor escape is possible. The mind feels far deeper contempt for the world than before, having learnt that nothing earthly can succour it in its torture; it is also much more detached from creatures, having learnt that no one but its Creator can bring it consolation and strength. It is more anxious and careful not to offend God, seeing that He can torment as well as comfort.†

11. (Two spiritual dangers to life). Two things in this spiritual state seem to me to endanger life,—one is what I have just spoken of, which is a real peril and no small one; the other is an excessive gladness and delight, which is so extreme that the soul appears to swoon away and seems on the point of leaving the body, which indeed would bring it no small joy.

12. (Courage needed here and given by our Lord). Now you see, sisters, whether I had not reason to tell you that courage was needed for these favours, and that when any one asks for them from our Lord He may well reply, as He did to the sons of Zebedee: "Can ye drink the chalice that I shall drink?"‡ I believe, sisters, we should all answer "Yes"—and we should be perfectly right, for His Majesty gives strength when He sees it needed: He ever defends such souls and answers for them when they are persecuted and slandered, as He did for the

---

* *Rel.* viii. 17.

† *Acta SS.* p. 64, n. 229.

‡ St. Matt. xx. 22: "Potestis bibere calicem quem ego bibiturus sum?"

Magdalen—if not in words, at least in deeds.* At last, ah, at last! before they die, He repays them for all they have suffered, as you shall now learn. May He be for ever blessed, and may all creatures praise Him! Amen.

---

* St. Matt. xxvi. 10; St. Mark xiv. 6; St. John xii. 7. *Way of Perf.* ch. xvi. 7; ch. xvii. 4. *Excl.* v. 2–4.

THE SEVENTH MANSIONS

1

God's Presence Chamber

Treats of the sublime favours God bestows on souls which have entered the seventh mansions. The author shows the difference she believes to exist between soul and spirit, although they are both one. This chapter contains some noteworthy things.

1. (Sublime mysteries of these mansions). YOU may think, sisters, that so much has been said of this spiritual journey that nothing remains to be added. That would be a great mistake: God's immensity has no limits, neither have His works; therefore, who can recount His mercies and His greatness?* It is impossible, so do not be amazed at what I write about them, which is but a cipher of what remains untold concerning God. He has shown great mercy in communicating these mysteries to one who could recount them to us, for as we learn more of His intercourse with creatures, we ought to praise Him more fervently, and to esteem more highly the soul in which He so delights. Each of us possesses

---

* Ps. cxliv. 3: "Magnitudinis ejus non est finis."

a soul, but we do not realise its value, as made in the image of God, therefore we fail to understand the important secrets it contains. May His Majesty be pleased to guide my pen, and to teach me to say *somewhat* of the *much* there is to tell of His revelations to the souls He leads into this mansion. I have begged Him earnestly to help me, since He sees that my object is to reveal His mercies, for the praise and glory of His name. I hope He will grant this favour, if not for my own sake, at least for yours, sisters—that you may discover how vital it is for you to put no obstacle in the way of the Spiritual Marriage of the Bridegroom with your soul, which brings, as you will learn, such signal blessings with it.

2. (St. Teresa abashed at treating such subjects). O great God! surely such a miserable creature as myself should tremble at the thought of speaking on a subject so far beyond anything I deserve to understand. Indeed I felt abashed, and doubted whether it would not be better to finish writing about this mansion in a few words lest people might imagine that I recounted my personal experience. I was overwhelmed with shame, for, knowing what I am, it is a terrible undertaking. On the other hand, this fear seemed but a temptation and weakness: even if I should be misjudged, so long as God is but a little better praised and known, let all the world hoot at me. Besides, I may be dead before this book is seen. May He Who lives and shall live to all eternity be praised! Amen.

3. (Our Lord introduces His bride into His presence chamber). When our Lord is pleased to take pity on the sufferings, both past and present, endured through her longing for Him by this soul which He has spiritually taken for His bride, He, before consummating the celestial marriage, brings her into

this His mansion or presence chamber. This is the seventh mansion, for as He has a dwelling-place in heaven, so has He in the soul, where none but He may abide, and which may be termed a second heaven.

4. (Darkness of a soul in mortal sin). It is important, sisters, that we should not fancy the soul to be in darkness. As we are accustomed to believe there is no light but that which is exterior, we imagine that the soul is wrapt in obscurity. This is indeed the case with a soul out of the state of grace,* not, however, through any defect in the Sun of Justice, which remains within it and gives it being, but the soul itself is incapable of receiving the light, as I think I said in speaking of the first mansion.† A certain person was given to understand that such unfortunate souls are, as it were, imprisoned in a gloomy dungeon, chained hand and foot, and unable to perform any meritorious action: they are also both blind and dumb. Well may we pity them, when we reflect that we ourselves were once in the same state and that God may show them mercy also.

5. (Intercession for sinners). Let us, then, sisters, be most zealous in interceding for them, and never neglect it. To pray for a soul in mortal sin is a far more profitable form of almsgiving than it would be to help a Christian whom we saw with hands strongly fettered behind his back, tied to a post and dying of hunger—not for want of food, because plenty of the choicest delicacies lay near him, but because he was unable to put them into his mouth—although he was extremely

---

* See the Saint's description of a soul in the state of sin, *Rel.* iii. 13 (towards the end).

† *Supra,* M. i. ch. ii. 1.

exhausted and on the point of dying, and that not a temporal death, but an eternal one. Would it not be extremely cruel of us to stand looking at him, and give him nothing to eat? What if by your prayers you could loose his bonds? Now you understand.

6. (The soul an interior world). For the love of God I implore you constantly to remember in your prayers souls in a like case. We are not speaking now of them, but of others who, by the mercy of God, have done penance for their sins and are in a state of grace. You must not think of the soul as insignificant and petty, but as an interior world, containing the number of beautiful mansions you have seen; as indeed it should, since in the centre of the soul there is a mansion reserved for God Himself.

7. (The spiritual nuptials). When His Majesty deigns to bestow on the soul the grace of these divine nuptials, He brings it into His presence chamber, and does not treat it as before, when He put it into a trance. I believe He then united it to Himself, as also during the prayer of union; but then only the superior part was affected, and the soul did not feel called to enter its own centre as it does in this mansion. Here it matters little whether it be in the one way or the other.

8. (Former favours differ from spiritual nuptials). In the former favours our Lord unites the spirit to Himself and makes it both blind and dumb, like St. Paul after his conversion,* thus preventing it from knowing whence or how it enjoys this grace, for the supreme delight of the spirit is to realise its

---

* Acts ix. 8: "Surrexit autem Saulus de terra; apertisque oculis nihil videbat." There is, however, nothing to imply that he was dumb as well as blind.

nearness to God. During the actual moment of divine union the soul feels nothing, all its powers being entirely lost. Now, however, He acts differently: our pitiful God removes the scales from its eyes,* that it may see and understand somewhat of the grace received, in a strange and wonderful manner in this mansion, by means of intellectual vision.

9. (The Blessed Trinity revealed to the soul). By some mysterious manifestation of the truth, the three Persons of the most Blessed Trinity reveal themselves, preceded by an illumination which shines on the spirit like a most dazzling cloud of light.† The three Persons are distinct from one another; a sublime knowledge is infused into the soul, imbuing it with a certainty of the truth that the Three are of one substance, power, and knowledge, and are one God. Thus that which we hold, as a doctrine of faith, the soul now, so to speak, understands by sight, although it beholds the Blessed Trinity neither by the eyes of the body nor of the soul, for this is no imaginary vision. All the three Persons here communicate Themselves to the soul, speak to it, and make it understand

---

* Acts ix. 18: "Et confestim ceciderunt ab oculis ejus tam-quam squamæ et visum recepit." *Way of Perf.* ch. xxviii. 11.

† *Rel.* iii. 6; v. 6–8; viii. 20, 21; ix. 12, 17, 19. Deposition by Fr. Giles Gonzalez, S.J., Provincial of Old Castile, afterwards Assistant-General in Rome: "While the holy Mother lived at the convent of the Incarnation of Avila, I often spoke with her, and once I remember she asked me: 'What am I to do, Father? Whenever I recollect myself I realise that already in this life the Three Persons of the Blessed Trinity may be seen, and that They accompany me and assist me in the management of my affairs'" (Fuente, *Obras,* vol. vi. p. 280). "Doña Maria Enriquez, duchess of Alva, said that St. Teresa made known to her many revelations she had received from our Lord, and that she (the duchess) held in her possession three paintings of the Blessed Trinity made according to the description of the holy Mother, who, while they were being done, effaced with her own hand those portions which the painter failed to design conformably to the vision she had had" (Fuente, *l.c.* p. 297).

the words of our Lord in the Gospel, that He and the Father and the Holy Ghost will come and make their abode with the soul which loves Him, and which keeps His commandments.*

10. (Permanence of Its presence in the soul). O my God, how different from merely hearing and believing these words is it to realise their truth in this way! Day by day a growing astonishment takes possession of this soul, for the three Persons of the Blessed Trinity seem never to depart; it sees with certainty, in the way I have described, that They dwell far within its own centre and depths; though unable to describe how, for want of learning, it is conscious of the indwelling of these divine Companions.

11. (The effects).You may fancy that such a person is beside herself and that her mind is too inebriated to care for anything else. On the contrary, she is far more active than before in all that concerns God's service, and when at leisure she enjoys this blessed companionship. Unless she first deserts God, I believe He will never cease to make her clearly sensible of His presence: she feels confident, as indeed she may, that He will never so fail her as to allow her to lose this favour, after once bestowing it; at the same time, she is more careful than before to avoid offending Him in any way.

12. (This presence is not always equally realised). This presence is not always so entirely realised, that is, so distinctly manifest, as at first, or as it is at times when God renews this favour, otherwise the recipient could not possibly attend to anything

---

* St. John xiv. 23: "Si quis diligit me, sermonem meum servabit, et Pater meus diliget eum, et ad eum veniemus et mansionem apud eum faciemus."

else, nor live in society. Although not always seen by so clear a light, yet whenever she reflects on it she feels the companionship of the Blessed Trinity. This is as if, when we were with other people in a very well lighted room, some one were to darken it by closing the shutters; we should feel certain that the others were still there, although unable to see them.*

13. (It is beyond the soul's control). You may ask: "Could she not bring back the light and see them again?"† This is not in her power; when our Lord chooses, He will open the shutters of the understanding: He shows her great mercy in never quitting her and in making her realise it so clearly. His divine Majesty seems to be preparing His bride for greater things by this divine companionship: which clearly helps perfection in every way, and makes her lose the fear she sometimes felt when other graces were granted her.

14. (The centre of the soul remains calm). Thus a certain person so favoured found she had improved in all the virtues: whatever were her trials or labours, the centre of her soul seemed to her never moved from its resting-place. Thus in a manner her soul seemed divided: a short time after God had done her this favour, when she was undergoing great sufferings, she

---

* One of the Saint's favourite comparisons. See *Life,* ch. xxvii. 7. *Castle,* M. vi. ch. viii. 3. *Rel.* vii. 26.

† "Though the soul be always in the high estate of marriage since God has placed it there, nevertheless, actual union in all its powers is not continuous, though the substantial union is. In this substantial union the powers of the soul are most frequently in union, and drink of His cellar, the understanding by knowledge, the will by love, etc. We are not therefore to suppose that the soul, when saying it went out, has ceased from its substantial or essential union with God, but only from the union of its faculties, which is not, and cannot be, permanent in this life" (St. John of the Cross, *Spiritual Canticle,* stanza xxvi. 9. On the words: "In the inner cellar of my Beloved have I drunk, and when I went forth").

complained of her soul as Martha did of Mary,* reproaching it with enjoying solitary peace while leaving her so full of troubles and occupations that she could not keep it company.

15. (The soul and the spirit distinct though united). This may seem extravagant to you, daughters, yet though the soul is known to be undivided, it is fact and no fancy, and often happens. Interior effects show for certain that there is a positive difference between the soul and the spirit, although they are one with each other.† There is an extremely subtle distinction between them, so that sometimes they seem to act in a different manner from one another, as does the knowledge given to them by God.

16. (The soul and its faculties not identical). It also appears to me that the soul and its faculties are not identical. There are so many and such transcendental mysteries within us, that it would be presumption for me to attempt to explain them. If by God's mercy we enter heaven we shall understand these secrets.

---

* St. Luke ch. x. 40. *Excl.* v. 2, 3; *Way of Perf.* ch. xv. 4; ch. xxxi. 4. *Rel.* viii. 6. *Concep.* ch. vii. 4.

† *Life,* ch. xviii. 4. The distinction between soul and spirit, to be found in the Epistle to the Hebrews, iv. 12, according to Cornelius a Lapide (*ad loc.*) consists in this, that the term *soul* comprises the faculties, senses, and passions, whereas the term *spirit* denotes the substance of the soul independently of its powers. In the inferior degrees of the Mystical life God operates through the faculties, while in the Mystical marriage He acts directly on the substance of the soul. St. Teresa is not quite consistent in the use of these terms, which is not surprising, as she owns that she does not quite understand this subtle distinction.

2

Spiritual Matrimony

Treats of the same subject: explains, by some delicately drawn comparisons, the difference between spiritual union and spiritual marriage.

1. (The spiritual nuptials introduced by an imaginary vision). WE now come to speak of divine and spiritual nuptials, although this sublime favour cannot be received in all its perfection during our present life, for by forsaking God this great good would be lost. The first time God bestows this grace, He, by an imaginary vision of His most sacred Humanity, reveals Himself to the soul, that it may understand and realise the sovereign gift it is receiving. He may manifest Himself in a different way to other people; the person I mentioned, after she had been to Holy Communion, beheld our Lord, full of splendour, beauty, and majesty, as He was after His Resurrection.* He told her that henceforth she was to care for His affairs as though they were her own, and He

---

* *Rel.* iii. 20; ix. 8 and 25.

would care for hers: He spoke other words, which she could understand better than repeat. This may seem to be nothing new, for our Lord had thus revealed Himself to her at other times;* yet this was so different that it left her bewildered and amazed, both on account of the vividness of what she saw and of the words heard at the time, and also because it took place in the interior of the soul, where, with the exception of the one last mentioned, no other vision had been seen.

2. (Spiritual espousals and marriage differ).You must understand that between the visions seen in this and in the former mansions there is a vast difference; there is the same distinction between spiritual espousals and spiritual marriage as between people who are only betrothed and others who are united for ever in holy matrimony. I have told you† that though I make this comparison because there is none more suitable, yet these espousals are no more related to our corporal condition than if the soul were a disembodied spirit. This is even more true of the spiritual marriage, for this secret union takes place in the innermost centre of the soul, where God Himself must dwell: I believe that no door is required to enter it. I say, "no door is required," for all I have hitherto described seems to come through the senses and faculties, as must the representation of our Lord's Humanity, but what passes in the union of the spiritual nuptials is very different. Here God appears in the soul's centre, not by an imaginary but by an intellectual vision, far more mystic than those seen before,

---

* *Life,* ch. xxxix. 29.

† *Castle,* M. v. ch. iv. 1.

just as He appeared to the Apostles without having entered through the door when He said: "Pax vobis."*

3. (Spiritual marriage lasting). So mysterious is the secret and so sublime the favour that God thus bestows instantaneously on the soul, that it feels a supreme delight, only to be described by saying that our Lord vouchsafes for the moment to reveal to it His own heavenly glory, in a far more subtle way than by any vision or spiritual delight. As far as can be understood, the soul, I mean the spirit of this soul, is made one with God,† Who is Himself a spirit, and Who has been pleased to show certain persons how far His love for us extends, that we may praise His greatness. He has thus deigned to unite Himself to His creature; He has bound Himself to her as firmly as two human beings are joined in wedlock, and will never separate Himself from her.

4. (Not so spiritual espousals). Spiritual espousals are different, and like the grace of union are often dissolved; for though two things are made one by union, separation is still possible, and each part then remains a thing by itself. This favour generally passes quickly, and afterwards the soul, as far as it is aware, remains without His company.

5. (Spiritual marriage permanent). This is not so in spiritual marriage with our Lord, where the soul always remains in its centre with its God. Union may be symbolised by two wax candles, the tips of which touch each other so closely that there is but one light; or again, the wick, the wax, and the

---

* St. John xx. 19.

† *Rel.* xi. 1 *sqq.*

light become one, but the one candle can again be separated from the other, and the two candles remain distinct; or the wick may be withdrawn from the wax. But spiritual marriage is like rain falling from heaven into a river or stream, becoming one and the same liquid, so that the river and the rain water cannot be divided; or it resembles a streamlet flowing into the ocean, which cannot afterwards be disunited from it. This marriage may also be likened to a room into which a bright light enters through two windows,—though divided when it enters, the light becomes one and the same.

6. (St. Paul and spiritual marriage). Perhaps when St. Paul said, "He who is joined to the Lord is one spirit,"* he meant this sovereign marriage, which presupposes His Majesty's having been joined to the soul by union. The same Apostle says: "To me, to live is Christ and to die is gain."† This, I think, might here be uttered by the soul, for now the little butterfly of which I spoke dies with supreme joy, for Christ is her life.

7. (The soul's jog in union). This becomes more manifest by its effects as time goes on, for the soul learns that it is God Who gives it "life," by certain secret intuitions too strong to be misunderstood, and keenly felt, although impossible to describe. These produce such overmastering feelings that the person experiencing them cannot refrain from amorous exclamations, such as, "O Life of my life, and Power which doth uphold me!" with other aspirations of the same kind.‡ For

---

* 1 Cor. vi. 17: "Qui adhæret Domino unus spiritus est."

† Phil. i. 21: "Mihi vivere Christus est et mori lucrum."

‡ Such exclamations, in considerable number, form the *Book of Exclamations* published by Fray Luis de Leon. De Fuente thinks it was written in 1569, but as St. Teresa's Spiritual Espousals took place on November 18, 1572, it seems, at least in parts, of a

from the bosom of the Divinity, where God seems ever to hold this soul fast clasped, issue streams of milk, which solace the servants of the castle. I think He wishes them to share, in some way, the riches the soul enjoys; therefore from the flowing river in which the little streamlet is swallowed up, some drops of water flow every now and then to sustain the bodily powers, the servants of the bride and Bridegroom.

8. (Its conviction of God's indwelling). A person who was unexpectedly plunged into water could not fail to be aware of it; here the case is the same, but even more evident. A quantity of water could not fall on us unless it came from some source—so the soul feels certain there must be some one within it who lances forth these darts and vivifies its own life, and that there is a Sun whence this brilliant light streams forth from the interior of the spirit to its faculties.

9. (Its peace). The soul itself, as I said, never moves from this centre, nor loses the peace He can give Who gave it to the Apostles when they were assembled together.* I think this salutation of our Lord contains far deeper meaning than the words convey, as also His bidding the glorious Magdalen to "go in peace."† Our Lord's words *act* within us,‡ and in these cases they must have wrought their effect in the souls already disposed to banish from within themselves all that is corporal and to retain only what is spiritual, in order to be joined in

---

later date. The Spiritual Nuptials must be placed between the aforementioned year and May 1575, but it is not possible to ascertain the exact date.

* St. John xx. 19.

† St. Luke vii. 50.

‡ *Supra,* M. vi. ch. iii. 6. *Life,* ch. xxv. 5.

this celestial union with the uncreated Spirit. Without doubt, if we empty ourselves of all that belongs to the creature, depriving ourselves of it for the love of God, that same Lord will fill us with Himself.

10. (Christ's prayer for the divine union of the soul). Our Lord Jesus Christ, praying for His Apostles, (I cannot remember the reference), asked that they might be made one with the Father and with Himself, as Jesus Christ our Lord is in the Father and the Father in Him!* I know not how love could be greater than this! Let none draw back from entering here, for His Majesty also said: "Not only for them do I pray, but for them also who through their word shall believe in Me";† and He said: "I am in them."‡

11. (Its fulfilment). God help me! how true these words are, and how clearly does the soul understand them which in this state of prayer finds them fulfilled in itself! And so should all of us, were it not through our own fault, for the words of Jesus Christ, our King and our Lord, cannot fail. It is *we* who fail, by not disposing ourselves fitly, nor removing all that can obstruct this light, so that we do not behold ourselves in this mirror wherein our image is engraved.§

---

* St. John xvii. 21: "Ut omnes unum sint, sicut tu, Pater, in me et ego in te, ut et ipsi in nobis unum sint."

† St. John xvii. 20: "Non pro eis autem rogo tantum, sed et pro eis qui credituri sunt per verbum eorum in me."

‡ St. John xvii. 23: "Ego in eis."

§ This idea is expressed in St. Teresa's poem, "Alma, buscarte has en Mi" (Poem 10, English version). Such is the power of love, O Soul, To paint thee in my heart No craftsman with such art Whate'er his skill might be, could there Thine image thus impart! 'Twas love that gave Thee life— Then, fair one, if thou be Lost to thyself, thou'lt see Thy portrait in my bosom stamped:— Soul, seek thyself in Me.

12. (Unalterable peace of the soul in Mansion VII). To return to what I was saying. God places the soul in His own mansion, which is in the very centre of the soul itself. They say the empyreal heavens, wherein our Lord dwells, do not revolve with the rest: so the accustomed movements of the faculties and imagination do not appear to take place in any way that can injure the soul or disturb its peace.

13. (Unless it offends God). Do I seem to imply that after God has brought the soul thus far it is certain to be saved, and cannot fall into sin again?* I do not mean this: whenever I say that the soul seems in security, I must be understood to imply for as long as His Majesty thus holds it in His care and it does not offend Him. At any rate I know for certain that though such a person realises the high state she is in, and has remained in it for several years, she does not consider herself safe, but is more careful than ever to avoid committing the least offence against God. As I shall explain later on, she is most anxious to serve Him, and feels a constant pain and confusion at seeing how little she can do for Him, compared with all she ought. This is no light cross, but a great

---

* In a letter dated May 1581, and addressed to Don Alonso Velasquez, then Bishop of Osma, St. Teresa writes as follows: "She [herself] has received such an assurance of coming one day to the fruition of God that she almost imagines she has already come into possession of Him, without, however, the joy that will accompany it. She is in the same position as one who by legal contract has received a splendid property which will become his, and whose fruit he will enjoy at a given date. Until then he only holds the title-deeds, without being able to take possession of the property. Nevertheless my soul would not like to come immediately into the possession of God, for it does not believe that it has deserved such a grace. It only desires to continue in His service, even at the cost of terrible sufferings. It would not mind thus serving Him to the end of the world, after having received such a pledge." St. John of the Cross, in treating of this subject (*Spir. Cant.* stanza xxii. 3) says: "I believe that no soul ever attains to this state without being confirmed in grace in it." See also Ribera, in the *Acta Ss.* p. 554, *circa finem*.

mortification, for the harder the penances she can perform, the better is she pleased. Her greatest penance is to be deprived by God of health and strength to perform any. I told you elsewhere what keen pain this caused her, but now it grieves her far more. This must be because she is like a tree grafted on a stock growing near a stream which makes it greener and more fruitful.* Why marvel at the longings of this soul, whose spirit has indeed become one with the celestial water I described?

14. (Struggles outside Mansion VII). To return to what I wrote about. It is not intended that the powers, senses, and passions should continually enjoy this peace. The soul does so, indeed, but in the other mansions there are still times of struggle, suffering, and fatigue, though as a general rule, peace is not lost by them. This "centre of the soul" or "spirit" is so hard to describe or even to believe in, that I think, sisters, my inability to explain my meaning saves you from being tempted to disbelieve me; it is difficult to understand how there can be crosses and sufferings, and yet peace in the soul.

15. (Comparisons explaining this.) Let me give you one or two comparisons,—God grant they may be of use; if not, I know that what I say is true. A king resides in his palace; many wars and disasters take place in his kingdom, but he remains on his throne. In the same way, although tumults and wild beasts rage with great uproar in the other mansions, yet nothing of this enters the seventh mansions, nor drives the soul from it. Although the mind regrets these troubles, they do not dis-

---

* Ps. i. 3: "Et erit tamquam lignum quod plantatum est secus decursus aquarum, quod fructum suum dabit in tempore suo."

turb it nor rob it of its peace, for the passions are too subdued to dare to enter here, where they would only suffer still
further defeat. Though the whole body is in pain, yet the
head, if it be sound, does not suffer with it. I smile at these
comparisons,—they do not please me—but I can find no
others. Think what you will about it—I have told you the
truth!

3

Its Effects

The great fruits produced by the above-mentioned prayer. The wonderful difference between these effects and those formerly spoken of should be carefully studied and remembered.

1. (Effects of the graces last received). THE little butterfly, then, has died with the greatest joy at having found rest at last, and now Christ lives in her.* Let us see the difference between her present and her former life, for the effects will prove whether what I told you was true. As far as can be ascertained they are these: first, a self-forgetfulness so complete that she really appears not to exist, as I said,† for such a transformation has been worked in her that she no longer recognises herself, nor does she remember that heaven, or life, or glory are to be hers, but seems entirely occupied in seeking God's interests. Apparently the words spoken by His Majesty have done their work: "that she was to care for His affairs, and He would care for hers."‡

---

* Phil. i. 21.

† *Castle,* M. vii. ch. i. 11 and 15.

‡ *Castle,* M. vii. ch. ii. 1. Compare the references there given.

2. (The soul only cares for God's honour). Thus she recks nothing, whatever may happen, but lives in such strange oblivion that, as I said, she seems no longer to exist, nor does she wish to be of any account in anything—*anything*! unless she sees that she can advance, however little, the honour and glory of God: for which she would most willingly die.

3. (But still performs its duties). Do not fancy I mean, daughters, that she neglects to eat and drink, though it brings no small torment to her, nor to perform the duties of her state. I am speaking of her interior; as regards her exterior actions, there is little to say, for her chief suffering is to see that she has hardly strength to do anything. For nothing in the world would she omit doing all in her power which she knows would honour our Lord.

4. (Other fruits of these favours). The second fruit is a strong desire for suffering, although it does not disturb her peace as formerly, because the fervent wish of such souls for the fulfilment of God's will in them makes them acquiesce in all He does. If He would have her suffer, she is content; if not, she does not torment herself to death about it as she used to do. She feels a great interior joy when persecuted, and is far more peaceful than in the former state under such circumstances: she bears no grudge against her enemies, nor wishes them any ill. Indeed she has a special love for them, is deeply grieved at seeing them in trouble, and does all she can to relieve them,* earnestly interceding with God on their behalf. She would be glad to forfeit the favours His Majesty shows

---

* Don Alvaro de Mendoza, Bishop of Avila, used to say that the best means of becoming befriended by Saint Teresa was to injure or insult her. *Acta Ss*. n. 1233. *Rel*. vii. 20.

her, if they might be given to her enemies instead, to prevent them offending our Lord.

5. (The soul's fervent desire to serve God). The most surprising thing to me is that the sorrow and distress which such souls felt because they could not die and enjoy our Lord's presence* is now exchanged for as fervent a desire of serving Him, of causing Him to be praised, and of helping others to the utmost of their power. Not only have they ceased to long for death, but they wish for a long life and most heavy crosses, if such would bring ever so little honour to our Lord. Thus, if they knew for certain that immediately on quitting their bodies their souls would enjoy God, it would make no difference to them, nor do they think of the glory enjoyed by the saints, and long to share it. Such souls hold that their glory consists in helping, in any way, Him Who was crucified, especially as they see how men offend against Him, and how few, detached from all else, care for His honour alone. True, people in this state forget this at times, and are seized with tender longings to enjoy God and to leave this land of exile, especially as they see how little they serve Him. Then, however, they return to themselves, reflecting how they possess Him continually in their souls, and so are satisfied, offering to His Majesty their willingness to live as the most costly oblation they can make.† They fear death no more than they would a delicious trance.

---

* *Rel.* viii. 15.

† Compare with the Saint's poem on Self-oblation, "Vuestro soy, para Vos naci" (Poem 1, English version): Long life bestow, or straightway let me die; Let health be mine, or pain and sickness send; Honour or foul dishonour—be my path Beset by

6. (Christ dwells within this soul). The fact is, that He Who gave them these torturing desires of death has exchanged them for the others. May He be for ever blessed and praised! Amen. In fact, such persons no longer wish for consolations nor delights, since they bear God Himself within them, and it is He Who lives in them. It is evident that His life was one continual torment: so would He have ours to be, at least in desire, for as to the rest He leads us mercifully as our weakness requires, though when He sees the need He imparts to us His strength.

7. (And recalls it to fervour if negligent). Such a soul, thoroughly detached from all things, wishes to be either always alone, or else occupied on what benefits the souls of others: she feels neither aridity nor any interior troubles, but a constant tender recollection of our Lord, Whom she wishes to praise unceasingly. When she grows negligent, the same Lord arouses her in the way that I told you, and it is easy to see that this impulse (I know not what term to use for it) comes from the interior of the soul, like the former impetuous desires.* It is now felt very sweetly, but is neither produced by the intellect nor the memory, nor is there any reason to believe the soul itself has any share in it. This is so usual and so frequent that any one who has been in this state must have noticed it. However large a fire may be, the flame never burns downwards, but upwards, and so this movement is seen to come from the centre of the soul whose powers it excites.

---

war or peaceful till the end. My strength or weakness be as Thou dost choose, Since naught Thou askest shall I e'er refuse. Say, Lord, what is it Thou dost will for me?

* *Castle,* M. vi. ch. vi. 6.

Indeed, were nothing else gained by this way of prayer but the knowledge of the special care God takes to communicate Himself to us, and how He entreats us to abide with Him (for indeed I can describe it in no other way), I think that for the sake of these sweet and penetrating touches of His love all our past pains were well spent.

8. (God's constant care of such souls). You will have learnt this by experience, sisters, for I think that when our Lord has brought us to the prayer of union, He watches over us in this way, unless we neglect to keep His commandments. When these impulses are given you, remember that they come from the innermost mansion, where God dwells in our souls. Praise Him fervently, for it is He Who sends you this message, or love letter, so tenderly written, and in a cipher that only you can understand and know what He asks. By no means neglect to answer His Majesty, even though you may be occupied exteriorly and engaged in conversation. Our Lord may often be pleased to show you this secret favour in public, and it is very easy, as the reply should be entirely interior, to respond by an act of love or to ask, with Saint Paul: "Lord, what wilt Thou have me to do?"* Jesus will show you in many ways how to please Him. It is a propitious moment, for He seems to be listening to us, and the soul is nearly always disposed by this delicate touch to respond with a generous determination.† As I told you, this mansion differs

---

* Acts ix. 6: "Domine, quid me vis facere?"

† The words from "know what He asks" to "as I told you" are not in the original manuscript, but must have been written on a separate slip, as is proved by a marginal note in the handwriting of the Saint: "Cuando dice aqui: os pide, léase luego este papel." This paper is now lost, but the passage it contained is preserved in the early

from the rest in that, as I said,* the dryness and disturbance felt in all the rest at times hardly ever enters here, where the soul is nearly always calm. It does not fear that this sublime favour can be counterfeited by the devil, but feels a settled conviction that it is of divine origin because, as above stated, nothing is here perceived by the senses or faculties, but His Majesty reveals Himself to the spirit, which He takes to be with Himself in a place where I doubt not the devil dare not enter, nor would our Lord ever permit him.

9. (Peace and silence of such souls). All the graces here divinely bestowed on the soul come, as I said, through no action of its own, save its total abandonment of itself to God. They are given in peace and silence, like the building of Solomon's Temple, where no sound was heard.† It is thus with this temple of God, this mansion of His where He and the soul rejoice in each other alone in profound silence. The mind need not act nor search for anything, as the Lord Who created it wishes it to be at rest, and only to watch, through a little chink, what passes within. Though at times it cannot see this, yet such intervals are very short, because, I believe, the powers are not here lost, but only cease to work, being, as it were, dazed with astonishment.

10. (Few ecstasies occur in Mansion VII). I, too, am astonished at

manuscript copies of Toledo, Cordova, and Salamanca, as well as in the first printed edition, and, through this, in the old translations; hence both Woodhead and Dalton have it in its proper place. It is, of course, not to be found in the autograph published in 1882, nor in Fuente's Spanish editions, nor in translations based upon these. The Spanish text will be found in *Œuvres*, vi. 297 note.

★ *Supra,* §§ 1 and 2.

† III Reg. vi. 7.

seeing that when the soul arrives at this state it does not go into ecstasies, except perhaps on rare occasions—even then they are not like the former trances and the flight of the spirit, and seldom take place in public as they did before.* They are no longer produced by any special calls to devotion, such as by the sight of a religious picture, by hearing a sermon (were it only the first few words), or by sacred music; formerly, like the poor little butterfly, the soul was so anxious that any thing used to alarm it and make it take flight. This may be either because the spirit has at last found repose, or that it has seen such wonders in this mansion that nothing can frighten it, or perhaps because it no longer feels solitary, since it rejoices in such Company.

11. (Probable reasons for this). In short, sisters, I cannot tell the reason, but as soon as God shows the soul what this mansion contains, bringing it to dwell within the precincts, the infirmity formerly so troublesome to the mind, and impossible to get over, disappears at once. Probably this is because our Lord has now strengthened, dilated, and developed the soul, or it may be that He wished to make public (for some end known only to Himself) what He was doing in secret within such souls, for His judgments are beyond our comprehension in this life.

12. (Allusions in Holy Scripture to this state). These effects, with all the other good fruits I have mentioned of the different degrees of prayer, are given by God to the soul when it draws

---

* "That is, so as to lose the senses" (marginal note in the Saint's handwriting). *Rel.* iii. 5.

near Him to receive that "kiss of His mouth" which the bride asked for,* and I believe her petition is now granted. Here the overflowing waters are given to the wounded hart: here she delights in the tabernacles of God†: here the dove sent out by Noah, to see whether the flood had subsided, has plucked the olive branch, showing that she has found firm land amongst the floods and tempests of this world.‡ O Jesus! who knows how much in Holy Scripture refers to this peace of soul! Since, O my God, Thou dost see of what grave import is this peace to us, do Thou incite Christians to strive to gain it! In Thy mercy do not deprive those of it on whom Thou hast bestowed it, for, indeed, until Thou hast given them true peace and brought them to where it is unending, they must ever live in fear.

13. (Watchfulness of such souls). I do not mean that peace is unreal on earth because I say "true peace," but that such souls might have to begin all their struggles over again if they forsook God. What must these persons feel at the thought that it is possible to lose so great a good? Their dread makes them more careful; they try to gather strength from their weakness lest, through their own fault, they should miss any opportunity of pleasing God better. The greater the favours they have received from His Majesty, the more diffident and mistrustful are they of themselves; the marvels they have witnessed having revealed more clearly to them their own miseries and the

---

* Cant. i. 1.

† Ps. xli. 2, 5.

‡ Gen. viii. 8, 9.

heinousness of their sins, so that often, like the Publican, they dare not so much as lift up their eyes.*

14. (Crosses suffered in this state). Sometimes they long to die and be in safety, but then, at once, their love makes them wish to live in order to serve God, as I told you, therefore they commit all that concerns them to His mercy.† At times they are more crushed than ever by the thought of the many graces they have received, lest, like an overladen ship, they sink beneath the burden. I assure you, sisters, such souls have their cross to bear, yet it does not trouble them, nor rob them of their peace, but is quickly gone, like a wave or a storm which is followed by a calm, for God's presence within them soon makes them forget all else. May He be for ever blessed and praised by all His creatures! Amen.

---

* St. Luke xviii. 13.

† *Rel.* ix. 19.

4

Martha and Mary

The conclusion sets forth what appears to be our Lord's principal intention in conferring these sublime favours on souls, and explains how necessary it is for Mary and Martha to go together. This chapter is very profitable.

1. (Vicissitudes of Mansion VII). You must not suppose, sisters, that the effects I mentioned always exist in the same degree in these souls, for, as far as I remember, I told you that in most cases our Lord occasionally leaves such persons to the weakness of their nature. The venomous creatures from the moat round the Castle and the other mansions at once join together to revenge themselves for the time when they were deprived of their power.

2. (Humility produced by them). True, this lasts but a short time—a day perhaps, or a little longer,—but during this disturbance, which generally arises from some passing event, these persons learn what benefits they derive from the holy Company they are in. Our Lord gives them great fortitude,

so that they never desert His service nor the good resolutions they have made, which only seem to gather strength by trial, nor do their hearts ever turn from them, even by a first slight movement of the will. This trouble but rarely happens; our Lord wishes the soul to keep in mind its natural condition, that it may be humble, and may better understand how much it owes Him, and how great is the grace it has received, and so may render Him praise.

3. (Such souls free from mortal and from wilful venial sins). Do not fancy that in spite of the strong desire and determination of these souls that they do not commit imperfections and even fall into many sins. (Not *wilfully*; for such people are given special grace from God on this point.) I mean, venial sins; as far as they are aware, they are free from mortal sins, although they do not feel certain they may not be guilty of some of which they are ignorant.

4. (The fate of Solomon). This grieves their hearts sorely, as does the sight of the souls perishing around them; although on the one hand they have strong hopes of not being themselves among the number of the lost, yet, remembering what we are told in Holy Scripture of the fate of the men who, like Solomon, seemed the special favourites of God,* and conversed so familiarly with His Majesty, they cannot help fearing for themselves.

5. (Holy fear). Let that one among you who feels most confidence on this point fear the most, for: "Blessed is the man who feareth the Lord," as David said.† May His Majesty ever

---

* III. Reg. xi.

† Ps. cxi. 1: "Beatus vir qui timet Dominum."

protect us! Let us beg Him never to permit us to offend Him: therein lies our greatest safety. May He be for ever praised! Amen.

6. (These favours strengthen souls to suffer). It would be well to tell you, sisters, the reason why God bestows such favours on souls in this world, although you must have learned this by the effects produced, if you have considered the matter. I return to the subject, that none of you may think it is only for the sake of the pleasure such persons feel, which would be a great mistake on your part, for His Majesty can bestow no greater favour on us than to give us a life such as was led by His beloved Son. Therefore, as I have often told you, I feel certain that these graces are sent to strengthen our weakness, that we may imitate Him by suffering much.

7. (Crosses borne by the saints). We always find that those nearest to Christ our Lord bear the heaviest cross: think of what His glorious Mother and the Apostles bore. How do you think St. Paul went through such immense labours?* We learn from his conduct the fruits of genuine visions and contemplation which come from our Lord and not from our own imagination, or the devil's fraud. Do you suppose that St. Paul hid himself to enjoy these spiritual consolations at leisure and did nothing else? You know that he never took a

---

* "Though thou shouldst have been rapt up to the third heaven with Saint Paul, thou art not thereby secured that thou shalt suffer no adversity. 'I,' said Jesus, 'will show him how great things he must suffer for My name's sake' (Acts. ix. 16). To suffer, therefore, is what waits for thee, if thou wilt love Jesus and constantly serve Him. . . . For our merit and the advancement of our state consist not in having many sweetnesses and consolations, but rather in bearing great afflictions and tribulations" (*Imitation*, bk. ii. ch. xii. 12).

day's rest, as far as we can learn, nor could he have slept much since he worked all night to get his living.*

8. (Effect of vision of our Lord on St. Peter). I am delighted with St. Peter, who, when fleeing from prison, was met by our Lord, Who told him He was going to Rome to be crucified again.† I never recite the Office in which this is commemorated without feeling a special joy. What effect did this vision have on Saint Peter, and what did he do? He went at once to meet his death—and our Lord did Him no small favour in finding him an executioner!

9. (Effects of these favours). Oh, my sisters! how forgetful of her ease, how unmindful of honours, and how far from seeking men's esteem should she be whose soul God thus chooses for His special dwelling-place! For if her mind is fixed on Him, as it ought to be, she must needs forget herself: all her thoughts are bent on how to please Him better, and when and how she can show the love she bears Him.

10. (Why the spiritual marriage takes place). *This* is the aim and end of prayer, my daughters; *this* is the reason for the spiritual marriage, whose children are always good works. *Works* are the unmistakable sign which shows these favours come from God, as I told you. It will do me little good to be deeply

---

* 1 Thess. ii. 9.

† The Antiphon of the Magnificat at first Vespers of the Feast of Saints Peter and Paul, June 29, in the Carmelite Breviary used by St. Teresa is: "Beatus Petrus Apostolus vidit sibi Christum occurrere. Adorans eum ait: 'Domine, quo vadis?'—'Venio Romam iterum crucifigi.'" "The Blessed Apostle Peter saw Christ come to meet him. Adoring Him, he asked 'Lord, where art Thou going?'—'I go to Rome to be crucified anew.'" The saint at once returned to Rome and was taken by the soldiers and crucified.

recollected when alone, making acts of the virtues, planning and promising to do wonders in God's service, if afterwards, when occasion offers, I do just the opposite. I did wrong in saying, "It will do me *little* good," for all the time we spend with God does us *great* good. Though, afterwards, we may weakly fail to perform our good intentions, yet some time or other His Majesty will find a way for us to practise them, although perhaps, much to our regret. Thus, when He sees a soul very cowardly, He often sends it some great affliction, much against its will, and brings it through this trial with profit to itself. When the soul has learnt this, it is less timid in offering itself to Him.

11. (Love for Christ proved by our deeds). I ought to have said, "will do us *little* good," in comparison with the far *greater* good we gain when our works fulfil our aspirations and our promises. She that cannot do all this at once should do it little by little, gradually dominating her will, if she would gain fruit from prayer. Even in this little nook she will find many a chance to practise this. Remember, this is of far more importance than I know how to express. Fix your eyes on the Crucified One, and all will seem easy. If His Majesty proved His love for us by such stupendous labours and sufferings, how can you seek to please Him by words alone?

12. (True spirituality). Do you know what it is to be truly spiritual? It is for men to make themselves the *slaves* of God— branded with His mark, which is the cross. Since they have given Him their freedom, He can sell them as slaves to the whole world, as He was, which would be doing them no wrong, but the greatest favour. Unless you make up your

minds to this, never expect to make much progress,* for humility, as I said, is the foundation of the whole building, and unless you are truly humble, our Lord, for your own sake, will never permit you to rear it very high, lest it should fall to the ground.

13. (Humility and the virtues must combine with prayer). Therefore, sisters, take care to lay a firm foundation, by seeking to be the least of all and the slave of others, watching how you can please and help them, for it will benefit you more than them. Built on such strong rocks, your Castle can never go to ruin. I insist again: your foundation must not consist of prayer and contemplation alone: unless you acquire the virtues and practise them, you will always be dwarfs; and please God no worse may befall you than making no progress, for you know that to *stop* is to go *back*—if you love, you will never be content to come to a standstill.

14. (Zeal of advanced souls). Perhaps you think I am speaking of beginners, and that one may rest later on, but, as I told you, the rest such souls feel is within them: they have less outwardly nor do they wish for it. Why, do you think, does the soul send from its centre these inspirations, or rather aspirations (the messages of which I spoke) to the dwellers in the precincts of the Castle, and to the surrounding mansions? To send them to sleep? No, no, no! The soul wages a fiercer war from thence to keep the powers, senses, and the whole body from being idle, than ever it did when it suffered in their company. Formerly it did not understand

---

* "If thou wilt stand upon self and wilt not offer thyself freely to My will, thine offering is not perfect, nor will there be entire union between us" (*Imitation*, bk. iv. ch. viii. 2).

the immense benefit its afflictions brought, though indeed they may have been the means God used to advance it to this state.

15. (Strengthened by the divine Presence within them). Besides, the Company it enjoys gives it far greater strength than ever before. If as David says: "With the holy Thou shalt be holy,* doubtless by its becoming one with the Almighty, by this sovereign union of spirit with spirit, the soul must gather strength, as we know the saints did, to suffer and to die. Beyond doubt, with the force thus gained, the soul succours all within the Castle, and even the very body itself, which often seems to have no feeling left in it. The vigour the soul derives from "the wine" drunk in the "cellar"† (into which the Spouse brought her and would not let her go) overflows into the feeble body, just as the food we eat nourishes both the head and the whole frame.

16. (Examples of the saints). Indeed the body suffers much while alive, for whatever work it may perform, the soul has energy for far greater tasks and goads it on to do more, for all it can perform appears as nothing. This must be the reason of the severe penances performed by many of the saints, especially the glorious Magdalen, who had always spent her life in luxury.‡ This caused the zeal felt by our Father Elias for

* Ps. xvii. 26: "Cum sancto sanctus eris."

† Cant. ii. 4.

‡ "St. Mary Magdalen gave herself up to penance and contemplation in a deep excavation of the rocks at La Baume, near Marseilles. In this wild spot there was neither bread, water, nor even herbage. Thus she lived for more than thirty-two years, without any kind of nourishment but that which was celestial, performing meanwhile most severe penances" (St. Vincent Ferrer).

the honour of God,* and the desires of St. Dominic,† and St. Francis‡ to draw souls to praise the Almighty. I assure you that, forgetful of themselves, they must have passed through no small trials.

17. (Both Martha and Mary must serve our Lord). This, my sisters, is what I would have us strive for—to offer our petitions and to practise prayer, not for our own enjoyment, but to gain strength to serve God. Let us seek no fresh path; we should lose ourselves in ways of ease. It would be a strange thing to fancy we should gain these graces by any other road than that by which Jesus and all His saints have gone before. Let us not dream of such a thing: believe me, both Martha and Mary must entertain our Lord and keep Him as their Guest, nor must they be so inhospitable as to offer Him no food. How can Mary do this while she sits at His feet, if her sister does not help her?§

18. (Christ's food). His food is, that in every possible way we

---

* III Reg. xix. 10.

† "There was one sentiment within him to which may almost be given the name of a passion: it was his ceaseless burning thirst for the salvation of souls. As his Divine Master had come into the world to save sinners and loved them even unto death, so he, too, gave up all that was most dear to him in his life to win souls to Christ. He was always giving himself: it was the very keynote of his existence. He would have sold himself as a slave, he would have been cut to pieces by the heretics, he would spare himself neither by day nor by night, if by any means he might save some" (from the *History of St. Dominic*, by Augusta Theodosia Drane. London, 1891, p. 256).

‡ "St. Francis of Assisi, at the very beginning of his Order, when he had only seven followers, said to them; 'Consider, my brethren, what is our vocation. It is not only for our own salvation that the mercy of God has called us, but for the salvation of many other souls. It is that we may go forth and exhort all men rather by our example than by our words, to do penance and keep the divine commands'" (*The Life of St. Francis of Assisi,* by a religious of the Order of Poor Clares, London, 1861, p. 32).

§ St. Luke x. 39, 40. *Life,* ch. xvii. 6. *Rel.* viii. 6. *Way of Perf.* ch. xxxi. 4. *Concep.* ch. vii. 4.

should draw souls to Him, that they may be saved and may praise Him for ever. You may offer two objections—first that I said that Mary had chosen the better part,* for she had already done Martha's work by waiting on our Lord, by washing His feet and by wiping them with her hair.

19. (Mary's mortification). Do you think it was a small mortification for a woman of rank, as she was, to go through the streets, perhaps by herself, for in her zeal she never thought of how she went? Then she entered a house where she was a stranger, and had to bear the railing of the Pharisee, and many other trials.† It was strange to see such a woman as she had been thus publicly change her life. With a wicked nation like the Jews, the sight of her love for our Lord, Whom they hated so bitterly, was enough to make them cast in her face her former life, and taunt her with wanting to become a saint. Doubtless she must have changed her rich robes and all the rest. Considering how men talk now of people far less well known than she was, what must have been said of her?

20. (Her grief at the Passion). I assure you, sisters, she won the better part, after many crosses and mortifications. Must not the mere sight of men's hatred of her Master have been an intolerable trial? Then, think of what she endured afterwards at our Lord's death! I believe, myself, that she did not suffer martyrdom because she was already a martyr by grief at witnessing the crucifixion.‡ Then what terrible pain His absence

---

* St. Luke x. 42: "Maria optimam partem elegit."

† St Luke vii. 37.

‡ Marginal note in the Saint's handwriting.

must have caused her* during the long years afterwards! You see, she was not always enjoying contemplation at the feet of our Saviour!

21. (Can we lead souls to God?). Secondly, you may say that you have neither the power nor the means to lead souls to God; though you would willingly do so, you do not know how, as you can neither teach nor preach as did the Apostles. I have often written an answer to this objection, though I cannot tell whether I have done so in connection with the Castle. However, as the difficulty probably often crosses your minds on account of the desires our Lord gives you of serving Him, I will now speak of it again.† I told you elsewhere how the devil frequently fills our thoughts with great schemes, so that instead of putting our hands to what work we can do to serve our Lord, we may rest satisfied with wishing to perform impossibilities.

22. (How to do so). You can do much by prayer; and then, do not try to help the whole world, but principally your companions; this work will be all the better because you are the more bound to it. Do you think it is a trifling matter that your humility and mortification, your readiness to serve your sisters, your fervent charity towards them, and your love of God, should be as a fire to enkindle their zeal, and that you should constantly incite them to practise the other virtues? This would be a great work, and one most pleasing to our Lord: by thus doing all that is in your power, you would prove to His Majesty your willingness to do still more, and

---

* *Life,* ch. xxi. 9.

† *Way of Perf.* ch. i. 1. *Found.* ch. i. 6, 7. *Supra,* M. vi. ch. vi. 2.

He would reward you as if you had won Him many souls. Do you answer:"This would not be converting my sisters, for they are very good already"? What business is that of yours? If they were still better, the praise they render God would please Him more, and their prayers would be more helpful to their neighbours.*

23. (Love gives value to our deeds). In short, my sisters, I will conclude with this advice; do not build towers without a foundation, for our Lord does not care so much for the importance of our works as for the love with which they are done. When we do all we can, His Majesty will enable us to do more every day. If we do not grow weary, but during the brief time this life lasts (and perhaps it will be shorter than any of you think) we give our Lord every sacrifice we can, both interior and exterior, His Majesty will unite them with that He offered to His Father for us on the Cross, that they may be worth the value given them by our love, however mean the works themselves may be.

24. (Conclusion). May it please His Majesty, my sisters and my daughters, that we may all meet together, where we may praise Him for ever, and may He give me grace to practise something of what I have taught you, by the merits of His Son, Who liveth and reigneth for ever! Amen. I assure you that I am filled with confusion at myself, and I beg you, for the sake of the same Lord, not to forget this poor sinner in your prayers.

---

* *Way of Perf.* ch. vii. 7.

Conclusion

ALTHOUGH, as I told you, I felt reluctant to begin this work, yet now it is finished I am very glad to have written it, and I think my trouble has been well spent, though I confess it has cost me but little. Considering your strict enclosure, the little recreation you have, my sisters, and how many conveniences are wanting in some of your convents, I think it may console you to enjoy yourselves in this interior Castle, where you can enter, and walk about at will, at any hour you please, without asking leave of your superiors. It is true you cannot enter all the mansions by your own power, however great it may appear to you, unless the Lord of the Castle Himself admit you. Therefore, I advise you to use no violence if you meet with any obstacle, for that would displease Him so much that He would never give you admission to them. He dearly loves humility:* if you think yourselves

---

* *Way of Perf.* ch. xvi. 1.

unworthy to enter the third mansion, He will grant you all the sooner the favour of entering the fifth. Then, if you serve Him well there, and often repair to it, He will draw you into the mansion where He dwells Himself, whence you need never depart, unless called away by the Prioress, whose commands this sovereign Master wishes you to obey as if they were His own. If, by her orders, you are often absent from His presence chamber, whenever you return He will hold the door open for you. When once you have learnt how to enjoy this Castle, you will always find rest, however painful your trials may be, in the hope of returning to your Lord, which no one can prevent. Although I have only mentioned seven mansions, yet each one contains many more rooms, above, below, and around it, with fair gardens, fountains, and labyrinths, besides other things so delightful that you will wish to consume yourself in praising the great God for them, Who has created the soul in His own image and likeness. If you find anything in the plan of this treatise which helps you to know Him better, be certain that it is sent by His Majesty to encourage you, and whatever you find amiss in it is my own. In return for my strong desire to aid you in serving Him, my God and my Lord, I implore you, whenever you read this, to praise His Majesty fervently in my name, and to beg Him to prosper His Church, to give light to the Lutherans, to pardon my sins and to free me from purgatory, where perhaps I shall be, by the mercy of God, when you see this book (if it is given to you after having been examined by theologians). If these writings contain any error, it is through my ignorance; I submit in all things to the teachings of the holy Catholic Roman Church, of which I am now a member, as I protest and promise both to live and die. May our Lord God be for ever praised and blessed! Amen, Amen.

I finished writing this book in the convent of St. Joseph of Avila, 1577, on the Vigil of St. Andrew, for the glory of God, Who liveth and reigneth for ever and ever! Amen.

FINIS

Index

Absalom, 72n

Acts of praise, love, etc., 93–94

Agnes, St., 213n

Alcantara, St. Peter of, 110, 221–22

Alva, Duchess of, 199, 277n

Amber, 207

Anthony, St., 211n

Antonius a Spiritu Sancto, 106n, 168n, 184n, 220n

Apostles: our Lord's prayer for, 286; sufferings of, 301

Augustine, St., 108n, 230

Avila, Blessed John of, 251n; St. Joseph's convent at, 222, 277n, 313

Awe, produced by visions, 246

Babe, likeness of, 114

Bañez, Fr. Dominic, 250n

Bee, likeness of, 47, 132

Beggar, likeness of, 110

Beginners, 49, 65, 85, 164, 304

Bethsaida, the blind man at the pool of, 40

Blindness, spiritual, 202

Body: the setting of the diamond, 37; the outer walls of the Castle, 37; care of, 80, 81, 117; strength of, necessary in prayer of Union, 122; effect of prayer of Union on, 122–23

Books, spiritual: insufficiency of, 109; use of, 132

Bride, in the Canticle, 129; and Bridegroom, 152

Butterfly, likeness of, 131, 132, 134–36, 141, 150, 195, 214, 216, 261, 284, 290, 296

Cæcilia, St., 151n

Call, God's, to the soul, 58–59, 107, 108

Carelessness in prayer, 40

Carmel, our Lady of, 29, 30; Order of, Constitutions, 45–46, 122; Rule of, 219

Carmelite nuns, discalced, 2, 8, 13, 29, 122

Castle, Interior, 3, 35–37, 42, 202; description, 46; entrance to, 39, 41; foundation of, 304; prayer and meditation, 40; precincts of, 41

Caterpillar, likeness of, 134

Cellar of wine, 129, 138

Certitude of the soul, a sign of Union, 127–29

Changes wrought in the soul by prayer of Union, 135, 137, 138

Charity, works of, only remedy in times of darkness, 170–71

Christ's face, 251–52; sufferings, our pains joined to, 133

Church, Holy Roman Catholic, 30, 232, 312; love of, 94

Clearness, a sign that locutions come from God, 190

Communion, Holy, 281

Complaints, loving, 173

Confession, regular, 132

Confessor: to be consulted on locutions, 189; and on visions, 250; if mistaken, 241–42; timorous, 166–67

Confidence, 64

Confirmation in grace, 287n

Conformity with the will of God, 62, 79, 80, 264

Consolations: divine (prayer of Quiet), 82, 91, 92, 100, 101, 102; earthly, no use, 170

Contempt, 79; for earthly things, an effect of raptures, 213

Contradiction, by good people, 163

Courage, necessary, 62, 81, 162, 195, 210, 213

Cross, 64; necessary in prayer of Union, 136; of saints, 301

Crystal, 35, 43–44

Darkness: dispelled by God, 169; different kinds of, 42, 275

David, King, 71, 258, 300, 305

Deaf mutes, 58, 59

Deception: fear of, 167; satanic, 153–55; where impossible, 175–76

Defects, impeding union, 144

Desires: of death, 267, 298; generous, 93; to serve God, better than visions, etc., 254, 292; of suffering, 291; sometimes to be checked, 217

Detachment, 75, 79–80

Detraction, 54

Devil, 43; like a file, 52; deceives by false favours, 115–17, 136; a good painter, 251; unable to interfere in prayer of Union, 124; and in intellectual visions, 256; wiles of, 49, 51, 53, 61, 115, 171

Devotion, sensible, see Sweetness in prayer

Diamond, soul likened to, 35, 37

Dilatation, of heart, 92, 101

Direction, necessary, 65, 84

Directors, learned and unlearned, 125, 167–68

Distractions, in prayer, 41, 95–97

Dominic, St., 153, 306

Dove, soul likened to, 141, 150, 172, 261

Drowsiness, 123, 124

Dryness, in prayer, 73, 75

Easter, trance on the feast of, 266
Ecstasies, rare in Seventh Mansions, 295–96
Elias, St., 229, 305–6
Energy, 81
Enriquez, Doña Maria, 199n, 277n
Entering within oneself, 107, 108, 109
Envy, spiritual, 38
Espousals, spiritual, 150–52; difference between, and matrimony, 282, 283
Exclamations, 284
Exterior works do not interfere with interior life, 291

Faculties: given to be used, 144; suspension of, 202
Faults, slight, 154
Favours, divine: not to be disbelieved, 38; value of, 83–84; how to be used, 114–15; false, 115–16, 136; distinction from divine, 116
Fear of illusions, 249
Ferrer, St. Vincent, 305n
Fervour, supernatural, 177, 304
File, devil likened to a, 52
Fire of burning coal, God likened to, 174
Flight of the spirit, 206, 207, 210, 211–13
Francis, St., 153, 221, 306
Fraternal charity, 148
Fretting under trials, 77–78
Friendship, spiritual, 61–62
Fuente, Don Vicente de, 284n

Gideon, 62n
Give all to God, 123
God compels the soul to listen when He speaks, 193

God's special care of souls most advanced, 294
Gonzalez, Giles, 277n
Gratian, Father Jerome, 54n, 72n, 96n, 128n
Grief, natural and supernatural, 137, 139, 145

Hart, wounded, 297
Heathen philosophers, 145
Hell, 265–66; fear of, lost, 225; torments of, smaller than those of the last Judgment, 247
Human praise and blame alike troublesome, 164–65
Humanity, sacred, of our Lord: meditation on, 226–35; vision of, 245, 281
Humility: effect of supernatural favours, 192, 208–9, 249; false, 48–49; always necessary, 47, 49, 58, 75, 78, 80, 103–4; from vision of a soul in mortal sin, 44; want of, 38, 81–82; humility and truth, 259–60
Hysteria, see Melancholia

Ignatius of Loyola, St., 153
Ignorance: injurious, 94, 97; of a priest, 126, 128
Imagination, 94–95, 117, 161; difference between it and visions, 247–48; locutions proceeding from, 188
Imitation of Christ, 39, 123, 142, 166, 301, 303
Impulses, 176
Incense, spiritual, 102, 177
Inebriation, spiritual, 203, 222–23
Insecurity, 70

Intellectual locutions, 189–91
Interior Castle, *see* Castle, Interior
Isabel of Jesus, 266n

Jacob, 198
Jerome, St., 247n
Jesus, 44; our model, 49; His Passion,
    see Passion of Christ
Jewels, 122, 213, 244
John of Avila, Blessed, 251n
John of the Cross, St., 35n, 37n, 108n,
    112n, 125n, 128n, 173n, 177n,
    184n, 185n, 204n, 207n, 228n,
    229n, 238n, 254n, 263n, 264n,
    265n, 279n, 287n
Jonas, prophet, 144, 188
Jordan, river, 216
Josue, 194
Joy at seeing locutions fulfilled, 187
Jubilation, 45, 220–23
Judas, 142, 154, 231
Judgment, last, 246

Kernel of palmito, 46
Kiss of the Bridegroom, 297

Lazarus, 70n, 143
Leon, Fray Luis de, 70n, 284n
Liberty of spirit, 46–47
Light, 50; supernatural, 210
Likeness of Christ, 251
Lizards, 124
Locutions, 182–94; "Be not
    troubled," 184, 185, 204; "It is I,"
    185, 238; "Be at peace," 185, 283;
    "To care for God's affairs," 281
Loss of highly favoured souls, 115
Lot's wife, 40
Love: of enemies, 165; of God, 93,
    145–46; of neighbour, 145–46

Ludolf of Saxony, 247n
Lutherans, 312

Mansions, 35, 37, 44, 46, 50, 299,
    311
Martha, 280, 306
Martin, St., 217
Mary, Blessed Virgin: our help, 50;
    meditation on, 227; sufferings of,
    301
Mary Magdalen, St., 38, 226, 268–69,
    285, 305–6
Matrimony, spiritual, 274, 276,
    281–89; difference between, and
    Espousals, 282, 283; effects of,
    302–3; in this state soul free from
    sin, 300; and confirmed in grace,
    287
Meditation, 226–32
Melancholia (hysteria), 73, 99–100,
    166, 182–83, 218, 223
Memento, 201
Mendoza, Don Alvaro de, 291n
Moses, 198–99
Mount Carmel, *see* Carmel, our
    Lady of
Music, 296
Mysteries, revealed during raptures,
    200–201

Noah's Ark, 297
Nuptials, spiritual, *see* Matrimony,
    spiritual

Obedience, 29, 35, 71, 84
Obligations: of a soul enraptured,
    208; on account of intellectual
    visions, 240
Odour, supernatural, 177
Olive branch, 297

Padranos, Juan de, Fr., 237n
Palace, God likened to, 257, 288
Palmito, 46
Passion of Christ, 139; becomes
    the property of the soul, 209;
    meditation on, 227–29, 231–33
Paul, St., 38, 75, 226, 248, 276, 284,
    301; hermit, 211n
Peace, 64; following upon Spiritual
    Matrimony, 285–86, 295, 297;
    "Peace be with you," 130, 283
Penances: indiscreet, 52; too discreet,
    80
Perfection, true, 53
Perfume, 102, 177
Perseverance, 64–65, 69
Peter, St., 75, 226n, 302
Phoenix, 196–97
Philippus a Ss. Trinitate, 90n, 104n,
    106n, 127n, 143n, 168n, 196n,
    198n, 207n, 212n, 220n
Pictures, holy, 296
Pilate, 259
Prayer: St. Teresa's writings on,
    29; books on, 39, 109–10; no
    difference between vocal and
    mental, 40; talking inconsiderately
    to God is not prayer, 40; need
    of guidance in, 45–46, 65;
    perseverance in, 65–66; prayer and
    mortification a great work, 308–9
Preparation for prayer of Union,
    133–34
Presence, spiritual: of our Lord,
    236–39, 293; of Saints, 239–40; of
    the Blessed Trinity, 277–79
Presence chamber, God's, 274, 276
Prioress, 117, 183, 234, 242, 243, 312
Prophecies, 186
Purgatory, 264

Quiet, prayer of, 112; difference from
    prayer of Union, 124; See also
    Consolations

Raptures, 195–205; effects of, 214;
    false, 115–16, 205; rare in Seventh
    Mansion, 295–96
Recollection, prayer of, 106–7,
    108–9; difference from prayer of
    Quiet, 112
Reptiles, 39, 41, 47, 49, 50, 59, 64, 75,
    90, 124
River of living waters, 42, 43

Sacrament, Blessed, 128
Samaritan woman, 264
Saul, King, 142, 253
Schram, Dom, 186n, 242n
Search for God, 230
Secrecy of raptures, 204, 243
Security, 69–70
Self-knowledge, 46–48, 97–98, 155,
    213
Senses, 44, 107, 202
Sepulchre, 129
Sermons, 132, 296
Seville, 81n
Siena, St. Catherine of, 207n
Silkworm, likeness of, 132–34, 141,
    144
Sin: mortal, 42–44; committed
    under the very eyes of God,
    257
Sinners in prison, 275
Slaves: of Christ, 303; of our
    neighbour, 304
Sleep of the soul in prayer of Union,
    123
Solitude, desire of, 214–15
Solomon, 72, 295, 300

Sorrow for sins increasing with
  graces, 224–26
Soul: likened to a castle, 35–36; to
  a crystal, 43–44; to a garden, 36;
  to a ship, 207–8; dignity of, 36; a
  soul that does not pray is lame, 39;
  soul in mortal sin, 42–45, 275–76;
  the soul and its faculties, 280
Spark from the fire of God,
  174–75
Standstill in virtue, 155–56
Struggles, interior, 60
Sufferings, bodily, 165–66
Sun, source of light, 42, 43–45, 46
Sweetness in prayer (sensible
  devotion), 91–93, 101

Tears, 91, 93, 137, 218, 219
Temptations: advantages of, 90;
  particularly fierce before
  Espousals, 153, 154–55
Teresa, St.: consoled by Christ, 209;
  cures a melancholy nun, 116;
  desires death, 225; desires others
  to serve God better, 142; her
  experience in spiritual matters,
  125–26, 152–53; feels no pain
  during ecstasies, 96; feels presence
  of our Lord, 236–39; of the Saints;
  239–40; former mistakes, 234–35;
  suffers from headaches, 29, 95;
  never suffered from hysteria,
  100; has more light now than
  formerly, 46, 89, 102; praises God
  for favours bestowed on others,
  83; profits by vision of a soul in
  mortal sin, 42–43, 44–45, 275;
  by heavenly visions, 279–80;
  readiness to suffer, 267–68; self-
  disparagement, 29–30, 45, 71,

72; submits her writings to the
  judgment of the Church, 312;
  suffers at the sight of sin, 139;
  transverberation, 262, 263, 266; is
  troubled by turmoil of thoughts,
  94; troubles she went through,
  163–71, 214, 243; her visions,
  254, 281; of the Blessed Trinity,
  277; wound of love, 175; writings,
  29–31, 45, 156–57
Theriac, 64
Thomas Aquinas, St., 125n, 210n
Toledo, St. Joseph's convent at, 30
Tortoise, 109
Trance: false, 115–16, 205; at Easter,
  266
Transverberation, 262, 263, 266
Tree of life, 42, 43
Trinity, Blessed: feast of, 30; vision of,
  277; presence of, 277–79
Troubles preceding perfect Union,
  162–69

Understanding, 94
Union: prayer of, difference from
  prayer of Quiet, 124; leads to
  Espousals, 151; with vanities of
  the world, 124–25; with the Will
  of God, 143–46, 264
Ursula, St., 153

Velasquez, Don Alonso, 287n
Virtues, real and imaginary,
  146–47
Visions: corporal, St. Teresa never
  saw one, 246; imaginary, 198, 200,
  210–11, 244–55; intellectual, 200,
  210, 236–43, 256–60; not to be
  sought or wished for, 252–54; of a
  soul in mortal sin, 42–43, 44–45

Watchfulness, 70, 155
Water, spiritual, 43, 100–101, 104–5,
    207–8, 264, 285, 287
Wax: soul likened to, 138; wax
    candles, 283–84
Will of God, Union with, 143–46, 264
Works, good, 66, 74, 75, 83, 147–48,
    170–71, 306–9

World, persons in the, 72, 78,
    79
Worldliness, 51, 59
Wound of love, 172–76, 262–64,
    267–68

Zeal, indiscreet, 52, 53, 85
Zebedee, sons of, 268

About St. Teresa of Avila

ST. TERESA OF AVILA was a Carmelite nun, mystic, and religious reformer who lived in sixteenth-century Spain. She is best known for her mystical writings and visions, her profound insights on prayer, and her work to reform the Carmelite order. She was canonized 40 years after her death and was made the first female Doctor of the Church in 1970.